KU-110-971

The Fine Art of Cooking

THE FINE ART OF COOKING

BY

HELEN JEROME, M.C.A.

FIRST CLASS DIPLOMAS LONDON AND PARIS (CORDON BLEU)
FORMERLY STAFF TEACHER OF COOKERY, THE POLYTECHNIC
REGENT STREET, LONDON
AUTHOR OF "THE ART OF PLAIN COOKING" AND "CONCERNING
CAKE MAKING"

LONDON
SIR ISAAC PITMAN & SONS, LTD.

First printed 1935
Revised impression 1942
Reprinted 1946
Reprinted 1947
Reprinted 1953
Reprinted 1956

SIR ISAAC PITMAN & SONS, LTD.
PITMAN HOUSE, PARKER STREET, KINGSWAY, LONDON, W.C.2
THE PITMAN PRESS, BATH
PITMAN HOUSE, BOUVERIE STREET, CARLTON, MELBOURNE
27 BECKETTS BUILDINGS, PRESIDENT STREET, JOHANNESBURG

ASSOCIATED COMPANIES

PITMAN MEDICAL PUBLISHING COMPANY, LTD.
45 NEW OXFORD STREET, LONDON, W.C.1

PITMAN PUBLISHING CORPORATION
2 WEST 45TH STREET, NEW YORK

SIR ISAAC PITMAN & SONS (CANADA), LTD.
(INCORPORATING THE COMMERCIAL TEXT BOOK COMPANY)
PITMAN HOUSE, 381–383 CHURCH STREET, TORONTO

FOREWORD

BY

MRS. VINCENT R. HOARE

President of the Women's Institute, The Polytechnic,
Regent Street, and Member of the Governing Body

IF Dr. Johnson is correct in declaring that "a man seldom thinks of anything with more earnestness than he does of his dinner," no apology can be needed for the publication of *The Fine Art of Cooking*. Mrs. Jerome has every qualification for giving practical help and advice to all who appreciate good cooking. She has had long and varied experience in teaching, as well as practical insight into Hotel and Trade work, and she is now in charge of the Advanced Cookery Classes at The Polytechnic, Regent Street.

By stressing the theoretical side of advanced cookery, her book meets a real need, for whereas there are many handbooks with simple recipes for household cookery, it is difficult to find a practical guide for those who wish to plan well-balanced, varied, and attractive menus. Mrs. Jerome's recipes are easy to follow, but they cannot have been easy to collect, for they include many which will be new to most English households.

I cordially recommend her book to teachers, to house-keepers, and to cooks, indeed to all who desire to provide their households and guests with fare which is attractive as well as wholesome.

" Louis XV was a great gourmet; and his reign saw many developments in the culinary art. . . . The very phrase ' cordon bleu ' (strictly applied only to a woman cook) arose from an enthusiastic recognition of female merit by the king himself.

" Madame du Barry, piqued at his opinion that only a man could cook to perfection, had a dinner prepared for him by a cuisinière with such success that the delighted monarch demanded that the artist should be named, in order that so precious a cuisinier might be engaged for the royal household. 'Allons donc, la France!' retorted the ex-grisette, ' have I caught you at last? It is no cuisinier at all, but a cuisinière and I demand a recompense for her worthy both of her and of your majesty. . . . I cannot accept less than a cordon bleu (the Royal Order of the Saint Esprit) for my cuisinière.' "

Encyclopaedia Britannica.
Eleventh Edition.

CONTENTS

CONTENTS

PAGE

ECONOMY ADAPTATIONS

THE aim of this book is to help those who wish to prepare dainty meals, and the notes on correct service and smart garnishing will be found very helpful.

Should some of the recipes be considered expensive, economies will occur to the practical mind, such as the substitution of evaporated milk for cream, and fresh margarine for butter —the cutting down of eggs, and so on. Richness in flavour must, of course, suffer, but the fundamentals are the same.

The artist in cookery will be well repaid for thought and time given to the production of attractive dishes.

H. J.

AUTHOR'S ACKNOWLEDGMENTS

The Author desires to express her grateful thanks to—

MRS. VINCENT HOARE for writing the Foreword to this book.

THE EDITOR of *The Yorkshire Post* for permission to reprint some of the recipes which have appeared in that paper.

THE EDITOR of *The Encyclopaedia Britannica* for the description of the first granting of the Cordon Bleu.

PATRICK JEROME for the help given in the French Chapters, and in proof correction.

THE FINE ART OF COOKING

THE PRELIMINARIES

QUANTITIES given in this book are for four people, unless otherwise stated, as this multiple is easily manipulated to any required figure.

OVEN TEMPERATURES are mentioned as approximate, because no two ovens require exactly the same degree, varying according to the size and capacity of retaining heat. The following is a comparative table of baking temperatures for an oven of average size—

Slow oven	. . .	250°–300°	Fahrenheit
Moderate oven	. .	300°–350°	,,
Hot oven	. .	350°–400°	,,
Quick oven	. .	400°–450°	,,
Very hot oven	. .	450°–500°	,,

THE NAMES OF DISHES are given in both French and English in many cases, and a comprehensive index of dishes is to be found at the end.

SOME PRELIMINARY PROCESSES

APPLE MARMALADE

Peel 1 lb. of apples, cut them in rough pieces, add a nut of butter, and about 3 oz. of sugar to sweeten. Add a suspicion of water if necessary, and cook over slow heat until pulped. Beat smooth.

APRICOT MARMALADE

Rub a 10 lb. tin of apricot pulp through a wire sieve. Dissolve 7 lb. of granulated sugar in it over gentle heat. Boil up, and cook for ½ hour, as for ordinary jam. Test in the usual way. Pass the marmalade through a coarse conical strainer into hot jars. Tie down as for jam, either at once or when quite cold.

ASPIC JELLY

A thin layer of aspic jelly is always poured on a silver dish (when cold food is to be served on it), to prevent the contact of food with metal.

BATTER FOR FRYING

1. *A crisp plain Batter.* 2 oz. of flour; a pinch of salt; 1 dessertspoonful of salad oil (or for economy 1 yolk); ½ gill of tepid water; a white of egg. Make a well in the flour, add the oil and water. Mix smoothly and beat well.

Leave in the cool for at least half an hour; add the stiffly whisked white of egg just before use.

2. *A richer Batter.* 2 oz. of flour; a pinch of salt; 1 dessertspoonful of salad oil; 2 yolks of eggs; 2 tablespoonfuls of milk, and 1 white of egg. Method as foregoing.

BEURRES

1. *Beurre Fondu.* Heat 2 oz. of fresh butter, and skim it. Add a few drops of lemon juice, salt, and cayenne.

2. *Beurre Noir.* Heat 2 oz. of butter in a frying-pan until of a rich brown colour, but not burnt. Add a teaspoonful of lemon juice, or vinegar, and serve.

3. *Beurre Noisette.* As the foregoing, but fried to a lighter colour.

BONING

I. *A Bird.* 1. Pluck and singe the bird, but do not draw it.

2. Cut off the head, remove the neck, crop, and windpipe.

3. Draw the sinews of the legs, and cut off the legs at the hock joints, and also the ends of the wings.

4. Turn the bird with the back upward, and cut through the skin on the backbone from neck to tail with a small sharp-pointed knife.

5. Remove the flesh as far as the centre front, working from right to left, as in filleting. Dislocate and remove the wing and thigh bones from the inside, scraping downward. Be careful not to cut through the skin over the breastbone.

6. Turn the bird round, and cut away the other half of the flesh.

7. Push the skin of the legs and wings inside. Cut away the tail, fold the bird in two, and wring a dishcloth out from very hot water and wipe the skin well.

Note. If it is required to keep the bird whole, work as above, omitting the centre cut, and turning the flesh of the bird backward like pulling off a glove inside out.

II. *A Joint.* Begin where the bone reaches, or is nearest to, the surface, according to the shape of the joint. Work round the bone with a small sharp knife, holding the bone as soon as it is possible with the left hand. If any meat should be left on the bone inadvertently, scrape it off and place it inside the boned meat, or place it with the stuffing.

BREAD SIPPETS (Shredded)

Cut off the corner of a firm sandwich loaf, about ¾ in.–1 in. from the corner point, making a triangular piece with the crust on two sides of it. Cut down in very thin slices, and dry these triangles to pale biscuit colour in the oven.

crust —— /\ —— crust

crumb

BUTTERS

1. *Anchovy*. Drain 6 fillets of Gorgona anchovy; cut them up, and place with 2 oz. of butter in a mortar. Pound well. Add the seasoning, a few drops of lemon juice, and (if desired) a suspicion of anchovy paste. Rub all through a hair sieve, and use as required.

2. *Green*. Wash 2 oz. of spinach well, together with 1 oz. of tarragon, 1 oz. of chervil, and a few sprigs of parsley. Blanch in a small saucepan. Drain, then pound well in a mortar. Chop 2 shallots finely; fry them golden brown in a little butter. Drain and add the shallots to the prepared green herbs, and add both to ¼ lb. of creamed butter by degrees, creaming well. Season, and pass through a hair sieve. Use for decorating or for flavouring.

3. *Maître d' Hôtel*. Cream 1 oz. of fresh butter on a plate, with a rounded knife. Add 1 teaspoonful of very finely chopped parsley, a teaspoonful of lemon juice, salt, and a few grains of cayenne. Spread in a flat cake, and set aside until firm. Roll up into tiny balls or cut into shapes. Use mainly for grills.

4. *Shrimp*. Pick ½ pint of shrimps; place the heads and trimmings in a mortar (omit the eyes and back shells), and pound with 2 oz. of butter thoroughly. Work in a little anchovy paste, pepper, and 1 drop of carmine, if desired. Pass through a hair sieve, and use as required.

5. *Tomato*. Sweat a chopped shallot in a little butter, and add ½ gill of tomato purée. Reduce until dry. When quite cold, place it in a mortar, and pound in ¼ lb. of butter by degrees. Pass through a sieve, and use as required.

CELERY, TO CURL

Cleanse white sticks of celery thoroughly, cut them into 2½ in. lengths, and shred finely lengthways. Place in ice-cold water for an hour or longer until they curl.

CREAM LINING

Mix together an equal quantity of cream and liquid cold jelly (either savoury or sweet, according to the nature of the dish); about 2 tablespoonfuls of each is sufficient for a $\frac{3}{4}$ pint mould. When it is quite cold, but still liquid, pour it into a tin mould, previously lined and decorated, and turn the mould round and round on some ice to make an opaque inner lining. When setting, run the surplus to an even layer at the bottom; or if much is left, pour it out of the mould.

CRÈME CHANTILLY

Whip some cream until it is thickening slightly and a trail is left when a little is dropped on the bulk. Add a level teaspoonful of castor sugar, and $\frac{1}{2}$ teaspoonful of vanilla essence to each $\frac{1}{2}$ gill of cream. Continue whisking until the cream hangs on the whisk.

FAGGOT OF HERBS

Take half a dozen parsley stalks of about $1\frac{1}{2}$ in. length, place a piece of bay leaf and a sprig of thyme in the middle of them, and tie round securely with thread.

FINES HERBES

Take equal quantities of parsley, tarragon, and chervil, and chop very finely, separately. Then chop well together, and use as desired.

GHERKIN FANS

Cut thin parallel slices of gherkin for almost its length, and spread out fanwise.

GILDING

This is to brush over with beaten egg—usually previous to heating in the oven, or under the griller, to give a golden brown gloss. Beaten egg so used is often termed "egg wash."

JELLY, TO CHOP

Allow some clear jelly to set quite firmly. Turn it on to a piece of damped greaseproof paper (preferably rubbed with a piece of ice), and chop with a slicing motion, using a sharp-pointed knife, previously damped, or rubbed with ice. Avoid over-chopping the jelly, or chopping before it is quite set. Both of these would cloud it. Use for decorating cold sweets.

MIREPOIX

1 oz. butter; 1 streaky bacon rasher; 2–3 large carrots and turnips; 2 large onions; 2–3 sticks celery; $\frac{1}{2}$–$\frac{3}{4}$ pint stock; a small bouquet garni (see page 281).

Melt the butter and fry the bacon in it to extract the fat. Add the prepared vegetables, cut in thick slices. Cook for 10 minutes without browning, covered with a lid, until the fat is absorbed. Add stock (sufficient to come to the top of the vegetables), the bouquet garni, and boil up. Use for braising.

OIL AND BUTTER FOR FRYING

For shallow fat frying this is a very successful combination of fats. The butter gives the best flavour possible in frying; but owing to its low melting point, burns very easily. Using oil in equal proportion minimizes the risk.

OMELETTE PAN, TO PROVE

Scatter some rough household salt over the bottom of the pan, and warm it through gently. Scour the pan heavily inside with this salt, using a piece of paper. Turn away the salt, and wipe out the pan inside with a soft dry cloth. Place in the pan a piece of lard the size of a walnut, melt and heat it until the fat darkens, tipping the pan so that it is thoroughly heated and greased inside. Pour away this fat, and add butter ready for frying the omelette.

OVEN STEAMING

A method of cooking used largely for boned fish in fillets or small cushions. Butter a Yorkshire pudding tin, or fireproof dish, lay the prepared fish in it, season, and sprinkle with lemon juice. Sprinkle further with water, fish stock, or white wine, and cover with a buttered paper. Cook, without browning, until the fish becomes white, opaque, and curd like. Remove the fish, reduce the liquor, strain it, and add to the sauce which accompanies the fish.

PANADA

A thick binding sauce. Usual proportions: 1 oz. butter or dripping, 1 oz. flour, 1 gill milk or stock.

Make as a white sauce, stirring well. If a specially thick panada is needed, and amount of flour to be used exceeds that of the fat, make it as for Choux Pastry (see page 221).

PASTA (Italian)

Under this heading are ranged all nouille paste mixtures from the thread-like vermicelli to cannelonni, which is a very large tube. Do not wash pasta, and cook it in boiling salted water, keeping the material from sticking to the bottom of the pan by occasional stirring with a metal spoon. An onion, stuck with two cloves, may be added to the water while cooking if desired to give flavour. Buy these pastes from a shop having a quick sale, and use them as fresh as possible. Macaroni takes on an average

20–25 minutes to cook, and longer when stale. When ready, the shape of the tube remains, but it will break quite easily with a fork.

PASTRY CREAM

1 egg, and 1 yolk; 2 oz. castor sugar; 1 oz. flour; flavouring essence; $\frac{1}{2}$ pint milk.

Beat the egg and yolk together, add the sugar, flour, and essence, and cream well together. Heat the milk slightly, stir it on to the mixture, return to the pan, and stir until boiling well. The flour prevents curdling.

PAYSANNE SHAPE

Root vegetables are cut into small barrels of $\frac{3}{4}$ in.–1 in. lengths, then sliced across thinly for use as garnish in soups, etc.

RADISH ROSES

Trim small red radishes, and cut from the tip towards the stem with two cross cuts, but without cutting right through. Drop into ice-cold water for a time, and the pieces will stand open like petals.

PIPING BAG

1. Start with a right-angled triangle of grease-proof paper, made from an exact square cut in half, diagonally (8"—12").

2. Twist corner C round to touch apex A on the inside. Be careful not to crease the paper.

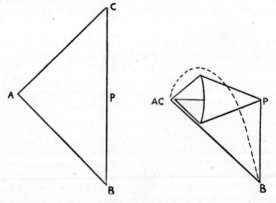

3. Twist corner B over the partly formed bag to touch apex A on the outside. The three corners of the triangle come together

at the apex and the point of the bag is in the centre of the long straight side.

4. Note that the point of the bag is perfectly sharp.

5. Fold down the corners inwards to secure the bag. Cut off point to allow pipe to protrude.

REFRESH

To refresh is to rinse any material in cold water (usually in a colander under a running cold water tap) until quite cold.

RICE, PLAIN BOILED

(About 2 oz. for 4 people.) Wash, blanch, and rinse. Sprinkle the rice into a pan of boiling salted water, containing 1 teaspoonful of white malt vinegar or 1 dessertspoonful of lemon juice to whiten. Boil until tender—about 10 minutes. Strain and rinse under a running hot water tap. Spread on a large dish, in a warm place, frequently teasling it with a fork to separate the grains and lighten them.

ROYALE

A steamed savoury custard, trimmed and cut into slices, then in fancy shapes when cold. Proportions: 2 yolks; $\frac{1}{2}$ white; $\frac{1}{2}$ gill white stock or milk; salt and pepper.

SAGE STUFFING

1 teaspoonful powdered sage leaves; $\frac{1}{2}$ lb. onions; 2 oz. breadcrumbs; 1 oz. butter; pepper and salt.

Cut the onions into quarters, and boil 25–30 minutes. Drain well, chop quickly, and add the butter while the onions are warm. Add the sage, pepper, and salt. Mix well, and use for stuffing ducks, geese, pork, etc.

SWEAT

This process is usually applied in the preparation of vegetables for sauces, soups, stews, etc. It implies the cooking of sliced vegetables in a small quantity of fat until the vegetables are softened but not browned.

VEAL STUFFING

3 piled tablespoonfuls fresh breadcrumbs; 1 tablespoonful dripping or finely chopped suet; 2 teaspoonfuls chopped parsley; a suspicion of grated lemon rind; $\frac{1}{2}$ teaspoonful powdered herbs; pepper and salt; beaten egg and milk.

Mix all the dry ingredients, and bind stiffly with the egg and milk. If the stuffing is to be used for forcemeat balls, use beaten eggs only for mixing; or if it is desired crumbly and soft, use milk only for mixing.

HORS D'ŒUVRES

(*Appetizers*)

RECENTLY Hors d'Œuvres have gained favour very much, and are served as a matter of course at luncheons, both formal and homely, and also at dinners and theatre suppers.

Hors d'Œuvres consist of a variety of relishes which will stimulate, but not satisfy, appetite. Hors d'Œuvres are of three kinds—

I. PLAIN. These are frequently the most appreciated and a selection of six varieties is usually served. (These frequently appear on the menu as Hors d'Œuvres Variés.) If the choice is given to such articles as Oysters, Grape-Fruit, etc., only one is served.

II. DRESSED. Usually three varieties are provided and good workmanship appears to great advantage in the preparation of these little dishes.

III. HOT. One variety is served as a rule and is of the nature of a savoury (e.g. Huîtres Mornay).

PREPARATION OF HORS D'ŒUVRES

1. Serve Hors d'Œuvres daintily and with effective garnishing, even when plain, placing them as a rule in a dish divided into compartments, or into separate small dishes arranged on a tray.

2. Serve them in small portions and as they are to create appetite, season them highly and have them piquante in flavour.

3. Hand small pats of butter separately (a small dinner roll will be already in place), serving them in small glass dishes in iced water and garnished with parsley.

SERVING OF HORS D'ŒUVRES

1. Hors d'Œuvres are placed on the table before the beginning of the meal, adding to its effective appearance, and as soon as the guests are seated they are handed to each.

2. In other cases the Hors d'Œuvres may be placed on the plates before the guests enter the dining-room. This is frequently done in the service of grape-fruit, melon, oysters, etc.

3. In many of the best and most popular restaurants and hotels, a variety of Hors d'Œuvres is served while dinner à la carte is being prepared.

18

OYSTERS. Usually served au naturel in their shells. Do not open until at the point of serving them or much of their aroma is lost. Hand chilli vinegar or cut lemon, brown bread and butter and cayenne separately. Oysters are a very popular Hors d'Œuvre when they are in season. They may appear on the menu as "Huîtres au Citron," "Huîtres au Naturel," "Huîtres de Whitstable," etc.

CAVIARE. This is prepared from sturgeon roes and is popular, though it is an acquired taste. Serve plain with very finely chopped shallot and lemon juice, sparingly used.

OLIVES. French and Spanish olives are both used, but the former are considered to have the finer flavour, though the Spanish variety are larger and more fleshy. Olives are allowed to remain on the table until dessert, and gourmets eat one between each course of a well cooked meal. They must appear firm and green. Steep them first in cold water, drain, and dry well.

SAVOURY BUTTERS. Made up into little pats, cubes, or balls and placed on canapés are popular.

SANDWICHES. These should be of diminutive size and wafer thinness, very daintily prepared and cut in fancy shapes.

CANAPÉS. This word is applied to the small "platform" on which many Hors d'Œuvres and Savouries are served. They are cut in small rounds, fingers, squares, and fancy shapes, and may consist of—

(a) Toast cut thinly and buttered while hot to ensure that it will not be hard.

(b) Bread, fried in butter or butter and olive oil until golden coloured.

(c) Cheese pastry cut in shapes and baked.

(d) Small plain biscuits commercially prepared.

(e) Brown bread, cut scant $\frac{1}{4}$ in. thick and spread with savoury butter.

FURTHER MATERIALS USED IN THE PREPARATION OF PLAIN HORS D'ŒUVRES

FISH. Fillets of smoked herrings, anchovy fillets, sardines brisling, lax, tunny fish, prawns, shrimps, etc.

SMOKED MEAT AND SAUSAGE. Ham; tongue; Bologna, liver, Lyons, or Strasbourg sausage may be sliced very thinly and served.

VEGETABLES AND SALADS. Cooked vegetable or potato salads, beetroot, tomatoes, radishes, gherkins, cucumber, etc. Two salads may be served in a variety of six hors d'œuvres.

FRUITS. Grape-fruit, melon, avocado pears, or pineapple, served with sugar, salt, and pepper, and sometimes ground ginger or cinnamon and oil and vinegar.

SUGGESTED VARIETY OF SIX PLAIN HORS D'ŒUVRES

1. Potato Salad.
2. Beetroot Salad.
3. Thin slices of liver sausage, garnished with parsley.
4. Sardines or anchovy fillets, drained from oil, neatly arranged, sprinkled with Vinaigrette dressing (see page 180) and garnished with capers.
5. Hard-boiled eggs coated with Mayonnaise.
6. Olives or gherkins.

A SELECTION OF THREE DRESSED HORS D'ŒUVRES

1. Olives à la Madras.
2. Sardines Piedmontaise.
3. Salade Caprice.

AMANDES SALÉES

¼ lb. Jordan almonds.	Fine salt.
2 tablespoonfuls salad oil.	

1. Blanch and skin the almonds, and rub them well in a cloth.
2. Heat the salad oil in a small frying-pan, and fry the almonds to a delicate biscuit shade.
3. Remove almonds with a metal spoon, and drain partially; while they are still warm and oily, spread them on a paper dredged with salt, and sprinkle the almonds by means of a salt dredger.
4. Lift on to a wire tray gently to remove superfluous salt.
5. Serve in small dishes, which are left on the table throughout the meal.

BONNES-BOUCHES DE SARDINES

1 oz. sardines (¼ tin small brisling).	1 hard-boiled egg. Thin slices brown bread.
1 oz. fresh butter.	Small cress to garnish.

1. Remove the tails and skins from the sardines, and break them up with a fork.
2. Mix them with the butter, and the hard-boiled egg yolk.
3. Pound all well together, and rub through a hair sieve.
4. Spread the bread with the sardine mixture, and scatter a little chopped cress over. Place another slice on top, previously spread with sardine butter, and sprinkle with finely chopped egg white, pressing it on well with the blade of a knife.
5. Cut into small fancy shapes, pipe a little of the remaining butter on top of each.
6. Garnish with small cress.

CANAPÉS VARIÉS

8 slices bread and butter (brown or white).
Savoury butter (see p. 13).

Liquid Aspic jelly (see p. 73).
Sprigs of parsley.

(*a*) 2 thin slices lean ham; Half a red pimento.

(*b*) 2 thin slices smoked salmon (lax); 2 gherkins.

(*c*) 8 fillets anchovy; 1 hard-boiled egg.

(*d*) 2 thin slices cooked tongue; Half a red pimento.

1. (*a*) Arrange the ham neatly on two of the slices of bread and butter. Cut in diamond or finger shapes. Lay a thin strip of pimento down the middle, and pipe savoury butter finely on the edges.

(*b*) Arrange thin slices of smoked salmon on two more slices of bread and butter, and cut in trefoils or rounds. Place a slice of gherkin in the centre, and surround with a piping of savoury butter.

(*c*) Arrange the fillets of anchovy side by side on two slices of bread and butter, and cut into spade shapes or crescents. Cover one half slantways with chopped white, and the other with sieved yolk of egg, pressing it well on to the fish. Pipe savoury butter at the edges.

(*d*) Arrange slices of tongue on the remaining two slices of bread and butter. Cut out heart-shaped or oval, put a round of pimento in the middle, and pipe the edges with savoury butter.

2. In all, cut out sixteen Canapés. Baste with liquid aspic to keep them moist.

3. Dish on a plain paper on a round dish (preferably silver), with tiny sprigs of parsley between.

Note. If the Canapés are cut into diamonds, spades, clubs, and hearts, they are suitable to serve at a little Bridge Dinner Party, or may be served as "snacks" for Bridge Party refreshments.

FILETS DE HARENG PORTUGAISE

1 large herring.
1 teaspoonful olive oil.
2 shallots.
2 tomatoes.

½ gill white wine vinegar.
½ pint fish stock.
½ gill tomato purée.

1. Remove the head, and fillet the fish. Place the fish on a board, and cut each fillet into about three pieces.

2. Put the olive oil in the bottom of a small saucepan, and add the shallots chopped small. Concass the tomatoes, and add them with the vinegar, fish stock, and purée.

3. Arrange the fish in the pan, season with salt and pepper, cover the fish with a round of greaseproof paper, cut to fit the saucepan.

4. Boil up, and allow to simmer for 12–15 minutes.

5. Arrange the fish on a fireproof dish, pouring the sauce over. Serve cold.

FRUIT COCKTAILS

1 grape-fruit, or a large orange.
1 piling tablespoonful chopped pineapple.
1 banana.
1 pear.
¾ gill maraschino cherries.
1 tablespoonful castor sugar.
1 small teaspoonful lemon juice.

1 tablespoonful sherry, or maraschino, optional.
1 teaspoonful slightly beaten egg white.
4 marshmallows.
1 teaspoonful finely chopped pistachios.

1. Cut the fruits into small pieces, and marinade with the sugar, lemon juice, and the sherry, or maraschino, if used.

2. Brush each edge of the marshmallows with slightly beaten egg white, and dip into the pistachios.

3. Arrange the fruit in a neat pattern in 4 coupé glasses, pour over any liquid from marinading, and put a marshmallow in the centre of each.

4. Stand each coupe glass on a tiny lace dessert paper on a small plate.

HORS D'ŒUVRES À LA RUSSE

Hors d'œuvres à la Russe are always mounted on toast Canapés, are piped with savoury butter, and glazed with liquid aspic. Caviare usually finds place, and the hors d'œuvres are dished flat on a large silver dish, filled in with sprigs of parsley.

CANAPÉS AUX SARDINES

1 slice buttered toast.
¼ tin small sardines.

2 teaspoonfuls butter.
Seasoning.

Liquid aspic.

1. Butter the toast while hot. Lay the drained skinned sardines on top, and cut out the toast exactly to fit each fish.

2. Cream the butter, seasoning it highly; put it into a paper cornet, cut off the extreme tip, and pipe a fine cable down the middle of each fish.

3. When the butter is quite firm, coat with the liquid cold aspic.

Note. Two fillets of anchovies, laid side by side, may take the place of the sardine.

CANAPÉS AUX OEUFS

1 slice buttered toast. | Green butter (see p. 13).
1 hard-boiled egg. | Liquid aspic.

1. Prepare the toast as above, and cut it in rounds, exactly to fit a slice of hard-boiled egg laid on each piece.
2. Pipe the green butter around the edge, and when set baste with cold liquid aspic.

CANAPÉS SAUMON FUMÉ

¼ tin smoked salmon fillets. | 1 slice toast.
1 oz. butter. | Tomato butter (see p. 13).

Cold liquid aspic.

1. Trim the fillets, cut them in small pieces, and pound the trimmings with the butter. Pass through a hair sieve, and butter a slice of hot toast with this.
2. Cut small squares or crescents from the toast, and arrange the fillets on these slightly overlapping.
3. Pipe the edges of the toast shapes with tomato butter, and baste with the aspic when the butter is set.

CANAPÉS AU CAVIARE

1 slice buttered toast. | 1 tablespoonful whipped cream.
1 small terrine of Russian | Lemon juice.
caviare. | Cold liquid aspic.
A few grains of cayenne. |

1. Prepare the toast, cut it in rounds of 1½ in. diameter, and butter them well.
2. When toast is cold, spread the caviare thickly on one side, and baste with the aspic.
3. On top pipe a little whipped cream, seasoned with cayenne, and slightly acidulated with lemon juice.

Note. If hot Canapés are required, put them, after spreading with caviare, in a hot oven for 2–3 minutes, and put a slice of heated stoned olive on each. The aspic is omitted in this case.

HORS D'ŒUVRES VARIÉS

BEETROOT SALAD

1 small beetroot. | 1 teaspoonful finely chopped
Vinaigrette dressing. | parsley.
1 teaspoonful finely chopped | Seasoning.
onion. |

1. Skin the beetroot and cut in thin slices; cut a fancy shape from each.

2. Chop the trimmings, mix them with the vinaigrette, and make into a mound in the hors d'œuvre dish.

3. Arrange fancifully cut pieces of beetroot over this, and decorate on top with the chopped onion and chopped parsley.

POTATO SALAD

4 new potatoes.	Seasoning.
1 tablespoonful vinaigrette.	1 pickled walnut.
½ gill mayonnaise.	

1. Cook the potatoes. While they are still hot, cut them in dice, and marinade with the vinaigrette dressing.

2. Season, arrange in a mound in the dish, and coat with thick mayonnaise.

3. Lay slices of pickled walnut on top.

EGG MAYONNAISE

2 hard-boiled eggs.	½ gill of mayonnaise.
2–3 leaves of lettuce.	Coralline pepper.

1. Slice the hard-boiled eggs in quarters lengthways, and arrange them in the dish on a little finely shredded lettuce.

2. Coat with the mayonnaise, and decorate with the coralline pepper.

SARDINES AU NATUREL

½ tin small sardines or brisling.	2 teaspoonfuls capers.
Vinaigrette dressing.	

Drain the small sardines or the brisling from their oil, and arrange neatly in the dish; garnish with capers.

VEGETABLE MACÉDOINE

2 heaped tablespoonfuls macé-doine of vegetables.	Mock mayonnaise salad dressing.
Seasoning.	½ a hard-boiled egg.

1. Prepare the macédoine, and leave to become quite cold, draining well.

2. Season, and mix with sufficient salad dressing to bind.

3. Make a small mound in the middle of the hors d'œuvre dish, sprinkle with the sieved egg yolk, and arrange chopped white at the edge separately.

PRAWN SALAD

6–12 large prawns.	Mustard dressing.
Small cress, or fine shreds of lettuce.	

1. Prepare the prawns, reserving some of the heads for garnish.
2. Arrange them neatly in the dish, coat with the dressing, and garnish with upstanding prawn heads, and small cress or lettuce shreds.

HUÎTRES MORNAY

(Hot hors d'œuvre)

1 gill white sauce.	Salt and pepper.
1 oz. grated parmesan and Cheddar cheeses together.	½ oz. butter.
Cayenne.	Sprigs parsley.
½ gill cream.	6 oysters in deep shells.

1. Prepare the Mornay sauce (see page 248).
2. Stand the oyster shells on a baking tin, holding them level with a little freezing-salt.
3. Place a little Mornay sauce in the deep shells, tear the beards off the oysters, and place an oyster in each shell. Coat with sauce.
4. Sprinkle with the grated cheese and oiled butter, and bake in the oven about 5 minutes. Place under a griller to glaze.
5. Dish on a paper on a round dish, with sprigs of parsley in the centre.

OLIVES À LA MADRAS

8 Spanish olives.	8 tiny rounds brown bread and butter.
8 strips anchovy fillets.	Small cress.

Savoury Butter—

2 teaspoonfuls butter.	1 hard-boiled yolk of egg.
1 small teaspoonful chutney.	Salt, pepper, cayenne.
1 teaspoonful anchovy paste.	

1. Make the savoury butter. Pound the butter, chutney, paste, and egg yolk together, seasoning highly. Rub the mixture through a hair sieve.
2. Stone the olives, cut strips of anchovy to fit round the base of each, and cut a round of thin brown bread and butter just large enough to support each olive.
3. Spread a little of the savoury butter on the round, and put the remainder in a small paper cornet, fitted with a coarse rosette icing pipe.

4. Fill the olives with the butter, put an olive on each round of the bread and butter, and curl a piece of anchovy around the base.

5. Pipe a tiny rosette of butter on top of each olive, and add an upstanding leaf of small cress.

6. Arrange the olives in an hors d'œuvre dish, garnish with the small cress, and serve.

Note. Olives à la Madras may be served as a Savoury, if preferred. In this case mount each on a croûton of baked cheese pastry.

PAMPLEMOUSSE AU GINGEMBRE
(Grape-fruit with Ginger)

2 large choice grape-fruit.	1 tablespoonful of chopped preserved ginger.
Sherry.	
A suspicion of ground ginger.	4 glacé cherries.

1. Prepare the grape-fruit in small sections, and divide it among 4 grape-fruit glasses or coupés.

2. Sprinkle the fruit with the sherry, and add a little grated nutmeg and ground ginger.

3. Sprinkle a little coarsely chopped preserved ginger over each, and place a glacé cherry, soaked in sherry, upstanding on top.

Note. Sugar may be dredged between each layer of fruit, if preferred.

SALADE CAPRICE

1 tomato.	Vinaigrette dressing (see p. 180).
1 stick white celery.	
1 cold cooked potato.	Chopped parsley.
1 dessert apple.	Pimento.
2–3 Spanish olives.	

1. Concass the tomato, and cut the celery, potato, and apple in julienne strips.

2. Marinade with the vinaigrette dressing, adding a little extra salt and pepper, and pile the mixture in a mound in an hors d'œuvre dish.

3. Remove the stones from the olives with a column cutter, and slice the fruit across into rings.

4. Decorate with these rings round the base of the mound, filling the centre with a tiny round of pimento.

5. Decorate the top with strips of the pimento, and sprinkle with the chopped parsley.

POTAGES

(*Soups*)

THE Soup Course is important in the Menu. A well seasoned soup, of good flavour and quality, is very appetizing; it starts the flow of the digestive juices and generates a feeling of well-being and of interest in the meal. Soup is indispensable in the correct dinner menu, but it may be omitted from a luncheon menu if desired.

RULES FOR SELECTING AND SERVING THE SOUP

The tendency being at present to shorten the meal, only one soup is served at small private dinner parties as a general rule.

2. If two soups are served, one is clear and the other thick, the former appearing first on the menu.

3. Whether the soup chosen is clear or thick depends on personal preference and the composition of the remainder of the menu. If there are solid dishes to follow, a clear soup is better, as it is less satisfying and will not impair appetite.

4. In choosing the soup, make sure that the chief ingredients do not consist of any that will be repeated in the menu in another course. It would be very incorrect to serve an artichoke purée and follow it later in the menu with a vegetable entremet consisting of artichokes; and Bisque de Homard should not, for example, be followed by Côtelettes de Homard.

5. Allow 1 gill of finished soup per person and an added gill or two for ease in serving.

6. Consider the season of the year when choosing the soup. Rich heavy soups are suitable only for winter, and in summer time clear soups, iced soups, and those of a light vegetable variety or prepared from fruit are most suitable.

7. In choosing the soup take its colour into consideration. A sequence of dishes of similar colour is to be avoided, and also the flavour of the soup should be distinctive from neighbouring dishes.

8. Serve the correct accompaniments. Dice of fried bread are always handed separately with a purée which has no garnish, unless it is composed of vegetables, when Cheese Straws may be served. Grated Parmesan Cheese may be handed with Consommés, and plain boiled rice must always accompany Mulligatawny Soup. Grisini may be handed with soup if desired.

VARIETIES OF SOUP

I. THIN SOUPS

(*a*) *Broths and Bouillons, which are unclarified.* Broth is the liquor in which meat and vegetables are cooked, and from which the nourishing properties are extracted by gentle simmering. Mutton, veal, and chicken are used for making broth, while beef broth is always known as Bouillon.

These broths are usually served (except for invalids) with a garnish of rice or pearl barley, and vegetables cut into dice or fancy shapes, and are specially suitable to serve at luncheons.

(*b*) *Consommés, which are the highest type of cleared soups.* Aim to produce a soup which is as clear and brilliant as possible.

In making consommés—

1. Have all utensils and materials perfectly free from grease.

2. Use egg whites of good quality for clearing (but the use of too much egg white impoverishes flavour).

3. Use good stock which is free from fat and sediment, and add finely shredded lean beef to improve flavour and help in clearing the soup.

4. Clear the stock by whisking it with the egg whites and shells and shredded beef. The albumen rises to the surface carrying impurities with it; and the crushed egg shell, together with the straining cloth, acts as a filter.

5. Avoid overcooking the garnish, and rinse it well before addition to the soup, as neglect of either of these points causes cloudiness.

II. PURÉES

These may be composed of meat, game, poultry, fish, vegetables, or pulse. The solid ingredients are passed through a sieve and retained to form a thickened whole. To prevent the separation of these ingredients a small quantity of some starchy matter is usually added as a liaison.

III. CREAM SOUPS AND THICKENED SOUPS OR POTAGES LIÉS

(*a*) Cream soups have the following characteristics—

1. Good veal or chicken stock is used in preparing them.

2. In some cases, some of the ingredients are retained in the form of a purée and are also used as the garnish.

3. Some farinaceous product may be added.

4. The liaison of cream and eggs is very usual, though some cream soups may be enriched with cream only.

(*b*) Thickened soups may be achieved by using the following thickenings—

1. A farinaceous product, such as flour, cornflour, fécule

tapioca, etc. The average proportion is ½ oz. or 2 teaspoonfuls to one pint.

2. A roux of butter and flour. ½ oz. of each ingredient thickens 1 pint of stock.

3. A liaison of cream and egg yolks.

IV. BISQUES

These soups are prepared from shellfish, fish stock, and the chosen thickening. They are not so thick as a cream soup or purée and are usually highly seasoned.

Bisques are suitable to serve in spring and summer, when shellfish are at their best.

CONSOMMÉ

A large number of consommés are made from this foundation, taking their distinguishing name from the garnish served in them.

½–¾ lb. minced lean beef.	A little salt.
2 whites of egg.	½ teaspoonful meat extract.
1 quart bone stock.	½ gill sherry.

1. Put the minced meat, freed from fat, skin, and sinews, into a saucepan.

2. Half whisk the whites and add with the salt. Mix thoroughly, adding the meat extract.

3. Add the cold stock gradually, stirring with a wooden spoon. Place saucepan over heat.

4. Whisk thoroughly until almost at boiling point. Boil up well.

5. Reduce the heat and simmer gently for 1 hour, when the meat will set together in a clot and sink to the bottom.

6. Strain carefully through a scalded jelly cloth and add the sherry.

Note. Consommé should be the clear deep amber colour of old sherry. Caramel ("Black Jack") may be used to colour it if preferred, in place of meat extract.

SIMPLE GARNISHES FOR CONSOMMÉ

When reckoning the amount of Consommé required, allowance must be made for evaporation during the time of simmering. A quart of stock would yield about 1½ pints of finished Consommé, which would be sufficient for four people.

CONSOMMÉ BRUNOISE

Prepare 1 level tablespoonful each of tiny dice of carrot, turnip, celery, and leek. Cook separately in small saucepans; rinse in hot water, place at the bottom of a hot tureen, and pour the soup over.

CONSOMMÉ AUX PETITS POIS

Cook 2–3 tablespoonfuls green peas with a little mint until tender but not broken. Rinse, place them at the bottom of a hot tureen, and pour the soup over.

CONSOMMÉ AUX POINTES D'ASPERGES

Use 2–3 tablespoonfuls cooked asparagus tips and proceed as above.

CONSOMMÉ ROYALE

Prepare a Royale (Steamed Custard, see page 16). When cold cut into slices, then in fancy shapes. Put these into a hot tureen and pour the hot soup over, just before serving.

CONSOMMÉ AU SAGOU

Boil up the Consommé. Shake $\frac{1}{2}$–$\frac{3}{4}$ oz. fine sago into it while stirring; stir and cook gently until the sago is quite clear. Pour into a hot tureen.

CONSOMMÉ AU TAPIOCA

As for Consommé au Sagou, using tapioca groult.

CONSOMMÉ AU VERMICELLE

Cook a scant $\frac{1}{2}$ oz. Vermicelli in stock until tender. Rinse well in hot water, place it in a hot tureen, and pour the soup over. Spaghetti may be used similarly; or a scant $\frac{1}{2}$ gill of Italian paste or rings of Macaroni may be used.

CONSOMMÉ CÉLESTINE

1$\frac{1}{2}$ pints consommé.

Savoury Pancakes—
$\frac{1}{2}$ oz. flour.
Small teaspoonful oiled butter.
$\frac{1}{2}$ egg.
$\frac{1}{4}$ gill milk.

1 teaspoonful grated Parmesan cheese.
$\frac{1}{2}$ teaspoonful finely chopped parsley.
Seasoning.

1. Make a batter with the flour, butter, egg, and milk.
2. Beat well, and add the cheese, parsley, and seasoning.
3. Make the batter into small thin pancakes, pressing them well with kitchen paper to remove all fat.
4. Roll up very firmly, as for swiss roll, and cut in fine shreds.
5. Put the shreds into a hot tureen, and pour the soup over gently.

CONSOMMÉ DOUBLE EN GELÉE FRAPPÉ

1 pint white stock made from knuckle of veal.	½ teaspoonful meat extract.
1 pint brown stock made from shin of beef.	1 tablespoonful sherry.
	Shell and white of one egg.
4 oz. lean shredded beef.	Pluche of chervil.
	Small piece gold leaf.

1. Remove all fat from the stock, add the shredded beef and leave to soak for ½ hour.

2. Add the washed crushed shell of egg, slightly whisked white, and meat extract. Whisk over steady heat until boiling point is almost reached.

3. Remove whisk, and boil up well. Cover the saucepan and leave at the side of the stove to infuse for ½ hour.

4. Strain carefully through a scalded cloth, adding the sherry.

5. Put the consommé into glass coupes and leave 12 hours to set, floating a tiny piece of gold leaf and chervil leaf on top.

6. Pack round with ice for 2 hours before serving.

7. To serve, stand each glass on a paper doily on a small plate with a spoon at the side.

Note. If the stock has been correctly made there should be sufficient natural gelatine in it to enable the soup to set.

CONSOMMÉ DE GIBIER

1½ pints consommé.	1 tablespoonful small balls of cooked carrot and turnip.
2–3 oz. cooked breast of game.	
1 tablespoonful cooked peas.	

1. Add the carcass of the game and the cleansed giblets to the stock to be used for making the consommé.

2. Clear the soup in the usual way.

3. Remove skin from the cooked game and cut it into small even-sized dice.

4. Add these to the soup and simmer for a minute or two.

5. Cook, strain, and rinse the peas and balls of carrot and turnip in hot water. Place them in a hot tureen.

6. Pour the consommé over.

CONSOMMÉ À LA JULIENNE

1½ pints consommé.

Carrot
Turnip
Leek   } 4½ oz. together.
Celery

A few leaves chervil.

1. Cut the vegetables into shreds $1\frac{1}{2}$ in. to 2 in. long (cabbage and lettuce may be added as well if desired).

2. Blanch these (with the exception of the celery), strain, and return to saucepan with a pinch of salt and pepper and $\frac{1}{2}$ oz. butter.

3. Cover with a buttered paper and lid. Place in the bottom of a moderate oven or on the lowest jet of gas until tender.

4. Remove and add a little consommé. Boil up, and remove all fat scrupulously.

5. Add all to the remainder of the consommé, together with a few points of chervil.

CONSOMMÉ MADRILÈNE

$1\frac{1}{2}$ pints Consommé.
1 large tomato.
1 teaspoonful tomato conserve.
Small nut of butter.

Fine shreds of nouilles (see p. 220).
Pluche of chervil.

1. Prepare 1 quart of stock and clear it for consommé (see page 29, points 1–5).

2. Concass the tomato and put it in a small saucepan with the conserve and butter. Reduce until the mixture leaves the sides of the pan.

3. Add it carefully at the side of the stock and leave to simmer 10–15 minutes.

4. Strain the soup in the usual way and reheat, adding sherry.

5. Prepare and cook the shreds of nouille paste. Rinse well and place in a hot tureen with the points of chervil.

6. Pour on the heated soup, which should be of clear tomato colour.

CONSOMMÉ MAIGRE

2 oz. carrot.
2 oz. leek.
2 oz. cabbage.
2 oz. onion.
$1\frac{1}{2}$ oz. turnip.
$\frac{1}{2}$ oz. celery.
Salt.

Pepper.
1 oz. butter.
1 quart water.
Small bouquet garni.
1 oz. seed tapioca.
Yeast extract.

1. Slice the vegetables thinly, blanch, and refresh with cold water.

2. Return to pan with salt, pepper, and butter, and sweat until tender over a glimmer of gas, covered with a buttered paper and lid.

3. Remove coverings, increase heat and allow vegetables to glaze to golden brown.

4. Cover with the water. Boil up, skim, and add the bouquet garni.

5. Simmer steadily for 1 hour. Add yeast extract. Correct seasoning and colour.

6. Strain the soup. Boil up, shake in tapioca, and cook until it is clear. Serve in a hot tureen.

CONSOMMÉ PROFITEROLES

1½ pints consommé.
Garnish—
   1 dessertspoonful choux pastry (unsweetened).

Few grains cayenne and salt.
1 teaspoonful Parmesan cheese.

1. Beat the choux pastry well, add the cheese and seasoning, and place it in a forcing bag fitted with a small plain forcing tube.

2. Pipe tiny pea-shaped pieces on to a greased baking sheet and bake until crisp in a moderate oven.

3. Place these in a hot tureen, pour the soup over, and serve at once before the garnish is soddened.

CONSOMMÉ DE TOMATES À LA ROYALE

(Clear Soup, with Savoury Custard Garnish)

6 oz. raw lean beef.
¼ teaspoonful salt.
A sprig of thyme.
A small bayleaf.
2 whites of egg.
1½ pints stock from bones.
½ tablespoonful French wine vinegar.

The green part of a small leek or sprouting onion.
A piece of carrot.
¼ lb. tomatoes.
¼ gill sherry.
White Royale garnish.
½ teaspoonful peppercorns.

1. Shred the beef very finely, and put it into a saucepan with the salt, herbs, peppercorns, and whisked white of egg. Mix well.

2. Add the stock, vinegar, vegetables, and the tomatoes cut in quarters, and whisk very thoroughly until boiling point is almost reached. Boil up, and allow to simmer very gently for 1 hour.

3. Prepare the garnish of steamed savoury custard (see page 16).

4. Strain the soup carefully through a scalded jelly cloth, adding the sherry while straining, and reheat.

5. Cut the steamed custard into thin slices, then rounds of the size of a sixpence, and put these in the bottom of a hot soup tureen.

6. Pour the soup over the garnish, and serve.

CONSOMMÉ VERT–PRÉ

1½ pints Consommé.
⅓ oz. tapioca groult.
1 heaped tablespoonful cooked green peas.

1 heaped tablespoonful cooked asparagus tips.

1. Prepare the consommé, and heat it to boiling point.
2. Shake in the tapioca, and cook while stirring until it is quite clear.
3. Cook the garnish and rinse well. Place it in the bottom of a hot tureen, pour the soup over, and serve.

THICKENED SOUPS

BISQUE DE HOMARD

Half a lobster. 1½ oz. butter.
¼ gill sherry. 1 oz. flour.
1 pint fish stock.
A piece each of carrot, turnip, and onion.
A small piece of mace.

Half a dozen peppercorns.
Salt.
1 teaspoonful anchovy essence.
A few grains of cayenne.
A few drops of lemon juice.
Carmine. ¼ gill cream.

1. Divide the lobster down the back, in order to take half of it. Remove the flesh, set aside some of the best pieces for garnish, and cut up the remainder quite small.
2. Remove the eye, and wash the shell, pounding the latter well with the butter.
3. Put the pounded shell and butter into a saucepan, with the pieces of flesh, allow the butter to melt, add the sherry, and then the flour. Mix well, and cook for a few minutes.
4. Add the stock, and stir until boiling; add the prepared vegetables, mace, peppercorns, and salt.
5. Simmer for ¾ hour, stirring occasionally.
6. Allow the soup to drip through a hair sieve, occasionally stirring it lightly.
7. Reheat; add the anchovy essence, cayenne, lemon juice, and carmine to bring up the colour.
8. Add the pieces of lobster and the cream, reheat thoroughly without boiling, and serve in a hot tureen.

BISQUE AUX HUÎTRES

1 doz. oysters.
1 shallot.
Slice of onion.
½ oz. butter.
Pinch curry powder.

1 dessertspoonful cornflour.
1 pint fish stock.
1 egg yolk } Liaison.
½ gill cream }
Salt, pepper, and nutmeg.

1. Beard half the oysters and reserve them for garnish. Pound the remainder in a mortar, with all of the beards, to a smooth paste, and rub through a fine wire sieve.

2. Sauté the chopped shallot and onion, without colouring, in the butter.

3. Add the mixed curry powder and cornflour, blend over gentle heat, then add the oyster purée and cook for a minute or two further.

4. Moisten with the liquor from the oysters and stock. Stir until boiling and simmer 20 min. Season with salt, pepper, and nutmeg.

5. Prepare liaison and blend with the soup, cooking carefully until thickened.

6. Wring the soup through a tammy cloth and return to pan; add the oysters cut in quarters, correct the seasoning, and reheat.

7. Serve in a warm tureen.

CRÈME DE CONCOMBRE

1 pint white stock.
1 small cucumber.
1 teaspoonful chopped shallot.
1 oz. butter.
$\frac{3}{4}$ oz. flour.

Salt and pepper.
Liquid green colouring.
Liaison: 2 yolks, $\frac{1}{2}$ gill milk, $\frac{1}{2}$ gill cream.
Croûtes of fried bread.

1. Boil up the strained stock, and add the cucumber, peeled and cut in $\frac{1}{2}$ in. slices, and the chopped shallot.

2. Simmer gently until the cucumber is soft (15–20 minutes) and rub through a hair sieve.

3. Rinse out the saucepan. Blend the butter and flour; add the sieved cucumber and stock. Stir until boiling, and simmer for 5 minutes.

4. Cool somewhat, add the liaison, and cook until the soup has thickened.

5. Colour delicately, correct the seasoning, and serve, handing the croûtes separately.

CRÈME DUBARRY

1 pint béchamel sauce (p. 244).
1 small cauliflower.
1 oz. leek (white part).
1 oz. onion.
1 oz. butter.
Veal or chicken stock, as required.

$\frac{1}{2}$ gill cream.
Garnish—
Cauliflower buds.
$\frac{1}{2}$ oz. butter.

1. Make the béchamel sauce.

2. Prepare the cauliflower; remove the sprigs, wash thoroughly, and put small pieces aside for the garnish.

3. Blanch the sprigs of cauliflower, and shred the leek and onion. Sweat the two latter in 1 oz. of butter until tender. Place with the cauliflower sprigs, and cover with a piece of buttered greaseproof paper. Cook until tender on a pin jet of gas, or in the oven.

4. Pass through a fine wire sieve, and add to the prepared béchamel sauce. Add a little stock, if necessary to make the soup of creamy consistency.

5. Boil up, and pass the soup through a hair sieve, or tammy it.

6. Reheat the soup, and garnish with the cauliflower buds, which have been prepared as follows—

Blanch, return them to the pan, and add the butter. Cover with a buttered paper, and cook on a pin jet of gas until tender.

POTAGE D'AMANDES

1½ oz. almonds.
A stick of celery, or ½ teaspoonful celery seeds.
½ a small onion.
½ pint milk.
¾ oz. butter.
¾ oz. flour.

¾ pint white stock.
Seasoning.
1 yolk of egg.
1 tablespoonful cream.
1 drop almond essence.
Croûtons of fried bread.

1. Blanch and pound the almonds, with a few drops of cold water to prevent oiling.

2. Cut up the celery and onion, and place with the almonds and milk in a small saucepan. Simmer gently for ½ hour.

3. Strain, pressing the almonds well to extract their flavour.

4. Blend the butter and flour. Add the white stock and stir until boiling. Simmer for 10 minutes, and correct the seasoning.

5. Add the almond milk, and bring just to boil.

6. Cool somewhat. Add the liaison of yolk and cream, and cook carefully until thickened. Add the one drop of almond essence, and stir in well.

7. Serve in a warm tureen, with croûtons of fried bread handed separately.

POTAGE CHANTILLY

½ pint lentils.
1 small carrot (2 oz.).
1 small onion (2 oz.).
1 clove.
A small bouquet garni.
1 egg yolk
A small nut of butter } Liaison.
2 tablespoonfuls cream

Salt, pepper, nutmeg, and cayenne.
Veal or chicken stock, as necessary.
Croûtons of fried bread.

1. Wash the lentils, put them into a saucepan well covered with water. Boil up, and skim. Add the carrot, onion stuck with the clove, and the bouquet garni.

2. Simmer steadily for about 1 hour, until the lentils are tender.

3. Remove the vegetables, and press the lentils through a hair sieve.

4. Return lentils to pan, adding the stock to make the purée of creamy consistency, boil, and skim for 15 minutes. Correct the seasoning.

5. Prepare the liaison in a basin, pour some of the hot soup on to it, and return all to rewarm.

6. Serve in a hot tureen, handing croûtes separately.

POTAGE À LA CHASSEUR

1 small game bird.	½ oz. flour.
Mirepoix—	1 oz. pearl barley.
A scant oz. of butter.	½ gill claret.
A rasher of streaky bacon.	1½ pints brown stock.
A sliced carrot, turnip, and	1 leek.
onion.	Garnish—
A small faggot of herbs.	Dice of cooked game.
1 oz. raw ham.	Shreds of mushrooms.

1. Truss the bird, and place it on the mirepoix on a tin, using half of the butter.

2. Roast until the bird is about three parts cooked.

3. Remove the fillets from the breast, and reserve for garnish.

4. Cut the carcass into small pieces, and fry with the mirepoix, adding the remainder of the butter, and the raw ham cut small.

5. Add the flour, and roast slowly until biscuit colour. Add the blanched barley, and cook all well together.

6. Moisten with the wine; add the stock and the leek (cleansed and sliced).

7. Stir until boiling, skim well, and simmer for 1½ hours.

8. Tammy the soup. Return to the pan, add the diced game, and simmer gently until quite cooked. Add the cooked mushrooms, and reheat. Correct the seasoning, and serve.

POTAGE PARMENTIER

2–3 leeks.	½ gill milk.
1½ oz. butter.	Seasoning.
1 lb. potatoes.	Powdered parsley.
1 pint white stock or water.	Croûtons of fried bread.
½ gill cream.	

1. Use the white part only of the leeks, cleanse thoroughly drain, and cut into pieces.

2. Melt half of the butter and sauté the pieces of leek in it for 7–8 minutes, without colouring.

3. Add the thickly sliced potatoes, liquid, and salt.

4. Cook about ½ hour, until the vegetables are quite soft. Press through a wire sieve.

5. Return all to the rinsed pan, correct the seasoning, and stir until boiling.

6. Put the remainder of the butter, the milk, and the cream at the bottom of a hot tureen.

7. Pour the boiling soup into it, stirring gently meanwhile.

8. Sprinkle with powdered parsley, and hand small dice of fried bread separately.

POTAGE ST. GERMAIN

1 lb. green peas.
1 small onion.
Scant 1 oz. butter.
A sprig of mint.
A sprig of parsley.
1 pint white stock.

Salt, and 6 white peppercorns.
1 teaspoonful flour.
½ gill milk.
½ gill cream.
Croûtes of fried bread.

1. Shell the peas and rinse them in cold water. Wash about a quarter of the best-coloured pods.

2. Sauté the peas and sliced onion in the butter, add the pods, mint and parsley, stock, salt, and peppercorns.

3. Simmer for about 1 hour, until the peas are tender.

4. Remove the mint, parsley, and onion, and rub the soup through a hair sieve.

5. Return it to the rinsed pan. Add the flour mixed smoothly with the milk. Boil well, and correct the seasoning.

6. Cool somewhat, add the cream, and rewarm without boiling. Pour into a hot tureen, and hand the croûtes separately.

POTAGE VELOUTÉ AGNES-SORELL

1½ oz. butter.
¾ oz. flour.
¾ oz. ground rice.
2 pints chicken stock.
Liaison—
    2 yolks.

½ gill cream.
Garnish—
    1 doz. preserved champignons.
    2 oz. cooked chicken and
        tongue.

1. Blend the butter with the flour and ground rice; add the stock. Stir until boiling, and simmer for ½ hour, skimming well.

2. Allow to cool, add the liaison, and cook carefully.

3. Shred the champignons into julienne (lengthways through cup and stem), and also the chicken and tongue.

4. Add the garnish to the soup, and continue cooking until the garnish will suspend in it.

5. Pour into a warm tureen and serve.

PURÉE D'ÉPINARDS

1 lb. spinach.	1 teaspoonful finely chopped shallot.
Salt.	
½ oz. butter.	¼ pint milk.
½ oz. flour.	Pepper and nutmeg.
¾ pint stock.	½ gill cream.
	Croûtons of fried bread.

1. Pick over, stalk, and wash the spinach in several waters. Put it wet into the saucepan, adding a little salt.

2. Boil gently until tender, adding a spoonful or two of water if it should be necessary. Drain well.

3. Blend the butter and flour; add the stock, and stir until boiling. Add the prepared spinach and chopped shallot.

4. Simmer gently for 20 minutes. Press through a fine hair sieve, or wring through a tammy cloth.

5. Return the soup to the saucepan. Add the milk to make it of creamy consistency.

6. Add the pepper, a suspicion of nutmeg, and the cream. Reheat, without boiling.

7. Serve in a hot tureen, handing the croûtons of bread separately.

PURÉE DE MARRONS

½ lb. chestnuts.	A few drops of carmine or browning.
1¼ pints white stock.	
2 oz. butter.	Seasoning.
½ a small onion.	2 tablespoonfuls cream.
1 tablespoonful flour.	Croûtons of fried bread.
2-3 sticks celery, or seeds.	

1. Prepare the chestnuts by making a small cut in each end of each nut. Drop the nuts into boiling water for 10 minutes. Remove the outer and inner skins.

2. Cook the chestnuts in a small saucepan, with half of the butter and sufficient stock to cover, for about ¾-1 hour.

3. When soft, pass the chestnuts through a hair or a fine wire sieve.

4. Melt the remaining butter in a saucepan and fry the onion without colouring. Add the flour and blend.

5. Add stock and stir until boiling. Add the purée, the sliced celery, or a teaspoonful of celery seeds tied in muslin, and the seasoning.

6. Simmer for 20 minutes; correct the seasoning, and colour.

7. Pass the boiling soup through a strainer on to the cream placed in a hot tureen.

8. Stir up, and serve with the croûtes of bread handed separately.

VELOUTÉ DE VOLAILLE

1 pint chicken stock.	Seasoning.
1 oz. cream of rice.	$\frac{1}{2}$ gill cream.
$\frac{1}{4}$ pint milk.	Cooked chicken to garnish.

1. Place the strained chicken stock in a saucepan, and boil up.

2. Mix the cream of rice smoothly with the milk, and thicken the stock with this.

3. Season, and simmer slowly for 1 hour, skimming if necessary.

4. Cut a piece of the cooked chicken into julienne strips, using sufficient to fill a gill measure loosely.

5. Pass the soup through a tammy strainer, or wring through a tammy cloth. Correct the seasoning and consistency.

6. Finish with the cream. Add the garnish and serve in a hot tureen, when it has been warmed through without boiling.

Note. The soup should be of the colour and consistency of good cream.

BROTHS AND BOUILLONS
BOUILLON EN TASSES

1$\frac{1}{2}$ pints strong beef stock.	Nutmeg, salt, and pepper.
A few drops caramel or a little meat extract.	Chopped parsley.

1. Prepare the stock, of good vegetable flavour and well skimmed. Remove every trace of fat.

2. Improve the colour with a little caramel or meat extract, and correct the seasoning.

3. Pour into heated soup cups, sprinkle a little chopped parsley on top, and serve.

Note. A well-beaten egg yolk may be placed at the bottom of each cup if it is liked, before the soup is poured in, or the soup may be flavoured with sherry.

COCK-A-LEEKIE

1 small fowl.	Salt and pepper.
2 quarts water or white stock.	1 teacupful rice.
1 bunch leeks.	1 teaspoonful chopped parsley.

1. Cook the trussed fowl in water or stock until tender (about 1½ hours) and remove.

2. Cleanse, trim, and blanch the white part of the leeks. Cut in neat pieces and place with the unblanched rice in the stock.

3. Simmer gently until the rice is cooked and the leeks are tender—about 1 hour. Frequently skim and stir while cooking.

4. Cut the breast of the fowl into small neat pieces, and add to the soup. Use remainder of bird for mince, friandines, etc.

5. Serve the soup in a hot tureen, sprinkled with finely chopped parsley.

MINESTRONE

6 oz. mixed vegetables: carrot, onion, leek, celery.	1 oz. scraped larding fat.
1 oz. butter.	Seasoning.
1 pint white stock or water.	A small clove of garlic.
1 oz. macaroni.	1 teaspoonful chopped parsley.
1 oz. cooked haricot beans.	Shredded bread sippets (see p. 13).
½ oz. rice.	Grated Parmesan cheese.
½ lb. tomatoes.	

1. Cut up the carrots in paysanne shape, and the remainder of the vegetables into small thin slices. Sweat them in the butter until tender, covered with a buttered greaseproof paper and lid.

2. Moisten with the stock or water.

3. Add the macaroni, broken into short lengths, and the haricot beans, which are barely cooked. Cook steadily for ½ hour.

4. Shower in the rice. Season, and cook for a further 30 minutes, until all the vegetables are tender. Correct the seasoning.

5. Stir in the larding fat, containing a small portion of garlic, finely chopped, and the chopped parsley, adding a small piece at a time.

6. Hand shredded bread sippets and the grated Parmesan cheese separately.

Note. Cabbage may be used in the mixed vegetables, if liked; also French beans, in season, cut into diamonds.

POT-AU-FEU

1 lb. lean beef (topside, breast, or shoulder).	Small thin squares stale bread.
1 quart cold water.	1 small parsnip.
1 carrot.	2–3 sticks celery.
Small teaspoonful salt.	Small bouquet garni.
1 turnip.	½ small cabbage.
1 onion.	Meat extract.
1 clove.	Chopped parsley.

1. Wipe the meat and tie it into shape. Put it into a pan (preferably earthenware) with the water and salt.

2. Bring quickly to boil, skim well, and add prepared vegetables two hours before serving. In all, simmer slowly for three hours. Scrupulous skimming and gentle simmering are essential to a good soup.

3. Again remove fat carefully. Colour the soup with meat extract or browning, correct seasoning, and boil up.

4. Pour the soup into a hot tureen at the bottom of which the squares of bread, baked fawn colour in the oven, have been placed. Sprinkle chopped parsley on the top.

Note. The meat can be served in slices, coated with Piquant or Tomato Sauce and garnished with the vegetables, or it is of excellent flavour for any réchauffé dishes. If preferred, the vegetables may be cut small and put into the soup, or the latter may be thickened with tapioca and the squares of toast omitted.

POISSON

(*Fish*)

IT is now the fashion at private dinners frequently to limit the number of dishes served in this course to one, although at a public function two may be served or even three.

Fish is served in two ways—

I. PLAINLY COOKED, SIMPLY GARNISHED, AND SERVED WITH A REALLY GOOD SAUCE

If it is served in this way, the fish chosen must be very choice, and its cooking must be perfection. It is a method of serving fish which finds favour with English folk.

Plainly boiled potatoes, trimmed to the shape of large marbles or of olives, and sprinkled with chopped parsley, should be handed with all fish served "au naturel," or may form part of its garnish. These are colloquially called "fish potatoes."

II. AS AN ENTRÉE

These can be either hot or cold and elaborate in composition and garnishing.

RULES FOR SERVING TWO KINDS OF FISH

1. It is usual to serve boiled fish first, such as salmon or turbot.
2. Serve cold fish after that which is hot.
3. When boiled fish appears first on the menu, it is frequently followed by some small fish, such as whitebait or smelts, cooked by frying or grilling.
4. When two fish sauces are to be served at a dinner, avoid similarity as to composition, colour, and flavour.

COLD FISH ENTRÉES

These dishes are suitable to be served at any kind of cold collation, such as a wedding reception, ball supper, or shooting party lunch, as well as at dinner parties.

CHARACTERISTICS OF COLD FISH ENTRÉES

(*a*) Aspic jelly, mayonnaise, and chaudfroid sauces are largely used in their composition and garnishing.

(*b*) The aspic jelly used in preparing fish entrées is made from good fish stock and is not over-acid.

(*c*) The fish is frequently moulded, aspic jelly and mayonnaise

43

being employed to set the mould, which is smoothly lined and smartly (though not necessarily elaborately) decorated.

(*d*) Further methods of serving are as a chaudfroid, consisting of one piece or of several, a salad or mayonnaise (salmon, lobster, etc.), soufflé or mousse.

NOTES ON SOME FISH USED IN THE RECIPES

CRABS

Cromer crabs are considered the best, but large numbers are also sent from the Isle of Wight. They are at their best in the summer and are obtainable from April to October.

The edible part of a crab is of two distinct varieties—

(*a*) The white flesh found in the claws and body.

(*b*) The dark-coloured soft meat found in the shell.

Choice—

1. See that the joints are stiff, that the crab is of good colour, and heavy for its size—if it is light it will be watery and stale.

2. The flesh of the male is considered to be the better. The male crab has larger claws and a smaller body than the female.

3. A medium-sized crab (about 8 in. across) is the best for flavour and texture, though small ones are useful to dress as individual portions.

4. Crabs are usually bought ready-boiled in towns, but if bought alive are cooked as are lobsters, allowing about $\frac{1}{2}$ hour for a medium-sized crab.

LOBSTERS

Lobsters are obtainable all the year round, but are best and cheapest from April to September.

Choice—

1. Buy at a shop having a quick sale, so that they are fresh and in good condition.

2. Medium-sized lobsters are best for flavour. Avoid any having thick encrusted shells.

3. When in good condition a lobster is heavy for its size and when the tail is lifted it springs rapidly back again.

4. As in the case of crabs, the flesh of the male is considered to have the better flavour, though the female lobster is useful for entrées because of her coral, or spawn. The male is smaller, narrower in the back, and has more claws.

5. If bought alive the lobster should be lively and heavy for its size.

To Boil a Lobster—

1. Tie up the claws securely.
2. Wash it and plunge headforemost into boiling water containing a faggot of herbs and a dash of vinegar.
3. Boil steadily 30–40 min. according to size, skimming from time to time. If overcooked the flesh is tough and indigestible, and also loses flavour.
4. When the lobster is cold, rub over the shell with a little oil to make it glossy.

MUSSELS

Mussels are used very largely in the preparation of fish entrées in France. They are seasonable all the year round but are best in winter, and a large Dutch variety is now obtainable. Discard at once any that are open, but if they are obtained from a reliable source and the shells are fast closed they are quite wholesome— though not very digestible.

To Prepare Mussels

Brush the shells well and scrape them to remove barnacles and weeds. Wash in several waters to remove sand. Put them while wet into a saucepan without added water, cover with a cloth, and steam until the shells open a little. If the liquor is to be used add (for 1 quart mussels): 2 oz. shredded blanched onion; $\frac{1}{2}$ gill white wine; juice of $\frac{1}{2}$ lemon and a faggot of herbs.

Decant this liquor through fine muslin, leaving any sand settled at the bottom. Remove the little beard which is found under the black tongue.

RED MULLET

These fish are not cleaned, hence the name "woodcock of the sea" frequently applied to them. Remove the eyes and fins and wipe the fish gently. They do not lend themselves particularly to variety, and the usual methods of cooking are to bake them in paper cases or a fireproof dish, to grill them, or to coat with egg and crumbs and fry them.

The grey mullet differs entirely from the red variety, belonging to another family. Its flavour is not so good and it is usually plainly cooked and served with sauce.

SALMON

When prepared by the simpler methods of cooking, such as boiling or grilling, the fine flavour of salmon may be savoured to the full. Perfect cooking and smart garnishing are essential. Salmon must always be well done or it is uneatable. The flesh is very rich in oil and not so digestible as the lighter kinds of fish; being very compact, a small amount of salmon is very satisfying. A steak from the middle of a salmon is called a "darne."

Choice—

1. Select a medium-sized fish which has a small head and tail with broad shoulders.
2. It may be cooked immediately it is drawn from the water, when between the flakes is found a creamy substance which disappears when the fish is kept.

It is at this stage that gourmets consider salmon to be in perfection.

3. Salmon may, however, be kept for two or three days, when it is considered to be more wholesome.

SOLES

Soles are a great stand-by in fish cookery, and lend themselves to infinite variety in preparation. They are obtainable all the year round, although they are not so good during February and March. When fresh they are firm to the touch, and cream-coloured on the under part, which is blue and flabby when the fish is stale.

TURBOT

Turbot is highly esteemed on account of its fine flavour and firm, although tender and gelatinous, texture. It often attains a very large size, though a turbotin, or chicken turbot, weighs only 2–3 lb. and is excellent when cooked whole. It has, as a characteristic, large uneven tubercles on the dark skin.

Leave turbot to soak for ½ hour in cold water with salt and lemon juice to whiten the flesh. If a whole fish is to be cooked, make a short incision across the tail, so that the blood will be drained from the spine.

For boiling, place the fish on the drainer, with the white side uppermost, and keep below boiling point for cooking. A slice of turbot ½ in. thick will take 8–10 minutes for cooking.

BLANCHAILLES AU NATUREL

1 pint whitebait.	ACCOMPANIMENTS
Fine salt.	**Thin brown bread and butter.**
Cayenne.	**Quarters of lemon.**

1. Have the whitebait perfectly fresh, as it is not drawn, and keep it cool before preparation—on ice, if possible.
2. Wash gently, removing all weeds, drain well, and spread on a cloth to dry, handling the fish as little as possible throughout.
3. Spread on another dry cloth, and dredge with flour.

4. Put the whitebait into a frying-basket in small batches, so that they do not touch one another, and shake the basket well to remove superfluous flour.

5. Plunge the fish into a fat bath which is just smoking in the usual way, and leave them until bubbling has ceased.

6. Remove. Either reheat the fat until smoking thoroughly or have a second bath of fat smoking (400° Fahr.), and plunge the whitebait into this.

7. This process is to crisp the whitebait, and they must be cooked through in about 1 minute. If the fat is not hot enough, and they are left in for some time to become crisp, the fish become overdone.

8. Several batches may be put together for the second frying. Drain thoroughly on soft kitchen paper.

9. Serve on a folded table-napkin, sprinkled with salt and a few grains of cayenne. Hand little rolls of thin brown bread and butter and quarters of lemon.

Note. When correctly cooked the whitebait are quite separate and crisp, but not dry.

CASSOLETTES D'ÉCREVISSES À LA RICHELIEU

10 oz. butter.
Beaten egg and coating crumbs.
Frying fat.
Fresh parsley.
Filling—
  1 oz. butter.
  1 oz. flour.
  ½ pint milk.

1 tablespoonful cream.
Salt and pepper.
A few grains of cayenne.
1 yolk of egg.
4 tablespoonfuls prepared shrimps.
2 teaspoonfuls lemon juice.

1. Divide the butter into five portions, and form each to a flat round cake (like a thick fish cake), using butter hands.

2. Allow the butter to set quite hard.

3. For the filling, make a white sauce with the butter, flour, and milk. Add the yolk and seasoning, recook, and add the shrimps and lemon juice. Keep hot until required.

4. Coat the pats of butter twice with egg and breadcrumbs, pressing the breadcrumbs on thoroughly. Mark a lid on the top of each with a 1 in. cutter.

5. Fry golden brown in smoking hot fat. Lift out on to crumpled paper, and at once remove the lids with a small sharp-pointed knife, and empty out the butter.

6. Turn the cassolettes upside down on soft crumpled paper to drain.

7. Divide the filling among the cassolettes. Put the lid on each one so that a little of the filling shows at one side.

8. Dish on a hot dish with sprigs of fresh parsley between.

COQUILLES AU GRATIN

8 scallops.	½ pint white coating sauce.
Juice of half a lemon.	A few shavings butter.
1 oz. butter.	1 tablespoonful browned crumbs.
2 tablespoonfuls fresh bread-crumbs.	Parsley.
	Fans of lemon.

1. Open the shells, remove any beards or black parts. Wash the fish well to remove sand.

2. Put the scallops while wet into a small saucepan and stew very gently for ½ hour, with 1 oz. of butter, and the juice of ½ lemon.

3. Scrub the deep shells of the scallops, dry them, and allow one for each two scallops. Butter the shells, then sprinkle with bread-crumbs.

4. Put two scallops in each shell, and cover with well-seasoned thick coating sauce.

5. Sprinkle brown crumbs over the surface, and add a few shavings of butter.

6. Brown under a griller or in a hot oven. Garnish with the parsley and lemon, and serve as an individual portion in the shell.

Note. Scallops must be very fresh when used. They somewhat resemble large oysters, but are yellow and white.

CÔTELETTES DE HOMARD

4 oz. cooked lobster.	Lemon juice.
Panada—	1 yolk of egg.
1 oz. butter.	Beaten egg and panurette to
1 oz. flour.	coat.
1 gill milk of fish stock.	Garnish—
A few grains cayenne.	Lobster feelers.
Salt.	Fried parsley.

1. Make the panada. Add the chopped lobster, the seasoning, and lemon juice. Add the yolk, and cook over gentle heat to bind.

2. Spread the mixture evenly on a plate to cool, and mark into 8 portions.

3. Form into cutlets. Coat with egg and panurette, and fry in deep fat.

4. Place a short piece of lobster feeler in the end of each, and dish the cutlets neatly, leaning one against the other on a dish paper, on a hot oval gratin dish, and garnish with fried parsley.

Note. If tinned lobster is used, drain it thoroughly from all liquid. Place an inch of macaroni in the narrow end of each cutlet before frying, or a piece of thick parsley stalk after frying.

CRABE GARNI

1 boiled crab of medium size.	1 teaspoonful finely chopped parsley.
2 tablespoonfuls mayonnaise.	
Seasoning.	$\frac{1}{2}$ hard-boiled egg.
1 tablespoonful breadcrumbs.	Shredded lettuce leaves.
	Lobster, or green, butter.

1. Twist off the large claws and smaller feelers of the lobster.

2. Separate the upper from the lower shell by pulling, and keep the latter intact for dishing.

3. Remove and discard—

    (a) The spongy gills known as "dead men's fingers."

    (b) The stomach—a little sac near the head.

    (c) The intestine, which is of greenish matter.

4. Crack the body, and pick out all the meat with a skewer.

5. Crack the claws and remove the meat. Chop all this firm flesh, season, and mix with the mayonnaise.

6. Mix the dark meat from the body with the breadcrumbs, and season it.

7. Scrub the body shell, and chip to the natural line by tapping gently with a skewer and small hammer.

8. Re-fill with the mixture, put the dark meat in a straight band down the middle, and the white mixture at each side.

9. Pipe the edge with lobster, or green, butter; sprinkle chopped parsley thickly down the middle, sieved egg yolk on one side, and chopped white on the other.

10. Serve on a bed of shredded lettuce, garnished with the small feelers.

Note. If hot crab is desired, substitute Béchamel Sauce for the mayonnaise, and cover the surface with breadcrumbs and butter shavings. Heat through and brown, in the oven. Omit lettuce, and garnish with sprigs of parsley.

CRÈME DE HOMARD

$\frac{1}{4}$ lb. cooked lobster.	Decoration—
1 gill cream.	Liquid aspic.
$\frac{1}{4}$ gill tomato pulp.	Lobster.
2 teaspoonfuls mayonnaise.	Truffle.
Cayenne, salt, and lemon juice.	Green salad plants or small cress.
$\frac{1}{4}$ oz. gelatine.	
$\frac{3}{4}$ gill aspic jelly.	Chopped aspic jelly.

1. Line a border mould with aspic jelly, and decorate with pieces of red lobster from the claws, truffle, etc.

2. Chop and pound the lobster, half whip the cream, and mix all the ingredients, adding last the gelatine dissolved in the aspic jelly.

3. When it thickens creamily, pour the mixture into the prepared mould.

4. Unmould when set, and decorate with lobster feelers and green salad plants, and pile aspic jelly in the centre of the mould.

Note. Prawns, crayfish, or cooked salmon may be substituted for the lobster.

DARNE DE SAUMON EN ASPIC

(for 8 portions)

1 steak of salmon—middle cut 2½ in.–3 in. wide.	½ gill liquid aspic jelly. ¼ oz. gelatine dissolved in it.
1 pint liquid aspic.	3 tablespoonfuls dice of cucumber.
Decoration—	
Cucumber skin.	1 hard-boiled egg.
Steamed egg white.	3 tablespoonfuls cooked peas.
Strips of pimento.	Garnish—
Aspic Mayonnaise—	Small cress.
1 gill mayonnaise (see p. 248).	Crimped cucumber.

1. Steam the salmon, skin, and bone it. Cut it in half through the middle, and make the steak even by placing one thick side on top of one thin one. Leave to become quite cold.

2. Line an oblong bread tin or oven glassware dish with liquid aspic, and arrange the decoration at the bottom. Cover with the liquid aspic.

3. Place the piece of salmon carefully in the middle, and pour in liquid aspic to come rather more than half way up the dish.

4. Prepare the aspic mayonnaise. Add the dice of cucumber, cooked peas, and hard-boiled egg cut in pieces, and the remainder of the egg from the decoration.

5. Arrange evenly at the sides and ends, filling level with the top of the fish.

6. Run a layer of liquid aspic over to fill the dish—leave to set.

7. Unmould—encircle with the small cress, and garnish further with crimped cucumber.

FILETS DE SOLE EN ASPIC

1 sole, filleted.	Decoration and Garnish—
Lobster cutlet mixture (see p. 48).	Steamed egg white.
	Truffle, Chervil, etc.
1 pint aspic jelly (see p. 73).	Small cress.

1. Prepare the fillets, and spread them with the lobster cutlet mixture. Roll them up neatly, and tie round loosely with thread.

2. Oven steam the fillets until cooked (10–12 minutes). Drain, and leave them to become cold.

3. Mask four dariole moulds with aspic, decorate them as desired, and set the decoration with a layer of aspic.

4. Put the fillets in the prepared moulds, and fill up with cold liquid aspic, adding it by degrees, and allowing each portion to set before adding the next.

5. Put a thin layer of aspic on an oval silver dish. Unmould the fillets, and dish them in a slanting line.

6. Put chopped aspic at one side and small cress at the other. Fans of crimped cucumber may be put among the aspic if desired.

Note. If the fillets are long they may be cut in half before they are rolled up, or the rolls may be cut in half transversely after cooking if they are too large.

HOMARD AU NATUREL

1 boiled lobster.
Parsley or green salad plants.

Mayonnaise, tarragon vinegar, salt, and pepper.
Brown bread and butter.

1. Twist off the large claws, and crack them carefully on each joint so that the flesh is not crushed.

2. Remove the small claws, and put on one side for garnishing.

3. Split the lobster through from head to tail along the back, using a heavy sharp-pointed knife.

4. Remove—
   (a) The intestine—a small tube running through the tail.
   (b) The stomach—a little sac to be found near the head.
   (c) The spongy gills.

5. Lay the two halves of the lobster on a flat dish with the cracked claws in the middle. Garnish with salad or parsley.

6. Hand brown bread and butter, mayonnaise, tarragon vinegar, and condiments separately.

HOMARD À LA NEWBURG

1 lobster.
1½ oz. butter.
1 tablespoonful cognac (or fish stock).
1 tablespoonful Madeira.
Seasoning.
1 tablespoonful chopped truffles or champignons.

1 tablespoonful Béchamel Sauce
Liaison—
   1 large tablespoonful cream.
   1 tablespoonful milk.
   2 yolks of eggs.
   Paprika and cayenne peppers.

1. Boil the lobster in court-bouillon (20 minutes for 1 lb. lobster). While it is still lukewarm, remove the head, and the flesh in one large piece (this can be accomplished by cracking the shell outside in many places).

2. Cut the flesh in slices. Crack the claws, and remove part of the shell, but leave the flesh in the claw at the tip.

3. Fry the pieces of lobster in butter, remove, and keep warm. Pour off some of the butter. Add the cognac, Madeira, and Béchamel Sauce.

4. Add the seasoning, a little fried paprika, and a few grains of cayenne. Add the chopped truffles, and heat all well.

5. Allow to cool somewhat, thicken with the liaison, add the lobster, and rewarm.

6. Serve on a round plated dish, with the claws opposite one another, the piece of head in the centre, and the smaller feelers around the edge.

KARI DE CREVETTES À LA FRANÇAISE

1 oz. chopped onion.
1 oz. butter.
1 heaped teaspoonful curry powder.
½ pint Béchamel or Velouté Sauce (see pp. 244 and 251).
½ gill cream.

Lemon juice and salt.
1 pint shelled prawns.
1 large peeled potato.
Fans of lemon.
Plain boiled rice.
Coralline pepper.

1. Fry the onion light golden colour in the heated butter. Add the curry powder and fry it to obtain full flavour and to prevent graining.

2. Add the prepared sauce. Boil up together, and add the cream, lemon juice, and salt to taste.

3. Add the prawns, tossing them lightly to avoid breaking them.

4. Prepare a border of straw potatoes (see page 122), on a gratin or fireproof glass dish. Pour the curry into the centre, and serve plain boiled rice separately, sprinkling the latter with coralline pepper.

5. Garnish the curry with fans of lemon.

Note. Curried prawns may be served cold, coated with a thin layer of aspic.

MAYONNAISE DE POISSON

1 small cabbage lettuce.
Vinaigrette dressing (see p. 180).
Cooked fish—½ lb.
1 gill thick mayonnaise.
6 anchovy fillets.

Capers.
2 gherkins.
4 olives.
Sliced beetroot or tomatoes.
1 hard-boiled egg.

1. Cleanse, dry, and cut the lettuce into julienne shreds. Season it lightly with vinaigrette dressing and drain again.

2. Pile dome-shaped in a salad bowl and cover with cooked fish, previously boned, skinned, and flaked.

3. Mask with mayonnaise. Garnish with a trellis of strips of anchovy and put a caper in the centre of each space.

4. Decorate at the edge with gherkin tassels, stoned olives, sliced beetroot or tomatoes, and quarters of hard-boiled egg.

5. Serve immediately.

Notes. (*a*) This method of preparation may be used for cooked chicken also.

(*b*) A few leaves from the heart of a lettuce may be used as an additional garnish.

MERLANS MEUNIÈRE

2 filleted whiting, ½ lb. each.	Beetroot, cut in diamonds.
Flour.	Juice of half a lemon.
3–3½ oz. butter.	2 teaspoonfuls chopped parsley.
Fans of lemon, and parsley.	Mignonette pepper.

1. Wash and dry the whiting fillets. Pass them through flour, and make a couple of slanting cuts on each fillet.

2. Melt 2 oz. of the butter in a frying-pan, and fry the fish, first on one side, then the other. The frying-pan may be put in the oven to finish the frying.

3. Decorate a silver or fireproof dish with the fans of lemon, the parsley, and the thin slices of beetroot cut into diamonds.

4. Place the whiting in the centre. Sprinkle with the lemon juice and the chopped parsley, and grind a little pepper over.

5. Brown the remainder of the butter carefully to noisette, pour it over the fish, and serve.

Note. The fish may be left whole, if preferred, or fillets of sole are often used in place of whiting.

POISSON EN CHAUDFROID

2 tail steaks of salmon, or cod.	Cucumber skin.
1 gill mayonnaise.	Truffle.
½ gill aspic jelly.	Small cress.
Decoration and Garnish—	4–5 stoned olives.
Liquid aspic for basting.	4–5 strips of anchovy fillet.
Chopped or piped aspic.	

1. Boil or oven steam the fish. Remove the skin and centre bone. Fill in the centre hole with crumbled bread, bind with muslin, and press the fish between two plates until cold.

2. Place the steaks on an icing rack. Add the cold liquid aspic to the mayonnaise, and when almost setting carefully coat the fish.

3. Decorate as desired with the cucumber skin and truffle, and baste with liquid aspic.

4. Put a thin layer of aspic on a silver dish. Lay the steaks on this, and put chopped or piped aspic round.

5. Garnish with bunches of small cress and stoned olives, with a strip of anchovy fillet around the base of each.

SAUMON BOUILLI À LA HOLLANDAISE

Fresh salmon.
Salt.
Fish potatoes (2 large raw potatoes).

Parsley sprigs.
Sliced cucumber.
Hollandaise Sauce.

1. Scrape the fish free from scales; clear it from blood by washing well.

2. Weigh the fish, and allow 10 minutes to the pound and 10 minutes over as the average time for cooking, but the thickness of the piece must be taken into consideration.

3. Place the fish on the drainer, and plunge it into sufficient fresh boiled salted water to cover. Avoid vinegar, which destroys the colour of the fish.

4. Skim well while cooking, the water being at simmering point.

5. Drain thoroughly, and dish on a folded table napkin, garnished with the potatoes and parsley.

6. Lay thin slices of cucumber overlapping on the fish, and hand the Hollandaise Sauce separately.

Fish Potatoes. Boil plainly, after cutting out with a large pea cutter or trimming into small barrel shapes.

SOLE À L'AMÉRICAINE

1 lb. sole, filleted.
1 small onion, cut in rings.
½ gill of sherry and fish stock.

1 truffle.
Sauce Américaine (see p. 252).

1. Fold the skinned fillets in flattened rolls. Place them on a buttered tin on the sliced onion.

2. Sprinkle with the wine and fish stock, and oven steam until ready.

3. Serve in individual cocotte pans, sauced over with Sauce Américaine.

4. Lay a slice of heated truffle on each and serve with a bunch of parsley sprigs in the centre of the dish.

SOLE MARGUERY

1 medium-size sole, filleted.
Juice of half a lemon.
½ gill white wine.
1–2 yolks of eggs.
1 oz. butter.

1 large tablespoonful peeled shrimps.
1 large tablespoonful shelled mussels or oysters.

1. Wash the fillets and lay them in a buttered seasoned sauté pan or Yorkshire pudding tin.

2. Fold the fillets flatly in half, if they are large, and moisten them with the lemon juice and white wine. Cover with a buttered paper, and oven steam until cooked.

3. Remove the fillets to a fireproof or silver dish, and reduce the fish essence in the tin.

4. Add the beaten yolks to the fumet, when it has cooled somewhat, and thicken the sauce to a cream.

5. Whisk in the butter in small pieces, taking care that the sauce is never more than just warm.

6. Garnish the dish at the sides with the shrimps, mussels, or oysters, and pour the sauce over all.

7. Pass the dish under a grill, sprinkle with coralline pepper, and serve.

SOLE AU VIN BLANC

1 lemon sole, approximately 1 lb., skinned and filleted.	Rounds of cooked carrot of the size of a shilling.
Seasoning.	Rounds of truffle of the size of a shilling.
Lemon juice.	
2 tablespoonfuls Sauterne or sherry.	Sauce au Vin Blanc (see p. 252).

1. Sprinkle each fillet with salt, pepper, and lemon juice, and fold it in half with the skinned side inside.

2. Place the fillets in a buttered seasoned Yorkshire pudding tin or fireproof dish. Sprinkle with lemon juice (to keep the fish white) and the wine.

3. Cover with a greased paper, and oven steam in a moderate oven 12–15 minutes, until the fish is opaque.

4. Dish the fillets neatly, leaning one against the other in a slanting line down an oval gratin dish, and arrange the garnish over it.

5. Prepare the sauce, adding the reduced fish essence from the tin.

6. Coat evenly with the sauce of semi-coating consistency, so that the garnish will show through.

SUPRÊMES DE SOLE MORNAY

1 lemon sole (1 lb.).	2 oz. grated cheese (Cheddar and Parmesan).
The juice of half a lemon.	Salt, pepper, cayenne.
About ½ pint fish stock.	1 tablespoonful fresh grated Cheddar cheese.
Duchesse potato mixture (6 oz. sieved potato, etc., see p. 119).	1 tablespoonful oiled butter.
½ pint thick Béchamel Sauce (see p. 244).	

1. Remove the black skin from the sole, and fillet it. Make two incisions on the back of the white skin, and fold each fillet over in half.

2. Put the fillets in a buttered seasoned fireproof dish. Add the lemon juice and fish stock to cover, and press a buttered paper on top. Boil up gently on the top of the stove, then place in the oven to poach for 5 minutes.

3. Decorate a fireproof dish with a cable of duchesse potato at the edge. Brush with egg, and allow to set in a brisk oven.

4. Drain the fish well, and place it in the prepared dish.

5. Reduce the fish liquor, and add it to the Béchamel Sauce. Have the sauce of thick consistency, add the grated cheese, and correct the seasoning.

6. Sprinkle the fish with freshly grated Cheddar cheese and the oiled butter, and glaze under a griller.

SUPRÊMES DE SOLE AUX RAISINS

(Fillets of Sole, garnished with grapes)

1 medium-size sole, filleted.	Suprême Sauce (see p. 251).
3 heaped tablespoonfuls skinned white grapes.	Salt, pepper, lemon juice. Coralline pepper.

1. Sprinkle the skinned side of each fillet of the sole with the salt, pepper, and lemon juice, and roll up.

2. Put the fillets into a greased Yorkshire pudding tin, sprinkle with a little water or fish stock, and cover with a buttered paper.

3. Oven steam until the fish is cooked, about 12–15 minutes.

4. Heat the pipped grapes in a little hot stock.

5. Remove the fillets to a hot gratin dish, dishing them in a straight line slantwise. Reduce the essence in the tin, strain, and add it to the Suprême Sauce.

6. Arrange the grapes at each side, towards opposite ends of the row of fillets.

7. See that the Suprême Sauce is of semi-coating consistency, and strain it over.

8. Sprinkle coralline pepper on each suprême.

TURBOT CAPRICE

1–1¼ lb. steak of turbot.	3 large tomatoes.
Seasoned flour.	1 large truffle cut in matches.
Oil and butter for frying.	1 teaspoonful chopped tarragon.
Garnish—	Sauce—
1 tablespoonful red part of carrot cut into match shapes.	½ gill cream.
Scant oz. butter.	¼ gill Madeira.
	¼ gill strong fish stock.

1. Prepare the Garnish—

(a) Toss the matches of carrot in a small saucepan in a little hot butter. Press a piece of buttered paper on top, and put on the lid. Cook for a few minutes without colouring on gentlest heat, then put the saucepan in the oven until the vegetable is quite tender.

(b) Cut the tomatoes in halves transversely, and put a nut of butter and a pinch of seasoning on each, and bake until tender but not broken.

(c) Chop the tarragon.

2. Fillet the fish and divide into six pieces. Wash, dry thoroughly, and roll in seasoned flour.

3. Fry golden brown on each side.

4. For the Sauce—

Pour off the fat, add the cream, Madeira, and stock. Heat with the matches of carrot and truffle, stirring lightly, and reduce.

5. Dishing—

(a) Place a spoonful of the shreds on each fillet of fish, and pour the remainder with the sauce round.

(b) Place half a tomato on each fillet, sprinkle with the chopped tarragon, and serve.

TURBOT À LA FLORENTINE

1 lb. steak of turbot.	$\frac{1}{2}$ pint Béchamel Sauce (see p. 244).
Seasoning.	
Lemon juice.	Browned crumbs.
1 tablespoonful white wine.	Grated cheese.
2 lb. spinach.	Oiled butter.

1. Divide the fish into fillets and oven steam them, sprinkling with seasoning, lemon juice, and white wine.

2. Prepare the spinach purée (see page 115), and arrange a layer in the bottom of a greased fireproof dish.

3. Arrange the pieces of fish on this, and coat with a layer of somewhat thick Béchamel Sauce, to which the reduced fish essence from the tin has been added.

4. Sprinkle with crumbs, grated cheese, and oiled butter.

5. Rewarm in the oven, then brown under a griller.

Note. The above dish can be served very attractively in scallop shells, either china or natural.

ENTRÉES

(Made Dishes)

THE ENTRÉE COURSE

ENTRÉES can be defined as "made" or "dressed" dishes, and are of great importance in the menu. A further definition of an entrée is that it is a dish complete in itself, i.e. the sauce and vegetable are both served in the same dish with the meat. The sauce is an important component of an entrée, and together with the dishing and garnishing can make or mar the dish.

When dishing an entrée have the sauces, purées, and garnishes quite ready before the actual dishing is begun. The dish may be placed in a baking-tin containing very hot water, while finishing touches are being given; or after dishing, the entrée may be placed in a hot oven for half a minute if it has become cooled during the process.

A successful entrée appeals first to the eye, and also delights the palate.

CLASSIFICATION OF ENTRÉES

I. HOT

(a) Solid Entrées, e.g.—

Cutlets.	Ragouts.	Salmis.
Fillets.	Sweetbreads.	Fricassées.
	Tournedos.	

(b) Light Entrées, e.g.—

Soufflés.	Bouchées.	Vol-au-Vents.
Timbales.	Beignets.	Petites Caisses.
	Croquettes.	

II. COLD, e.g.—

Chaudfroids.	Galantines.	Mousses.
Soufflés.	Timbales.	Darioles.

CHARACTERISTICS OF ENTRÉES

1. They are always served in small portions, so that each guest can help himself or herself quite easily. Entrées are never served from the sideboard.

2. The dish is more or less elaborate, two or more processes of cooking being introduced into its preparation.

3. The sauce is always well flavoured and seasoned, and is only handed separately in the case of soufflés, etc., when it is not possible to serve it in the dish.

4. The garnish is very dainty, and skilfully prepared.

5. If two entrées are to be served in a menu—

(a) An entrée consisting of small birds would precede one prepared from large birds or from meat.

(b) A hot entrée is served before a cold one.

(c) One is usually chosen of light colour and the other is dark. The entrée placed first on the menu depends entirely on the dishes preceding and following.

COLD ENTRÉES

These belong to a most artistic portion of cooking, and are elaborately dressed. Cold entrées are much in favour in the Dinner Menu in hot weather, and are served also at Ball or Dance Suppers, Banquets, Shooting Party Luncheons, Wedding Receptions, Smart Luncheons, etc.

Characteristics of Cold Entrées—

1. In their preparation chaudfroid sauces, aspic jelly, aspic cream, and mayonnaise are largely used.

2. The aspic jelly, which is a prominent feature of cold entrées, must be full flavoured and very clear.

3. Hâtelets, or silver skewers, ornamented with fancifully cut vegetables, and a garnish of aspic are often used in building up large elaborate dishes.

4. Time must be allowed for good craftsmanship on these dishes, although it is not necessarily the most elaborate pattern in decoration which shows to the best advantage.

BRAISING

Braising is a compound method of cooking, being a combination of steaming and of baking, which develops a particularly fine flavour. It is a method of cooking which is very popular in France.

A Braisoire is the correct utensil to use for this purpose. It is a strong, somewhat shallow stewpan, which has a concave overlapping lid, to accommodate the glowing charcoal which is the orthodox way of providing top heat. The lid overlaps the lower part of the pan, fitting it very closely to prevent the loss of steam. Charcoal is used because it has neither smoke nor smell, but in this country it is usual to use a stewpan or casserole with a close fitting lid, placing it in the oven when top heat is required.

In braising meat there is less loss of weight by evaporation, as steaming prevents this; also an excellent flavour is developed from the mirepoix or bed of vegetables on which the article to be braised is placed. It is suitable for small pieces of meat, such as fillets, cutlets, etc.

Foods which have a somewhat insipid flavour are suitable, either white or red meats; but white meat, such as veal, is more usually employed. The joint is boned and frequently stuffed. Poultry, sweetbreads, rabbits, and pigeons are often braised, and also vegetables of delicate flavour, such as cauliflower, artichokes, lettuce, etc.

THE PROCESS OF BRAISING

(a) BARDING OR LARDING

Joints of meat are usually barded or larded with fat bacon, otherwise they would often be deficient in fat. The bacon also imparts a pleasant flavour, and prevents meat from becoming dry. Larding bacon is prepared without the use of saltpetre.

If the joint is barded, a piece of larding bacon covers the surface.

If larded, small pieces of larding bacon termed "lardoons" are sewn into the joint with a larding needle. These lardoons are cut match shaped, and about $1\frac{1}{2}$ in. long.

(b) MIREPOIX

The Mirepoix is a bed of stewed vegetables on which the food to be braised is placed. It is this mirepoix which imparts its special flavour to the braise. To prepare it see page 14.

Lay the prepared joint or other food to be braised on the mirepoix, cover it with a greased greaseproof paper, and the tight-fitting lid. Baste from time to time with the stock from the mirepoix.

(c) COOKING

Cook over heat for two-thirds of the time necessary. Then remove the pan to a moderate oven, and take off the lid for the last 15–20 minutes to crisp the larding bacon.

THE TIME REQUIRED varies with the size and thickness of the meat; the average time to allow for joints is: 25 minutes per lb. and 25 minutes over. For fillets and cutlets allow 30–35 minutes in all.

SAUTÉING

The name of this process is derived from the French *sauter*, meaning to jump, and as a culinary term implies tossing the food in a little hot fat over brisk heat until the fat is absorbed. It is used—

(a) To cook thin slices of food completely, e.g. kidneys, cooked potatoes.

(*b*) To provide the initial stage of cooking for vegetables in the case of many sauces and soups.

(*c*) To finish the cooking of garnishes for certain dishes. In this case butter is the fat usually employed, as it enriches the flavour.

HOT ENTRÉE RECIPES

CASSEROLE DE VOLAILLE

(Casserole of Chicken)

¾ pint **Espagnole Sauce** (see p. 246).	1 doz. **champignons** (bottled or tinned).
1 tender young **chicken** (drawn).	2 **truffles** cut in batons.
Oil and **butter** for frying.	1 teaspoonful finely chopped **parsley**.

1. Make the Espagnole Sauce.

2. While the sauce is simmering, divide the chicken into joints, and remove skin from all but the wings. Fry the joints pale golden colour in the smoking fat, using a large frying-pan. Drain well.

3. Strain the Espagnole Sauce into a casserole. Put in the joints and baste them with the sauce. Cover with a piece of buttered paper and a lid.

4. Stand the casserole in a small baking-tin with a little water in it, and cook in a moderate oven for 1½ hours.

5. Heat the stemmed champignons and batons of truffle in a little hot stock.

6. When dishing, remove the back of the fowl, which is only added to improve the flavour. Arrange the joints neatly in another hot casserole and strain the sauce over.

7. Pile the heated champignons in the centre and arrange the batons of truffle round the edge.

8. Sprinkle with a little finely chopped parsley, put on the lid, and serve very hot.

CÔTELETTES D'AGNEAU EN CUIRASSES

Rough puff pastry, made with 6 oz. flour, etc.	2 teaspoonfuls **tomato conserve**.
5 small trimmed **lamb cutlets**.	Seasoning.
Oil and 2 oz. **butter** for frying.	1 teaspoonful finely chopped **parsley** or **tarragon**.
Farce—	1 tablespoonful **oil** for frying.
3 oz. **mushrooms**.	Beaten **egg** to brush over.
1 slice **onion**.	Slices fried **aubergine**.
1 large tablespoonful light **white wine**.	

1. Make the pastry, and put it aside to chill and relax.

2. Trim the cutlets closely, sprinkle with salt, and bat them into shape.

3. Fry the cutlets on both sides in a little butter and oil.

4. Place the cutlets aside to become quite cold, pressed between two dishes.

5. Prepare the Farce—

(a) Chop the mushrooms finely, and fry the chopped onion in some of the oil. Add the chopped mushrooms, and fry all well together.

(b) Add the white wine, tomato conserve, and seasoning, and blend all together over gentle heat.

(c) Remove, stir in the chopped parsley or tarragon lightly, and spread to cool.

6. Roll out the pastry to a long oblong strip.

7. Brush lightly with water, and put a small spoonful of farce on the end nearest. Lay a cutlet with the lean on the farce, and spread another spoonful on top.

8. Roll the pastry over, leaving the bone protruding, and cut off the required amount of pastry.

9. Join the pastry well down the side, pinching it up around the bone, which is left protruding.

10. Roll out the pastry at the other end a little, and slant off the corners with a knife. Damp underneath, and fold the wrapping under.

11. Place on a baking-tin, and put a ring from the rolled-up trimmings of pastry on each.

12. Brush with beaten egg, and bake until the pastry is well cooked and golden brown.

13. Dish in a circle with the bones protruding, and a cutlet frill on each.

14. Fill in the centre with slices of fried aubergine and serve *hot*.

CÔTELETTES À LA RÉFORME

A piece of best end of neck of small mutton, with five bones.

Garnish—
  1 medium-sized carrot.
  3 gherkins.
  2 truffles.
  1 white of egg (steamed).
  4 preserved champignons.

Coating—
  2 oz. lean cooked ham.
  3 tablespoonfuls white coating crumbs.
  1 egg.

For Frying—
  Butter and oil.
  ½ pint of Sauce Réforme (see p. 250).

1. Divide the meat into neat cutlets and trim them.

2. Prepare the sauce.

3. Prepare the Garnish—

(a) Cut the carrot in 1 in. lengths, and from them cut small batons about ⅛ in. square at the ends. Cook in boiling salted water until tender, and drain.

(b) Cut the gherkins, truffles, and slices of steamed egg white into similar batons.

(c) Remove the stems from the champignons, and cut the cups into three strips.

(d) Heat the garnish in a little stock, drain well, and toss in a nut of butter, with salt and pepper, just before it is required for use.

4. Add the chopped ham to the coating crumbs, and use with the beaten egg to coat the cutlets in the usual way.

5. Fry the cutlets golden brown in smoking oil and butter, 10–12 minutes in all. Drain.

6. Dish the cutlets in a circle on a round entrée dish. Pile the prepared garnish in the centre, and pour the sauce around.

CÔTELETTES D'AGNEAU BRAISÉS À LA SOUBISE

(Braised lamb cutlets, Soubise Sauce)

5 trimmed lamb cutlets. | **Jus lié** (see p. 247).
Mirepoix to braise (see p. 14). | **Soubise Sauce** (see p. 251).

1. Braise the cutlets for about ¾ hour, until quite tender.

2. Dish the cutlets, leaning one against the other, in a flattened half circle on a hot dish.

3. Coat with the jus lié and garnish with cutlet frills.

4. Pile thick Soubise Sauce in the curve of the cutlets. Sprinkle with a suspicion of finely chopped parsley and serve.

ESCALOPES DE RIS DE VEAU MILANAISE

(Veal scallops, with spaghetti)

1 large heart sweetbread. | **1 oz. lean cooked ham.**
½ pint white veal stock. | **1 oz. preserved champignons.**
Tomato sauce. | **Scant 1 oz. of grated Parmesan.**
Mirepoix for braising. |
Garnish— | **Coating—**
    2 oz. spaghetti. | Egg and white breadcrumbs.

1. Cleanse and blanch the sweetbread. Refresh and trim. Press between two dishes for an hour.

2. Braise the sweetbread for ¾ hour, and slice it slantways into scallops.

3. Coat the scallops with egg and breadcrumbs, and fry to a golden colour.

Garnish.

Garnish—

(*a*) Parboil the spaghetti in boiling salted water for 3 minutes. Strain, and cover with the white veal stock. Simmer until cooked, allowing the stock to evaporate.

(*b*) Add the cheese, strips of ham and truffle, and the mushrooms.

To serve—

(*a*) Pour the prepared tomato sauce into a hot round dish.

(*b*) Arrange the scallops overlapping in a circle.

(*c*) Place the garnish in the middle.

ESCALOPES À LA VIENNOISE (WIENER SCHNITZEL)

5 large thin veal fillets.
Beaten egg.
Coating crumbs.
Oil and butter for frying.
Lemon juice.
Beurre Noisette (see p. 12).

Garnish—
1 hard-boiled egg.
1 tablespoonful chopped parsley.
1 doz. slices lemon.
5 stoned olives.
5 anchovy fillets.
A few capers.

1. Prepare the escalopes. Sprinkle with seasoning, dip in flour, and coat with egg and breadcrumbs.

2. Prepare the garnish—

Remove the yolk from the white of the hard-boiled egg, sieve the former, and chop the latter, separately.

Chop the parsley.

Cut thin slices from a crimped lemon; stand a stoned olive, with a strip of anchovy fillet rolled round its base, on each. Arrange the remaining slices of lemon cut in half at the sides of a flat dish.

3. Fry the escalopes, and arrange them slightly overlapping on the dish. Sprinkle with lemon juice and pour nut-brown butter over.

4. Place a quarter circle of egg yolk at each end of the dish in a line, chopped parsley in a line against it, and the chopped egg white inside that.

5. Arrange olives, etc., on the meat and sprinkle with the capers.

FILETS DE BŒUF À LA GODARD

1 lb. middle fillet of beef.
1 tablespoonful finely chopped shallot.
½ tablespoonful finely chopped parsley.
5 small rounds lean ham.
Farce—
  2 oz. raw lean veal.
  1½ tablespoonfuls cream.
  Seasoning.

½ pint jus lié (see p. 247).
Clarified butter and oil for frying.
Duchesse Potato Mixture, 6–8 oz. potato, etc. (see p. 119).
Garnish—
  ½ doz. mushroom heads.
  ½ doz. stoned Spanish olives.
  1 truffle cut in batons.

1. Trim the fillets, using a round cutter, four large or five smaller ones. Dip them in the chopped shallot and parsley, and leave them for one hour.

2. Grease some tiny bouche moulds, put a small round of ham in the bottom of each, and sprinkle the sides with parsley.

3. Mince and sieve the veal through a wire sieve. Add the cream and seasoning.

4. Fill the little tins with the farce, using a hot spoon to make the mixture quite smooth, and press it against the side of the tins. Steam gently 10–15 minutes in a bain-marie.

5. Prepare the jus lié, making it thick enough to coat the fillets.

6. Fry the fillets briskly in clarified butter and oil, lessen the heat, and allow the fillets to cook through.

7. Pipe a line of duchesse potato down a hot fireproof dish, and lay the fillets flat on this, seeing that each is quite flat.

8. Unmould a bouche on to each, strain the sauce over, and put a little pile of garnish (heated in stock, and strained) at each side towards opposite ends.

FILETS DE BŒUF AUX BANANES

(Small beef fillets, with fried bananas)

1 lb. fillet of beef.
Meat glaze.
Duchesse Potato Mixture II (see p. 120).
Beaten egg and white coating crumbs.

Quarters of bananas.
Butter and oil for frying.
Tomato or Demi-glace Sauce (see pp. 252, 245).
A few champignons or scraped horseradish.

1. Trim the meat into small fillets.

2. Prepare the duchesse potato mixture, spread it on a plate to cool, and divide it into the same number of portions as the fillets. Shape them into flat cakes. Coat them with egg and breadcrumbs, and fry; or brush with egg, and bake (see page 120). Keep them hot.

3. Cut the bananas into halves, then quarters lengthways, and coat the pieces with egg and breadcrumbs.

4. Fry the fillets in smoking hot butter and oil for 6–7 minutes; they should be slightly underdone.

5. Dish the fillets on the potato cakes, and arrange them in a circle on a hot dish.

6. Arrange the bananas in the centre, and pour the sauce around.

7. Place the head of a preserved champignon (which has been heated in stock and well drained) on each fillet, which has been brushed with meat glaze.

JAMBON À LA MAILLOT

(Ham, Madeira Sauce, Maillot Garnish)

6 slices cooked ham.	Garnish A La Maillot—
A scant ½ gill Madeira.	Carrots.
Sauce Madère (see p. 248).	Turnips.
Parsley.	Potatoes.
	Green Peas.

1. Prepare the sauce, making it of semi-coating consistency.

2. Prepare the garnish—

(a) Trim the carrots, turnips, and potatoes to the size of large olives.

(b) Cook the carrots and turnips in boiling salted water.

(c) Blanch the potatoes, and fry them golden brown in deep fat.

(d) Prepare and cook the green peas in the usual way.

3. Arrange the slices of ham on an oval gratin dish, overlapping somewhat. Pour the Madeira wine over, and place the dish in the oven to heat the meat and evaporate the wine.

4. Coat the meat with the sauce.

5. Arrange the peas in a pile at each end of the dish, and the remainder of the garnish in alternate heaps in pairs facing one another, and sprinkled with a suspicion of the finely chopped parsley.

LANGUES D'AGNEAU AUX ÉPINARDS

4 lambs' tongues.	½ gill brown sauce.
2 oz. carrot.	5 small skinned tomatoes.
2 oz. onion.	2 large peeled potatoes.
1 faggot of herbs.	Oil and butter to sauté.
6 white peppercorns.	1 teaspoonful finely chopped
½ pint brown stock.	parsley.
½ gill tomato sauce.	2½ lb. spinach (see p. 115).

1. Blanch, refresh, and stew the tongues, simmering them slowly $1\frac{1}{4}$–$1\frac{1}{2}$ hours. Put them into a bowl of cold water and skin them. Trim the sides and cut away the root.

2. Slice the carrot and onion about $\frac{1}{4}$ in. thick, and put them with the herbs, peppercorns, and stock in the saucepan. Heat all up, put in the tongues, cover with a greased paper and lid, and place the pan in the oven to braise, basting from time to time for 30 minutes. This process is to improve flavour.

3. Remove the tongues. Pass the stock through a strainer and add the sauces. Boil up together and put in the tongues to keep hot.

4. Skin the tomatoes, and put each in a narrow band of buttered seasoned paper. Poach them in the oven.

5. Wash the potatoes, peel, and cut them into dice. Sauté them golden brown in butter and oil, and put them into the oven to finish cooking.

6. Make a firm mound of the prepared hot spinach in the middle of a round silver dish. Dress the tongues against this, standing up, with the thick part to the bottom.

7. Put a tomato between each two, sprinkled with the parsley, and one on the top.

8. Pour the sauce round, and arrange the potatoes in little heaps round the edge.

NOISETTES DE MOUTON AUX CHAMPIGNONS
(Boned Mutton Cutlets, Mushroom Patties)

5 oval patty cases of puff pastry —6–8 oz. flour, etc. (see p. 218).
1 gill Velouté Sauce (see p. 251).
4 flap mushrooms, medium size.
Maître d'hôtel butter—$\frac{1}{2}$ oz. butter, etc. (see p. 13).

Small potato croquettes, coated with panurette (see p. 119).
Pieces of endive to garnish.
A piece of best end of neck of small mutton, with 5 bones on it, not chopped.

1. Prepare the puff pastry. Shape the patty cases, chill them, and bake in a quick oven.

2. Prepare the Velouté Sauce.

3. Cleanse and chop the mushrooms, removing if necessary any dark part which would spoil the colour of the sauce. Fry them in butter and keep hot.

4. Prepare the maître d'hôtel butter and put to chill.

5. Prepare and fry the potato croquettes.

6. Cleanse, soak, and drain the endive.

7. Cut the roll of meat from the bone, remove the fat, and cut across into 5 noisettes. Grill briskly.

8. Dishing—

(*a*) Drain the mushrooms, add them to the sauce, and fill it into the patty cases. Place a noisette with a small pat of maître d'hôtel butter on top on each case.

(*b*) Dish on a plain dish paper on a hot round gratin dish in the form of a star.

(*c*) Fill in the centre of the dish with potato croquettes and put sprigs of endive between the patties.

PAUPIETTES DE BŒUF

(Beef Rolls)

1 lb. lean beef, cut thickly.	Mirepoix for braising (see p. 14).
4–6 oz. sausage meat.	Riz pilaf or nouilles (see pp.
2 or 3 slices of larding bacon.	201 and 220).

1. Cut the beef into very thin slices, 2 in. by 6 in. Make two small holes at each end of each slice, about ½ in. from each corner point diagonally, and thread a strip of larding bacon through lengthways.

2. Make a farce with the minced trimmings of the beef and sausage meat, well seasoned.

3. Divide the farce between the slices and roll up. Tie round with string.

4. Braise for about 1 hour until tender.

5. Strain the stock and thicken with a little roux.

6. Arrange the paupiettes in a slanting line on a hot dish, strain the sauce over, and garnish with the riz pilaf or nouilles.

POULET À L'INDIENNE

(Curried Fowl)

1 young fowl.	Gherkin tassels.
Oil and butter for frying.	Accompaniments—
1 pint Curry Sauce (see p. 247).	Chutney.
Boiled Rice—	Bombay duck.
4 oz. Patna Rice.	Poppadums.
Coralline pepper.	Fresh grated coco-nut.
Garnish—	Gherkins.
Fans of lemon.	Pickled pimentos.
Chilli skin.	

1. Divide the chicken into joints, remove the skin, and fry the joints lightly in the butter and oil. Drain well on crumpled paper.

2. Prepare the sauce, add the joints to it, and simmer gently for an hour.

3. Pile the joints in a fireproof dish, strain the sauce over, and

garnish with fans of lemon, strips of chilli skin, and gherkin tassels.

4. Serve the plainly boiled rice in a separate dish, sprinkled lightly with coralline pepper.

5. Hand the accompaniments in separate small glass or china dishes, arranged on a tray.

POULET SAUTÉ À LA MARENGO

1 tender young fowl.
Clarified butter, and oil.
Tomato Sauce (½ lb. tomatoes, 1 gill stock, etc., see p. 252).
Brown Sauce (1 oz. dripping and flour, ½ pint stock).
1 doz. champignons.
1–2 truffles.

Garnish—
Heart-shaped croûtons of fried bread.
1 tablespoonful finely chopped parsley.
4–5 fried eggs à l'Américaine (see below).

1. Make the sauces.

2. Divide the chicken into joints; fry them lightly in the clarified butter and oil, and drain well. Trim the joints again if necessary.

3. Heat the sauces in a casserole or stewpan, add the chicken joints, mushrooms, and the truffles cut into batons. Stew gently 1¼–1½ hours.

4. Fry the croûtons of bread, and dip the points to the depth of half an inch in the sauces, then into chopped parsley.

5. Pile the joints in the middle of a flat round dish (silver preferably). Pour the sauce over, arranging the mushrooms and truffles evenly.

6. Arrange the croûtons, with the points outward, and a fried egg on each.

FRIED EGGS À L'AMÉRICAINE

1. Put some olive oil into a small deep frying-pan, and into it also place a crust of bread and a small wooden spoon to evaporate moisture.

2. Break each egg into a saucer, and remove half of the white.

3. Tilt the pan slightly towards yourself, and fry the eggs so that the white surrounds the yolk, using two small wooden spoons to complete the process.

4. Remove the eggs with a small fish slice.

Note. These eggs may be served separately as a Luncheon Dish if garnished with bacon rolls, grilled tomatoes, and fried parsley.

POULET MARYLAND

(To serve 6 persons)

1 steamed chicken.
Potato croquettes (see p. 119).
Horseradish Sauce (see p. 249).
Thickened brown gravy.
Corn Fritters—
  Half a tin of Sweet Corn.
  Half a pint thick Béchamel
  Sauce (see p. 244).

1 egg yolk.
Egg and coating crumbs.
Butter and oil for frying.
3 bananas.
6 small tomatoes.
6 bacon rashers.
Coating batter (see p. 12).

1. Prepare the potato croquettes, Horseradish Sauce, and slightly thickened brown gravy, the latter prepared with chicken stock.

2. CORN FRITTERS. Drain the Sweet Corn, and boil it with the Béchamel Sauce. Bind these with yolk of egg. Place the mixture on a greased dish and leave to become cold. Cut in small rounds, using a floured cutter, and coat with egg and breadcrumbs. Fry golden colour in the butter and oil.

3. FRIED BANANAS. Split the bananas lengthways and across, pass them in flour, then egg and coating crumbs, and fry in shallow fat.

4. TOMATOES. Grill these whole, and finish cooking in the oven, Slightly nick the skin across the top before grilling.

5. BACON. Grill the rashers.

6. CHICKEN. Cut up the chicken when cold, leaving a part of the breast on each wing, and removing the bones from the thigh joint and drumsticks. Flatten each piece, season well on both sides, dip in the coating batter, and fry in deep fat.

7. DISHING. Arrange the chicken piled up on an entrée dish. Place slices of banana on the chicken, the tomatoes at one end of the dish, and the potato croquettes at the other. Place the corn fritters at each side, with the grilled rashers of bacon on top. Hand the Horseradish Sauce and the brown gravy separately.

RIS RE VEAU À LA SUPRÊME

(Braised sweetbreads, Suprême Sauce)

1 large heart sweetbread.
Mirepoix (see p. 14).
1 croûte of fried bread.

½ pint Suprême Sauce (see p. 251).
Preserved champignons or cooked green peas to garnish.

1. Soak the sweetbread in cold salted water for 1 hour.

2. Blanch briskly, and put again into cold water to check cooking.

3. Skin the sweetbread and press between plates until cold. Remove any gristle or fat.

4. Braise gently for $\frac{3}{4}$ hour. Prepare the sauce.

5. Cut the sweetbread into $\frac{1}{2}$ in. slices; arrange these leaning one against the other on an oblong croûte of fried bread, placed on an oval or oblong entrée dish.

6. Coat with Suprême Sauce and garnish with the heated vegetable chosen.

SALMIS DE GIBIER

4 oz. streaky bacon.	Salt and pepper.
1 onion.	2 tablespoonfuls claret.
2 small game birds.	Croûte of fried bread.
3 oz. butter.	Garnish—
1 oz. flour.	1 doz. stoned olives.
1 pint stock.	Fleurons of pastry.
A tiny bouquet garni.	

1. Cut the bacon rashers across in strips, place them on a baking tin, and partly cook them.

2. Place the sliced onion on top, with the trussed birds on that.

3. Place slightly more than half the butter on the birds, and bake in a fairly hot oven for 20 minutes.

4. Untruss the birds, and cut them in half down the middle.

5. Fry the flour brown in a stewpan in the remaining butter, add the stock, bouquet garni, salt, and pepper.

6. Add a few pieces each of well-drained onion and bacon.

7. Stew gently until quite tender, about $1\frac{1}{2}$ hours. Add the claret about 20 minutes before the birds are cooked.

8. Dish the halves of birds on a croûte of fried bread.

9. Correct the seasoning, strain the sauce over, arrange the fleurons on the game, and pile heated stoned olives at one end.

TOURNEDOS À LA PARISIENNE

Croûtes of fried bread.	$1\frac{1}{4}$ lb. middle fillet of beef.
Green asparagus tips or French beans.	$\frac{1}{2}$ pint jus lié (see p. 247).
Parisienne potatoes (see p. 123).	$\frac{1}{2}$ gill of Béarnaise Sauce (see p. 244).

1. Make the jus lié and Béarnaise Sauce and keep hot. Cut a croûton of bread to fit each tournedos. Fry these and keep them hot.

2. Cook the asparagus or French beans, and keep hot in stock until required.

3. Trim the fillet of beef, and cut it into rounds (tournedos) of about 2 in. diameter and 1 in. thick.

4. Prepare the Parisienne potatoes.

5. Grill the tournedos briskly on each side.

6. Dishing—

(a) Place each tournedos on a croûton, with a spoonful of thick Béarnaise Sauce on top.

(b) Dish in a circle, with the asparagus tips or French beans in the centre.

(c) Pour the jus lié around, and arrange the potatoes in small piles between the tournedos.

VEAU SAUTÉ À LA MILANAISE

1 lb. fillet of veal.	1 large tomato (or $\frac{1}{2}$ gill tomato
2 oz. lard and butter (together).	purée).
$\frac{3}{4}$ pint Brown Sauce.	2 oz. spaghetti.
1 rasher of bacon.	Garnish—
1 shallot.	Stoned olives.
1 large teaspoonful sherry.	

1. Cut the meat into neat strips, and fry lightly in clarified lard and butter. Drain well.

2. Make the Brown Sauce, and pour it into a casserole.

3. Add the veal, the bacon (blanched and cut into strips), the sliced shallot, sherry, and skinned sliced tomato.

4. Simmer gently $1\frac{1}{2}$–2 hours.

5. Cook the spaghetti until tender in boiling salted water—about 15 minutes.

6. Pile the meat in the centre of a hot entrée dish, arrange the spaghetti around, and strain the sauce over the whole, after correcting the consistency and seasoning.

7. Garnish with the heated stoned olives and serve.

CHAUDFROIDS

A Chaudfroid consists of cooked meat, game, poultry, or fish which is coated with a well-flavoured and seasoned Chaudfroid Sauce, decorated tastefully, glazed with aspic, and dished smartly.

The pieces used for building up a Chaudfroid must be neatly shaped and trimmed, and quite cold, or one large piece can be prepared, such as a galantine, whole fowl, etc.

A CHAUDFROID SAUCE is prepared from one of the foundation sauces. The ingredients for the sauce depend on the colour required, and the purpose for which it is to be used. The following varieties can be made—

White Chaudfroid Sauces from Béchamel or Velouté Sauce.

Brown Chaudfroid Sauce from Espagnole Sauce.

Fawn Chaudfroid Sauce from half Béchamel and half Espagnole Sauce.

Mayonnaise Chaudfroid Sauce from Mayonnaise.

Terra-cotta Chaudfroid Sauce from half Espagnole and half Tomato Sauce.

Cardinal Chaudfroid Sauce from Béchamel Sauce and Lobster Coral.

Green Chaudfroid Sauce from green vegetable purée or colouring, added to Béchamel or Velouté Sauce.

NOTES ON CHAUDFROID SAUCES

1. The sauce should be of the consistency of a coating sauce. When ready, the sauce should flow over the article to be coated yet be thick enough to mask it entirely. The correct temperature should be ascertained before coating.

2. The sauce should be rendered glossy by the addition of aspic jelly and gelatine, these causing the sauce to set when cold.

Proportion—

1 gill Aspic to 1 pint Sauce, and 4 sheets or $\frac{1}{4}$ oz. gelatine.

3. The gelatine should be slowly dissolved in the aspic and added to the sauce, which has been warmed, and well beaten to remove any lumps.

4. The sauce should then be tammied and cream added if it is a white chaudfroid.

5. When a number of pieces are to be coated, the sauce, when of the right consistency, should be placed in a bowl of hot water. This prevents the sauce from setting before all the pieces are coated.

COLD ENTRÉE RECIPES
ASPIC JELLY

1½ pints stock.	Rind of 1 lemon.
1½ gills sherry and water.	1 onion.
½ gill mixed vinegars (use 1 teaspoonful Chilli vinegar, 1 dessertspoonful tarragon vinegar, and make up the remainder in French wine and white malt vinegars).	1 small carrot.
	½ teaspoonful salt.
	1 stick celery.
	2 oz. gelatine.
	10 white peppercorns.
	Shells and whites of 2 eggs.

As for lemon jelly (see page 136). Leave the vegetables in large pieces, so that they do not break up and cloud the jelly. Aspic jelly is always used a little stiffer than any sweet jelly.

CHARTREUSE DE GIBIER

(Moulded Minced Game)

Filling—
6 oz. cooked game.
1 oz. cooked ham.
1 gill Espagnole Sauce.
½ tablespoonful chopped truffle.
4 chopped champignons.
1 tablespoonful sherry.
¾ gill stiff aspic.
½ gill cream.
Salt and pepper.

Decoration—
Aspic jelly.
Truffle.
White of egg (steamed).
Brown Lining—
½ gill stiff aspic jelly.
¾ gill Espagnole Sauce.
Garnish—
Chopped aspic.
Crimped cucumber or small cress.

1. Mask a plain oval charlotte mould with aspic jelly, and decorate with fancy shapes of truffle and steamed egg white cut in slices.

2. Mask again with aspic, and cover the decoration. Coat with brown lining.

3. Mince, pound, and sieve the game and ham. Mix them with the sauce, truffle, champignons, and sherry, and add the liquid aspic.

4. Fold in the half-whipped cream lightly, season highly with salt and pepper, and pour into the prepared mould.

5. When set, unmould and garnish with chopped aspic and crimped cucumber, or small cress.

Notes. (*a*) If necessary, add a little browning to the sauce for the brown lining, and also tammy it before use.

(*b*) Any kind of game, or mixed game, may be used for this dish.

CHAUDFROID DE VOLAILLE AU MOUSSE DE TOMATES GLACÉS

Half a cooked fowl.
½ pint Chaudfroid Sauce (see p. 73).
Slices of truffle.
Aspic jelly.
Mousse de tomates—
1 finely sliced carrot.

3 button onions.
1 oz. butter.
¾ lb. tomatoes.
½ tin tomato conserve.
Salt and pepper.
½ oz. gelatine.
¾ gill whipped cream.

1. FOR THE MOUSSE—

(*a*) Sauté the carrot and onions in the butter, without browning. Add the tomatoes, cut in quarters. Boil up in their own juice and cook all until pulpy.

(*b*) Drain the tomato mixture and press it through a hair

sieve. Add the tomato conserve, the salt and pepper, and a few drops of carmine if necessary. Add the gelatine, dissolved in a little water.

(c) Place the mixture on ice and add the half-whipped cream.

(d) When it is quite thick, spread the mousse smoothly with a palette knife to the shape of a round dish (silver if possible), raising the mixture slightly in the centre.

2. Divide the fowl into joints, and coat it with the chaudfroid sauce in the usual way (see p. 73).

3. Put a round of truffle on each, and arrange the joints on the tomato mousse.

4. Coat the whole with cold liquid aspic.

5. Pipe round the edge of each joint with chopped aspic, in which some chopped truffle trimmings have been lightly incorporated.

CÔTELETTES D'AGNEAU EN ASPIC

(Lamb Cutlets in Aspic)

A piece of best end of neck of lamb with five bones.	1 pint aspic jelly.
	1 small lettuce.
Salt and pepper.	$\frac{1}{4}$ pint macedoine of vegetables.
Oil and butter for frying.	$\frac{1}{2}-\frac{3}{4}$ gill mayonnaise.

1. Divide the lamb into cutlets, trim them neatly, sprinkle them with salt and pepper, and fry in smoking hot oil and butter.

2. Press between two dishes with a weight on top until quite cold.

3. Dissolve the aspic and pour one-third of it into a sauté pan or a baking-tin rinsed out with cold water.

4. Brush the cutlets with aspic, and lay them about $\frac{1}{2}$ in. apart in the jelly with the bones all curving the same way.

5. Pour the remaining jelly gently over and leave to set.

6. Wash the lettuce well and, when crisp, shred it into fine strips with a sharp knife; form a circle of the shredded lettuce in a round entrée dish.

7. With a sharp knife, dipped in cold water, cut out the cutlets from the jelly, turning the whole thing out on a piece of greaseproof paper rubbed with ice. Arrange the cutlets in a circle on the lettuce with the bones to the inside of the circle.

8. Fill up the centre with the macedoine of vegetables, mixed with the mayonnaise.

9. Chop the remainder of the aspic, and arrange small piles of it around the dish.

CÔTELETTES D'AGNEAU À LA POMPADOUR

5 lamb cutlets, braised and trimmed.

1½ gills White Chaudfroid Sauce (see p. 73).

Green Chaudfroid Sauce—
¼ gill green pea purée.
¼ gill white sauce.

¼ gill aspic jelly, with 2 sheets of gelatine dissolved in it.

Truffle and pimento to decorate.

Aspic jelly, some liquid, and some for piping.

Small cress.

1. Prepare and braise the cutlets for ¾ hour. Press between two dishes, weighted, for 24 hours.

2. Trim the cutlets, and place them on an icing-rack with the bones to the left.

3. Coat 3 cutlets with the White Chaudfroid Sauce, and 2 with the Green Sauce. Decorate the former with pimento and the latter with truffle. Baste with the liquid aspic.

4. Pour some liquid aspic on to a silver dish. When it is set, arrange the cutlets flat upon it in the shape of a fan.

5. Pipe chopped aspic around the edge of each cutlet, and place small cress at the points of the bones.

CÔTELETTES D'AGNEAU À LA RUSSE

(Glazed Lamb Cutlets)

5 lamb cutlets, braised and trimmed.

Meat glaze.

Chopped pistachios, shaken through a wire sieve.

Aspic jelly.

Rounds of potato cut after cooking.

French salad dressing.

Small cress.

1. Prepare the cutlets and braise for ¾ hour. Press them between two dishes, weighted, for 24 hours.

2. Trim the cutlets, then place them on an icing-rack with the bones to the left.

3. Brush the cutlets with the glaze, and dip the sides into the chopped pistachio nuts at once.

4. Pour some liquid aspic on to a flat dish, preferably silver. When it is set, arrange the cutlets flat on it in the shape of a fan.

5. Arrange, at the points of the bones, a small mound of the potato rounds, tossed in French salad dressing and garnished with small cress.

CORNETS DE JAMBON VÉNITIENNE

Aspic jelly.

1 gill mayonnaise.

Slices of cooked ham, about 6 oz.

½ oz. gelatine, dissolved in ½ gill aspic.

Scant ½ pint vegetable macedoine.

Seasoning.

Crescents cut from stiff aspic.

Rounds of truffle.

1. Make the jelly and mayonnaise.
2. Cut the ham in triangular pieces. Dip each piece in liquid aspic jelly and slip inside a cornet mould.
3. Trim round the ends of the cornets with a pair of scissors.
4. Stand the prepared cornets upright, embedded in ice.
5. Dissolve the gelatine in the aspic and strain it into the mayonnaise.
6. Add the macedoine, which has been well seasoned, and fill some of the mixture into each cornet.
7. Make a mound of the remaining mayonnaise and macedoine, in the middle of a round dish, silver preferably. Then spread it to a neat round ¼ in. thick.
8. Unmould the cornets and dish them on the macedoine, placing the points of the cornets to the centre.
9. Arrange crescents cut out from stiff aspic on the flat edge of the dish, and arrange a small mound of chopped aspic in the centre of the points of the cornets.
10. Place the smallest cornet upstanding in it, and a little chopped aspic between each.
11. Brush each cornet with aspic jelly and pipe round the edge with chopped aspic.
12. Place a small round of truffle at the middle of the macedoine, at the end of each cornet.

CRÈME DE VOLAILLE AUX TOMATES

(Chicken and Tomato Cream)

Tomato Jelly—
  ¾ lb. tomatoes.
  ⅓ oz. butter.
  3 tablespoonfuls aspic jelly.
  ¼ oz. gelatine.
Filling—
  ½ lb. cooked chicken, weighed after boning.
  2 tablespoonfuls white sauce.

Seasoning.
  ½ oz. gelatine.
  A scant ½ gill of aspic.
  1 gill cream.
Decoration—
  Aspic jelly.
  Truffle.
  Green salad plants.

The Mould

Line a plain charlotte with aspic jelly, and decorate at the sides and bottom with a bold pattern cut from the truffle. Line the mould a second time with aspic jelly.

Tomato Jelly

1. Slice the tomatoes and cook them in a frying-pan with the butter.

2. Season and rub through a hair sieve. Add the aspic with the gelatine melted in it.

3. When it is quite cold, but not set, line the prepared mould thickly with this jelly. Leave to set.

Mixture

1. Put the chicken and ham twice through a mincer, pound well, and pass through a wire sieve.

2. Add the white sauce, seasoning, and dissolved gelatine.

3. Add the half-whipped cream.

4. When this mixture is quite cold, fill the inside of the prepared mould with it.

5. Unmould when set, and dish on a bed of green salad plants.

CRÈMES DE VOLAILLE À L'ÉCARLATE

Aspic jelly.
Cucumber skin.
Truffle or steamed white of egg.
Small cress.
First Mixture—
 ½ lb. tomatoes.
 ½ oz. butter.
 Seasoning.

½ gill stiff aspic jelly.
⅛ oz. powdered gelatine.
Second Mixture—
 3 oz. cooked chicken or veal
 1 oz. cooked tongue.
 ½ gill Béchamel Sauce.
 ½ gill cream.
 ½ gill stiff aspic.

First Mixture

Slice the tomatoes, and heat them in a small saucepan with the butter and seasoning. Rub through a hair sieve. Add the aspic, in which the gelatine is dissolved.

Second Mixture

Pass the chicken twice through the mincer with the tongue. Pound well with the sauce, and rub all through a wire sieve. Add the half-whipped cream and season well.

Method

1. Line some small plain oval or bouche moulds with aspic. Decorate half with cucumber skin, and the other half with truffle or steamed egg white.

2. Fill the cucumber-decorated moulds half full with the first mixture, and remainder half full with the second mixture. Spread each quite flat, taking care to obtain a sharp clean edge.

3. When these mixtures are set, complete the filling of the moulds with the alternate coloured mixture.

4. Dish in a slanting line on an oval dish. Arrange a little chopped aspic on one side, and small cress on the other.

GALANTINE DE VEAU EN CHAUDFROID

½ lb. lean veal—minced.
¼ lb. pork sausages.
¼ lb. streaky bacon—blanched.
3 oz. breadcrumbs.
Salt, pepper, nutmeg.
½ teaspoonful powdered herbs—
  sieved.
1 raw egg.
2–3 hard-boiled eggs.
½ gill stock.
2 oz. cooked ham or tongue.

½ oz. pistachios and a few
  blocks truffle (optional).
Chaudfroid Sauce—
  ½ pint Béchamel Sauce.
  ½ gill aspic.
  ¼ oz. gelatine (scant).
  Liquid aspic.
Garnish—
  Cucumber skin.
  Red pimento.
  Green salad plants.
  Chopped aspic.

1. Make the Galantine mixture—

(a) Place the minced veal in a basin, together with the skinned sausages, and blanched bacon rashers cut across in fine strips.

(b) Add the breadcrumbs, and season well with the salt, pepper, nutmeg, and herbs.

(c) Beat up the egg, add the stock, and mix all well.

2. Spread the mixture on a pudding cloth, and arrange the whole hard-boiled eggs, and the strips of ham or tongue with their length to the length of the galantine. Also the blocks of truffle and whole pistachio kernels, if used.

3. Form into a short thick roll. Tie up firmly in the pudding cloth, boil for 2 hours, and press in the usual way.

4. Next day remove the cloth, and place the galantine on an icing-rack.

5. Coat with the prepared Chaudfroid Sauce. Decorate as desired, and baste with liquid aspic.

6. Dish on a flat dish, after trimming the ends. Arrange green salad plants on one side, and chopped aspic on the other.

GALANTINE DE VOLAILLE EN CHAUDFROID

(Galantine of Chicken)

1 boiling fowl.
A cupful of sliced potherbs.
Bouquet garni.
Stuffing—
  ¾ lb. sausage meat.
  3 oz. cooked ham.
  3 oz. cooked tongue.
  1 tablespoonful parsley.
  2–3 truffles.

½ oz. pistachios.
Chaudfroid Sauce: ¾ pint
  Béchamel Sauce, etc. (see p.
  244).
Green salad plants.
1–2 tomatoes.
Truffle, pimento, or cucumber
  skin to decorate.
Aspic jelly.

1. Choose a large, somewhat older bird, which has smooth unbroken skin, and is undrawn.

2. Bone the bird (see p. 12), then place it on one side while preparing the stuffing, and the stock for cooking the galantine.

3. For the Stock—

(a) Remove the inside from the carcass of the fowl. Reserve and clean the gizzard, heart, and liver, and burn the intestines.

(b) Break up the bones and neck and cleanse well.

(c) Place all these in a large saucepan (except the liver, which may be used for a savoury), add some salt, and boil up.

(d) Skim and add the potherbs and bouquet garni. Allow to simmer until the galantine is ready.

4. For the Stuffing—

(a) Mix the parsley with seasoning.

(b) Cut the ham and tongue in strips, also the truffle. Blanch the pistachios and leave them whole.

(c) Spread the fowl on the board with the skin side down, and level out the flesh as much as possible. Spread with half the sausage meat in a layer.

(d) Sprinkle with the parsley, and arrange the strips of ham and tongue, truffle, and the pistachios down the middle lengthways from head to tail.

(e) Sprinkle again with the seasoning, and spread over the remaining half of the sausage meat.

(f) Fold up the fowl from each side, and secure with a few stitches with a darning needle and thread.

(g) Tie the galantine in a cloth very tightly, as for roly-poly pudding.

5. For the Cooking—

(a) Place the galantine in the prepared stock, and cook for 2–3 hours, according to the size and age of the bird; turn it over once.

(b) When ready, lift out the galantine, and roll it tightly in a clean dry cloth.

(c) Place the galantine between two dishes or tins, and place about 4 lb. in weight on top.

Finishing—

(a) The next day, remove the cloth and stitches.

(b) Place the galantine on a wire icing-rack, and coat with the chaudfroid sauce.

(c) Decorate, and baste with aspic jelly.

(d) Arrange the galantine on a flat dish on the green salad plants, with piles of chopped aspic around.

LANGUE DE BŒUF AUX CERISES

6 oz. cooked sliced tongue.
½ tin bright red cherries.

1 pint liquid aspic (see p. 73).
Green salad (see p. 181).

1. Arrange the slices of tongue neatly overlapping in an entrée dish.

2. Arrange a circle of well-drained tinned cherries around.

3. Baste with the aspic, which is perfectly cold but still liquid, using just sufficient jelly to come to the top of the cherries.

4. When set, serve with the salad.

Note. Slices carved from the breast of a cold cooked duck or cooked ham may take the place of the tongue.

MAYONNAISE DE VOLAILLE

Half a tender young fowl, boiled or steamed.
1 gill mayonnaise (see p. 248).
2 tablespoonfuls liquid aspic.
Liquid aspic for basting.
Green salad.

Garnish—
1 truffle.
Chopped aspic.
Watercress or small cress.
12 dried walnut halves.

1. Divide the chicken into joints, remove as much skin as possible, chopping away any out-sticking pieces of bone.

2. Lay the joints with the best side uppermost on an icing-rack.

3. Coat each piece evenly with mayonnaise to which the two tablespoonfuls of cold liquid aspic have been added.

4. Decorate each joint with a small round of truffle. Baste with cold liquid aspic, and leave to set.

5. Arrange some carefully prepared green salad plants on an oval flat dish, and in a slanting line, and lay the joints of the chicken on it.

6. Garnish on one side with the chopped aspic, and on the other with the cress. Scatter the walnuts, broken in pieces, at the edges of the aspic.

MOUSSE DE JAMBON BÉCHAMEL

(For 6 portions)

½ lb. cooked ham.
1 tablespoonful tomato conserve.
1 gill aspic.
½ oz. gelatine.
1 gill Béchamel Sauce (see p. 244).
1 gill cream.
Salt, pepper, and cayenne.

2 stiffly whisked whites of egg.
Decoration—
   Truffle, cucumber skin, etc.
Accompaniments—
   Green salad (see p. 181).
   Cumberland Sauce (see p. 244).

1. Pass the ham twice through the mincer, pound it with the tomato conserve, and press through a wire sieve.

2. Dissolve the gelatine in the aspic, and add the sieved ham to it, together with the Béchamel Sauce, the half-whipped cream, salt, pepper, and cayenne.

3. Fold in the whites of eggs, which have been whisked very stiff and dry.

4. When the mixture is thickening creamily, pour it into a large soufflé case, round which a band of stiff paper has been tied.

5. When set, pour on a thin layer of aspic and decorate. Cover the decoration with aspic and leave to set.

6. Remove the paper carefully, and serve with green salad and Cumberland Sauce, handed separately.

MOUSSE DE JAMBON ESPAGNOLE

(For 6 portions)

½ lb. cooked ham.	Carmine.
Salt, pepper, nutmeg.	1½ gills cream.
½ pint Espagnole Sauce (see p. 246).	Decoration—
	½ gill pale-coloured aspic jelly.
½ oz. gelatine.	
1 gill aspic jelly.	1 tablespoonful chopped truffle.
2 tablespoonfuls white stock.	

1. Tie a band of stiff paper around a china soufflé case of 5 in. diameter.

2. Pass the ham twice through a mincer, pound, and sieve it.

3. Season with the salt, pepper, and nutmeg, and add the Espagnole Sauce, which is well coloured and flavoured with tomato.

4. Dissolve the gelatine in the aspic, together with the stock, colour with the carmine, and add.

5. Half whip the cream and fold lightly into the mixture.

6. When it is setting creamily, pour it into the prepared soufflé case, and allow to set.

7. Add the chopped truffle to the aspic, and pour it on the top of the mould when the jelly is cold but not set.

8. Again put aside to set, then remove the paper, and serve. A green salad and Cumberland Sauce are suitable accompaniments.

· *Note.* A mousse of game (Mousse de Gibier Espagnole) can be prepared similarly; either one kind or trimmings from a variety of game can be used.

PIÈCE DE BŒUF EN BERCEAU

(To serve 6 portions)

1 lb. piece of beef fillet, braised.
1 tin foie gras, or pâte pepperium.
½ oz. butter.
Seasoning.
Aspic jelly—about 1 pint.
Carrots and turnips.

Green peas.
French beans.
1 small cauliflower.
1 gill mayonnaise.
¼ oz. gelatine.
Scant ½ gill aspic.
Parsley.

1. Braise the beef fillet, and leave it to become cold.
Next day, trim and slice it.
Then put the foie gras into a little basin with the butter and seasoning, spread a little on each slice of the beef, and put slices together again as a joint.

2. Prepare the garnish—

(a) Cut the carrots and turnips into 1 in. lengths, and stamp out with a column cutter (second size). Cook each separately in boiling salted water, refresh, and drain.

(b) Cook, refresh, and drain the peas.

(c) Trim the French beans, cut them in diamond shapes, and cook, refresh, and drain.

3. Line and decorate a bread tin or oblong ovenware dish, and run a thin layer of aspic at the bottom. Arrange each kind of vegetable in a line lengthways in the tin, and alternately, until the whole of the tin is covered.

4. Cover the vegetables with the aspic jelly to the depth of ½ in. and leave to set.

5. Place the piece of beef in the prepared tin.

6. Make the cooked cauliflower into small balls by squeezing in a cloth.

7. Dissolve the gelatine in ½ gill of aspic, and add it to the mayonnaise. Add half of this to 2–3 tablespoonfuls remains of vegetable garnish, and fill in each end of the mould.

8. Coat the cauliflower balls with the remaining aspic mayonnaise.

9. Fill up the mould with liquid cold aspic and allow the dish to set.

10. Unmould on to an oval dish—silver, if possible— and encircle with chopped jelly.

11. Put a tiny scrap of parsley in the middle of each cauliflower ball, baste with aspic; when they are set, arrange them evenly around the meat.

TIMBALE DE POULET TOULOUSE

4 oz. cooked chicken or veal.
1 oz. cooked ham or tongue.
1 teaspoonful anchovy essence.
½ gherkin—chopped.
1 teaspoonful truffle trimmings.
Salt, pepper, cayenne.
¾ gill aspic.
¼ oz. gelatine.
1 gill cream or good white sauce.
Decoration—
    Aspic jelly.

Truffle.
Cucumber skin, chilli skin,
    or pimento.
Cream Lining—
    4 tablespoonfuls cream.
    2 tablespoonfuls liquid aspic.
Garnish—
    Chopped aspic.
    Small cress.
    Crimped cucumber.

1. Line a plain oval charlotte mould with aspic, and decorate it at the bottom edge with a neat design of truffle and cucumber skin, chilli skin, or pimento. Put a little of the decoration on the sides of the tin also.

2. Set the decoration in aspic to the depth of a scant ½ in. When it is set, line with the cream lining (see p. 14).

3. Mince and pound the chicken and ham. Add anchovy essence, seasoning, chopped gherkin, and truffle.

4. Add the aspic in which the gelatine has been dissolved, and lastly the whipped cream or white sauce.

5. Fill up the mould and make it quite level.

6. When it is set, unmould on to a silver or gratin dish. Garnish with chopped aspic, small cress, and crimped cucumber.

RELEVÉS AND RÔTIS

(Removes and Roast Game, Poultry, or Birds)

THE RELEVÉ

THE Relevé is the most solid dish of the whole meal, and consists of a joint of meat, cooked by braising, roasting, or boiling. Occasionally on the Continent this course is served after the hors d'œuvre or fish, and in England formerly this dish was brought in as soon as the soup tureen was removed—hence its English designation.

CHARACTERISTICS

1. Favourite joints for serving as Relevés are: Saddle of Lamb or Mutton; Leg of Lamb or Mutton; Fricandeau of Veal (braised fillet of Veal); whole Fillet, Ribs, or Sirloin of Beef; Braised Ham or Tongue; Venison, etc. A boiled Turkey or large Fowl might be served in this course; and also, in a Lenten menu, a whole boiled fish.

2. If there are two Relevés on the menu, poultry is served before butcher's meat.

3. A Relevé consists of the whole joint: if carved partially beforehand for ease in service, it must be put together again to appear whole.

4. Have the Relevé quite distinct in character from the entrée and roast.

5. Serve it on a large flat dish with a garnish of vegetables cut rather larger than for an Entrée.

Some typical garnishes for Relevés appear on p. 258.

BŒUF À LA JARDINIÈRE

2½ lb. fresh silverside of beef.	1 pint jus lié (see p. 247).
Spinach purée (see p. 115).	Sprigs of cooked cauliflower.
¾ lb. potatoes, cut in dice, or small new potatoes.	1–2 oz. butter.
	Browned crumbs.

1. Cook the beef by boiling; prepare the Spinach Purée. Cut the potatoes into dice, and cook carefully. Prepare the gravy.

2. Cook a small cauliflower in the usual manner, and divide it into sprigs. Put these on a buttered Yorkshire pudding tin, with a few tiny pieces of butter. Season, sprinkle with the browned crumbs, and dry off in the oven.

3. Dish the meat on a large dish, and strain some of the jus

lié over it. Mound the spinach at one side of the dish, and the potatoes mixed with gravy at the other. Pour round the dish any remaining gravy.

4. Put the prepared cauliflower sprigs in small piles at the ends.

Note. For service as an Entrée, carve some small slices of the meat, and put them overlapping in a crescent on a large silver dish. Place the spinach purée in a mound in the remaining space, and the potatoes and cauliflower on each side.

FILET DE BŒUF À LA DUBARRY

(Fillet of Beef, with Cauliflower Balls)

2 lb. piece of beef fillet.	½ pint Brown Sauce (flowing).
Larding fat.	1 small cauliflower.
Butter and oil.	¼ pint Mornay Sauce (see p. 248).
1 carrot. 1 onion.	1 tablespoonful grated cheese.
½–1 gill Madeira.	Château potatoes (see p. 118).

1. Prepare the fillet of beef and lard it well. Tie it into shape, and place in a saucepan, larded side downward, which has some smoking butter and oil in it.

2. Add the sliced carrot and onion.

3. When all is nicely brown, pour off all the fat, and add the Madeira and Brown Sauce. Bring to boil, and simmer gently for 1½ hours.

4. Cook the cauliflower and squeeze it into small balls in a cloth.

5. Coat each ball on a plate with Sauce Mornay and sprinkle with grated cheese. Brown lightly under the griller.

6. Place the meat on an oval dish, pour the sauce round after skimming well, and arrange the balls of cauliflower at each side.

7. Pile the Château Potatoes at each end of the dish.

FRICANDEAU DE VEAU AUX NOUILLES

(Braised Cushion of Veal)

Mirepoix (see p. 14).	Larding bacon.
3 tablespoonfuls veal stuffing (see p. 17).	Glaze.
	Tomato Sauce (see p. 252).
2 lb. slice fillet of veal.	Nouilles (see p. 220).

1. Prepare the mirepoix.

2. Spread the veal stuffing on the meat, roll up, and tie round securely in three or four places.

3. Lard the roll with small strips of the larding bacon.

4. Place the meat on the mirepoix; cover with a buttered paper and the lid.

5. Cook over gentle heat for 1 hour or a little longer, basting occasionally with the stock.

6. Place the pan in the oven for $\frac{1}{4}$ hour. Remove the meat, place it on a greased tin, and cook for a further $\frac{1}{4}$ hour to crisp the lardoons.

7. Remove the meat to a hot dish and brush with the glaze.

8. Pour the prepared tomato sauce around the meat, and garnish with the cooked nouilles, tossed in a little butter.

GIGOT D'AGNEAU BRAISÉ À LA SOUBISE

1 small leg of lamb.	1½ gills stock.
½ clove garlic.	Seasoning.
3 oz. dripping.	A small bouquet garni.
1 small onion.	½ pint jus lié (see p. 247).
1 clove.	½ pint Soubise Sauce (see p. 251).

1. Bone the leg of lamb, and insert the garlic in the centre. Tie it up firmly into its original shape, using fine string and skewers.

2. Melt the dripping in a braising- or stew-pan. Add the onion stuffed with the clove, place in the meat, and allow it to take golden brown colour over quick heat.

3. Pour off the fat. Add the stock, seasoning, and the bouquet garni.

4. Cover the pan, boil up, then place in the oven to cook 2½–2¾ hours, basting well every 20 minutes.

5. Add the jus lié to the pan 20 minutes before the meat is cooked.

6. Dish up the lamb. Boil up and skim the gravy, and strain it over the meat.

7. Garnish with small mounds of Soubise Sauce, placed round the dish.

GIGOT BRAISÉ BRETONNE

(Braised Leg of Mutton, with Haricots)

1 small leg of mutton, or a leg of lamb.	½ pint good stock.
1 clove garlic.	Garnish—
1 oz. butter.	1 pint haricots (after cooking).
1 tablespoonful olive oil.	1 teaspoonful chopped parsley.
2 carrots, 2 turnips, 2 onions.	Soubise Sauce (see p. 251).
2–3 sticks of celery.	Browned, or Château, Potatoes (see p. 118).
Small bouquet garni.	
½ bottle claret.	

1. Bone the joint, and stick the clove of garlic into the thick part.

2. Melt the butter in a braising pan; add the oil, and heat until smoking.

3. Brown the meat, turning the joint frequently, and set on one side.

4. Add the vegetables, thickly sliced, and brown them lightly. Pour off all superfluous fat.

5. Lay the meat on the vegetables, add the claret, stock, and seasoning. Simmer very gently for $3\frac{1}{2}$ hours.

6. Dish the meat on a large brown earthenware dish. Pour over the gravy (this may be thickened with a little arrowroot if liked), and garnish with the prepared haricots, sprinkled with the parsley.

7. Hand Soubise Sauce and potatoes separately.

LONGE DE MOUTON DEMI-GLACE

2–3 lb. boned loin of mutton.
1 large tablespoonful veal stuffing (see p. 17).
Mirepoix for braising (see p. 14).
Glaze.

Jus lié (see p. 247).
Garnish—
    3 large tomatoes; dice of raw potatoes.

1. Bone the loin of mutton, and stuff it with the well-seasoned veal stuffing. Roll up and tie into shape.

2. Prepare the mirepoix, lay the meat on it, and cover with a buttered paper. Braise for 2 hours.

3. Remove the joint to a hot dish or plate and brush it with glaze. Put it on the serving-dish and pour the jus lié round.

4. Garnish with shells of baked tomato, filled with small dice of fried potatoes, and piled up well.

Note. In Summer time the tomato cases may be filled with freshly cooked green peas.

LONGE DE VEAU BRAISÉ BOUQUETIÈRE

2 lb. loin veal.
1 oz. dripping.
1 carrot.
1 onion.
Sprigs of parsley.
$1\frac{1}{2}$ pints brown veal stock.
$\frac{1}{2}$ lb. tomatoes.
$\frac{1}{2}$ pint jus lié (see p. 247).
Garnish Bouquetière—
    $\frac{1}{4}$ lb. carrots.

$\frac{1}{4}$ lb. turnips.
8–10 button onions.
$\frac{1}{4}$ lb. French beans.
$\frac{1}{2}$ small tin peas.
$\frac{1}{2}$ small cauliflower.
$\frac{1}{4}$ lb. butter.
Sugar. Salt.
1 tablespoonful chopped parsley.

1. Bone the veal and tie round with string in three places.

2. Place dripping in a stewpan, slice carrot and onion coarsely, and add with the veal bones.

3. Lay the salted and peppered meat on top; place 2 or 3 sprigs of parsley at the side. Place the pan in the oven to roast the meat brown.

4. Drain off the superfluous fat, then add the stock. Boil up, adding the tomatoes cut in halves, and finish cooking in the oven, basting well occasionally. Cook about 1½ hours in all, removing the lid when the meat is nearly cooked.

5. Prepare the garnish and keep all hot together in one pan, in separate piles.

6. Place the meat in the centre of a large flat dish (preferably silver) and coat with jus lié. Arrange the garnish in small piles around, to balance on opposite sides of the dish. If desired, a few slices of the meat may be cut.

Garnish Bouquetière—

CARROTS. Peel and cut into small barrels (paysanne). Cook in a small saucepan in a little water with a large nut of butter, about a teaspoonful sugar, and a little salt. By the time the carrots are cooked, the water should be absorbed, and they should look shiny.

Sprinkle with finely chopped parsley when in position on the dish. Also sprinkle turnips, onions, and cauliflower.

TURNIPS. As for carrots.

ONIONS. Treat similarly, but do not cut them.

CAULIFLOWER. Take four large buds and wash them very well. Boil quickly. Refresh with cold water, toss in a little butter, and keep warm.

BEANS. Trim, and slice in long strips. Cook as on p. 105 and heat up in butter. Arrange the beans in bundles with one across the centre.

NOIX DE VEAU AUX ÉPINARDS
(Fillet of Veal, Spinach)

A slice of veal fillet, 1½–2 lb.
1 oz. butter.
1 tablespoonful olive oil.
1 small carrot, and onion.
½–¾ pint Demi-glace Sauce (see p. 245).

Spinach Bouchées—
1 cup cooked sieved spinach.
1 cup stiff white sauce.
½–1 yolk of egg.
Seasoning.
Duchesse potatoes (see p. 119).

1. Tie the veal into shape and brown it in the butter and oil.

2. Add the sliced carrot and onion, brown lightly, and pour off all fat.

3. Pour in the Demi-glace Sauce, and when hot add the meat,

bring up to boiling-point, place the lid on the pan, and cook gently for 1½ hours.

4. Lift out the veal and place it on a hot dish.

5. Correct the seasoning and consistency of the sauce and strain it over the meat.

6. Arrange baked duchesse potatoes at each end of the dish, and the Spinach Bouchées around.

For the Spinach Bouchées—

Mix the ingredients required, and place them in small greased bouche moulds. Stand them in a Yorkshire pudding tin and steam gently until set.

SELLE DE PRÉ-SALÉ DUCHESSE

Piece of loin of mutton, 2 lb., not chopped.	Glaze.
	A little butter.
Duchesse potato mixture (½ lb. cooked potatoes, etc., see p. 119).	Pinch of sugar.
	Sauce—
Green peas, about 1 gill after shelling.	1 tablespoonful tomato conserve.
	1 tablespoonful Madeira.
Slices from 1 medium-sized carrot.	½ gill stock.
	½ teaspoonful arrowroot.

1. Tie the mutton into shape and roast it in the usual way.

2. Pipe the duchesse potato mixture into circles, about the size of tartlets, spirally for two or three turns. Drip some beaten egg over, and bake golden brown in a hot oven.

3. Cook the green peas and keep them hot.

4. Peel the carrot, cut in half lengthways, remove the yellow centre, and slice across finely. Cook these slices in boiling salted water, to which a little butter and a pinch of sugar have been added.

When the water has been quite absorbed, add a little more butter.

5. Remove the roll of meat from the bone, also the undercut, and carve in slices lengthways.

6. Place the bone back on the dish to hold up the meat, and place the slices of meat back on it in position as far as possible. Brush with glaze.

7. Pour off all fat from the meat tin, add the tomato conserve, the wine, and stock mixed with a little arrowroot. Season and boil up, and pour round the meat.

8. Arrange the circles of potato down each side of the dish, piled up alternately with the peas and carrot slices.

THE RÔTI

RULES FOR THE SERVICE OF THE RÔTI

1. The article of food served in this course, whether Game, Poultry, or Birds, must be roasted either before the fire or in the oven. When meat is roasted and served in a dinner, it appears in the Relevé course.

2. When Game is out of season, poultry, such as chickens, capons, ducks, ducklings, goslings, young turkeys, guinea fowls, etc., may be served as game.

3. Game and Poultry are always served with certain accompaniments, viz. good gravy, bread sauce, browned crumbs, chip potatoes, and a green salad dressed with French salad dressing. When serving roast fowl, substitute bacon rolls for browned crumbs; and in the case of roast turkey, substitute bacon rolls and grilled sausages for the browned crumbs.

4. Small birds, such as pigeons or ptarmigan, are served on a croûte of fried bread, and birds which are not drawn (woodcock, snipe, landrail, and golden plover) have a slice of lightly toasted bread placed under them whilst cooking "to catch the trail." This is served with the bird.

POULTRY

In this category come those domestic birds which are suitable for food—fowls, turkeys, geese; ducks; guinea fowls; and pigeons. Poultry is at its best in the Spring and early Summer, when it is young and the flesh is tender and delicate in flavour. The white meat of the breast and wings is the most choice part, the dark meat of the legs being more muscular and of coarser fibre.

To Choose Poultry

In the choice of poultry, age and freshness are the two points to note in addition to plumpness.

1. *If young*—

(a) The legs are smooth and pliable, the scales on them are not thick, and are only slightly overlapping, and the spurs of the male bird are hardly developed.

(b) The feet are supple, and the beak and breastbone pliable—the tip of the latter, being gristle, bends easily.

(c) The skin is white and unwrinkled, the breast plump and white.

(d) The quills on the wings can be easily pulled out, and there should be no long hairs, especially on the thighs.

(*e*) There should be down under the wings and over the body, and the combs and wattles should be small.

2. *If fresh—*

(*a*) There should be no unpleasant smell, and flesh should be firm and show no greenish tinge.

(*b*) The eyes should be clear and not shrunk into the head.

(*c*) The feet should be soft and limp, and the feathers soft and full.

STORAGE

1. Poultry, like meat, must be hung until the time of rigor mortis is past, when the muscles relax, and flesh becomes tender. As an alternative, cook the bird immediately it is killed, plucked, and prepared, and before it is cold.

2. After 36–48 hours the bird can be cooked, although the time for further hanging depends on weather conditions and larder accommodation.

3. If the bird is not to be cooked immediately after purchase, hang it by the feet in a cool, well-ventilated larder. It must not be overhung, and the slightest green tinge on any part of the flesh denotes that it should be cooked at once.

4. The bird should be plucked, but it keeps better if not drawn.

5. Poultry should not be overhung. If there should be any suspicion of taint, wash out the body with cold water, to which a little salt and vinegar have been added; rinse and dry thoroughly with a clean cloth. But it is much better not to use such birds.

THE ECONOMICAL USE OF POULTRY

However carefully and economically it may be prepared and cooked, poultry is dearer in comparison with the average joint, because there is a large proportion of waste in the head, carcass, and other inedible parts.

It is frequently, however, not used to the best advantage. The carcass bones, skin, and trimmings can be made into stock, which will give good flavour for a small quantity of soup or sauce. Remnants of cooked fowl with various additions will form good salads or light entrées, while tiny scraps and trimmings can be made into appetizing savouries, as can also the livers of fowls.

A fowl divided into joints in the kitchen and made into an entrée will "go further" than when plainly roasted or boiled, and also a stuffed roasted fowl is a slightly more economical proposition.

GAME

KINDS

1. *Winged Game.* This includes—

(*a*) Game which is preserved—partridges, pheasants, and grouse.

(*b*) Wild birds—woodcock, plover, ptarmigan, etc., and the smaller wheatears, ortolans, quails, etc.

(*c*) Waterfowl—moorhens, wild duck, etc.

All these birds are roasted and served in the same way in the rôti course.

2. Ground, or four-footed, game includes venison (deer flesh), hares, and rabbits.

WINGED GAME

Choice. Game requires more careful examination than poultry, because it needs more hanging, and is usually sold unplucked.

. In buying birds for roasting, it is necessary to prove that they are young, and for these a higher price may be given. For many entrées, soups, etc., older birds are equally suitable, and less should be paid for these.

The age of birds is denoted by the plumage, beak, and legs, especially at the beginning of the season, when the feathers are not fully developed.

(*a*) In young birds the long quills in the wings are soft.

(*b*) The lower beak is brittle; when the bird is lifted by it, it will break off.

(*c*) The legs will be smooth.

Birds are in good condition if the breasts are firm and well covered with flesh.

(*a*) The eyes should not be shrunken and the plumage should be well conditioned, and the birds should not be badly shot.

(*b*) Special points are that young grouse should have short spurs and "V" shaped quills, and young partridges have yellow legs and a dark bill.

To Keep Winged Game

1. Game requires much care in keeping, as it is tough and tasteless when fresh, and its flavour is usually more appreciated when a certain amount of putrefaction has set in. The time for which it can be kept depends on the state of the atmosphere, as well as on the taste of the consumer.

2. Game should be hung in its feathers in a current of air, and should not be drawn until required for use.

3. Protect it from flies.

4. Game is ready for cooking when the tail feathers come out easily when pulled—unless it is desired very "high."

To Prepare for Cooking

Care should be taken in removing the feathers that the skin is unbroken. Draw carefully, and wipe the inside, but never wash it.

Certain birds should not be drawn before cooking. These are woodcock, snipe, landrail, and golden plover. These birds are often served with the head left on, and are always served on a piece of toast or fried bread that is placed under them while roasting to catch the gravy that falls while cooking.

To Distinguish Between English and Foreign Game

Much foreign game is sold when British game is out of season.

With foreign game the claws are usually hard and dry, the birds are larger, cheaper, and coarser, the skin is sometimes broken, and the breast is hard. The head and plumage are more crushed, and the eyes are shrunken.

VENISON

Venison must be well hung to be tender—a fortnight is not too long in clear cold weather. Dredge with black pepper and ground ginger as a preservative, washing it off before roasting. The haunch is considered to be the choice joint, and roast venison is served as a relevé. It is possible to obtain venison practically all the year round, as buck venison is in season from June to the end of September, and doe venison from November to February.

RABBITS

Rabbits are not wholesome unless perfectly fresh, and should not be hung longer than for one day. In young rabbits the claws are smooth, yet sharp and pointed. The ears are soft and thin and will tear easily, while the cleft in the lip is narrow and the teeth are small and white. Young rabbits are suitable for roasting, and older ones for boiling, stewing, soup, or broth.

HARES

Points for the choice of hares are as for rabbits; but unlike rabbits, hares must be well hung. Hang a hare in its fur by the hind legs for six or seven days with a cup over the mouth to catch the blood, which should be utilized if the hare is to be jugged, or made into soup.

Young hares (up to about 1 year old) are called leverets and will be of about 5 lb. weight; they are suitable for roasting or jugging. Old hares should be used only for soups and forcemeat.

TABLE FOR COOKING POULTRY

Kind	Time for Cooking	Special Points
Turkey.	2½ hours for Turkey about 16 lb.	Male bird is the better for roasting. Bird should weigh not less than 9 lb. or it will be very lean and small—16–18 lb. in weight is good. Hang for a week in cold weather.
Guinea Fowl.	1–1¼ hours according to size.	Flesh very savoury and digestible. Seasonable from Feb. to June, so is a useful substitute for Game, though it may be stuffed as ordinary fowl if preferred. Truss like game.
Fowl.	1 hour; or for a large bird 25 min. to each lb.	See special recipe.
Duck.	About 1½ hours.	Choose two young ducks rather than one very large one. Hang for 2 days. Froth the breast like Game. May be served with Cranberry Sauce or Jelly, or Orange Sauce if preferred. Usually not stuffed in these cases.
Goose.	1½ hours; or up to 2½ hours if large.	Must be well cooked, or is unpalatable and indigestible. Stuff with sage and onion or chestnut stuffing. Serve with gravy, and browned or Château potatoes.

TABLE FOR COOKING GAME

Kind of Game	Time for Roasting	Special Points
Blackcock.	¾ hr.	Have this well hung, or it is rather tasteless. Forcemeat balls may be handed with it.
Golden Plover.	25–30 min.	Do not draw. Place toast under while cooking, and baste constantly with butter. Send to table on the toast, which should be well saturated with the basting and the trail.
Grouse.	35 min.	Hang unplucked for at least 2 days, and further days plucked, according to weather conditions. If it is served "high" be sure to cook it very well.
Partridge.	30 min.	In cool weather this may hang up to a fortnight.
Pheasant (large).	45–55 min.	Hang at least 5 days, or 10–14 days in good weather conditions. A few strips of juicy steak may be placed inside the bird before trussing. Half a dozen of the best tail feathers are usually stuck into the tail end of the bird when dished.
Ptarmigan.	35 min.	Has, when well hung and carefully cooked, a rather bitter, appetizing flavour, which is much esteemed by epicures.
Quail.	20–25 min.	Wrap in vine leaves, if available, placed under fat bacon, or cover with a plain crust. May be cooked undrawn if preferred.
Snipe.	20–25 min.	Do not draw. Serve very hot, and avoid over-roasting. The thigh is considered the best part, and lemon sippets sometimes accompany the bird.
Teal.	25 min.	A waterfowl of delicate flesh. Treat as wild duck.
Widgeon.	25 min.	Waterfowl should not hang longer than 1 day. Serve with orange salad or orange sauce.

TABLE FOR COOKING GAME—(*Contd.*)

Kind of Game	Time for Roasting	Special Points
Wild Duck.	30–35 min.	Sometimes has a slightly fishy flavour, as it feeds largely on fish. It may be trussed like domesticated duck if preferred. Should be crisp and brown on the surface, but rather underdone. The breast is the best part. Serve with orange salad or orange sauce.
Woodcock.	30 min. (Well cooked.)	Frequently preferred very underdone. Serve with orange sauce or orange salad.

CANETON RÔTI

(Roast Duckling)

1 duckling.
Sage and onion stuffing (see p. 17).

Apple Sauce.
½ pint thickened brown gravy.

1. Prepare the stuffing.

2. Pluck, singe, and draw the duck. Cleanse the giblets, and simmer for ½ hour for the gravy.

3. Wipe the inside and outside of the bird with a damp cloth. Scald, and scrape the feet.

4. Cut off the claws and remove the wings at the first joint from the body.

5. Place the stuffing in the body of the bird.

6. Truss the duck with the feet placed across the back, and the ends of the wings caught in behind the legs. Alternatively, the legs may be cut off at the hock joint, then skewered to the sides of the bird.

7. Bake for about 1½ hours in a hot oven at first.

8. Serve with a little of the gravy poured round, the remainder in a sauce-boat, and the apple sauce also served separately in a sauce-boat.

Note. Green peas and new potatoes are the usual accompaniments of duck.

DINDON RÔTI

(Roast Turkey)

1 turkey, 14–18 lb. preferably. Stuffing, see below.	Dripping, or butter and bacon fat, for basting. Accompaniments, see below.

1. Draw and truss the turkey as for Roast Fowl. It may be served unstuffed, with accompaniments as for Game—in this way the full flavour of the turkey may be savoured.

2. When it is to be stuffed, place veal forcemeat in the crop, and, if liked, sausage meat or chestnut stuffing in the body. Serve grilled or baked sausages if sausage-meat stuffing is not served.

3. Tie a buttered paper over the breast, and baste thoroughly and frequently.

4. Hand gravy and bread sauce separately. When turkey is stuffed, it is more usual to serve it with a suitable vegetable and browned or Château potatoes; though it may be served with chipped potatoes and a green salad.

POULET RÔTI

(Roast Fowl)

1 tender fowl.	Gravy.
Dripping and butter for basting.	Watercress to garnish.
1 slice fat bacon.	Bread Sauce.
Veal forcemeat, if liked.	Green salad (see p. 181).
4–5 streaky bacon rashers.	Chip potatoes (see p. 118).

Drawing. Have two bowls of water at hand—one warm for cleansing the fingers, and the other cold to receive the giblets. Place a double thickness of kitchen paper on a board.

1. Hold up the bird by the legs and singe it. Cut off the head, leaving 3 in.–4 in. of neck.

2. Turn the bird over, insert a small sharp-pointed knife at the end of the spine, and slit up the neck. Pull away all loose skin and, gathering it up in the left hand, cut off the neck very close to the top of the spine.

3. From this end remove the crop and windpipe, and any fat which may be present.

4. Turn the bird round, and make a short cut between the tail and the vent. Place the two long fingers of each hand inside the bird at each end to loosen the inside, keeping the fingers high under the breastbone to avoid breaking the gall bladder attached to the liver at the back of the bird.

5. Withdraw the left hand, and hold the bird firmly while taking hold of the gizzard and drawing down all the inside. Be

careful not to break the gall bladder when cutting it off the liver.

6. Place liver, gizzard, which has been cleaned out, heart, and kidneys in the bowl with the neck. Cleanse and use for making stock for gravy. Wrap all remaining in the paper and burn it. Wipe out inside of bird with a damp cloth.

7. Cut round the skin at the hock joint, and draw out the sinews. Cut off the feet; scald and scrape the scaly skin off the remaining piece of leg.

Trussing

1. Fold the flap of skin smoothly over the back at the neck end, and fold the ends of the pinions backward and under to secure it. If the bird is to be stuffed, place the stuffing in the neck end before folding over the flap.

2. Place the bird on its back, and press the legs well down into the sides to plump up the breast. Pass the tail through the vent. Place the bird with the neck end to the right of the worker.

3. Thread a trussing needle with string. Pass it through the first wing joint, through the bird, and out in a similar position on the other side.

4. Insert the needle in the second joint, leaving a stitch of about 1 in. showing. Catch in the legs, and return to similar joint. Tie the string in a bow, making the bird taut and trim, but being very careful not to drag the wing bones under the bird.

5. Re-thread the needle, and pass it through the back of the bird under the hock joints. Pass the string round twice, and tie in a bow at the side.

6. Cover the breast with a piece of fat bacon and a buttered paper. Wrap the legs in greased paper.

Cooking

1. Place the bird on a grid in a meat tin.

2. Bake (in a hot oven at first) basting frequently, 1–1¼ hours.

3. While bird is cooking prepare the accompaniments, and remove the bacon and paper from the bird for the last 10 minutes to colour the breast to an attractive golden colour.

Dishing

1. Remove the string and place the bird on a hot dish.

2. Place the baked rolls of bacon on top, and garnish at the tail end with the watercress.

3. Prepare a thin gravy, pour a little round, and the remainder into a sauce-boat.

4. Serve the Bread Sauce, chipped potatoes, and green salad separately.

Note. If the bird is to be stuffed and served as the only meat course in a dinner, serve a suitable vegetable and browned or Château potatoes with it.

GIBIER RÔTI AU CRESSON

(Roast Game)

1 tender, plump game bird. Fat bacon for barding the breast. Butter and oil for basting. Flour for dredging. Croûte of fried bread.	Accompaniments— Thin gravy. Watercress. Chipped potatoes (see p. 118). Bread Sauce. Green salad (see p. 181). Fried crumbs.

PREPARATION

1. Choose well-hung game—the time for hanging depends on weather conditions and on the taste of the consumer. Wipe the bird inside and out with a damp cloth.
2. Cleanse the giblets and simmer them $\frac{1}{2}$ hour for gravy.
3. Truss the bird as for Roast Fowl (see p. 98), but cut off the ends of the wings, securing the wings with the legs to the sides of the body by means of a skewer.
4. Place a small lump of butter inside the bird, and avoid breaking the skin. Tie a slice of fat bacon over the breast.

COOKING

1. Bake the bird in a moderately hot oven, basting well each 10–15 minutes. Allow time according to the table on p. 96.
2. 10 minutes before the bird is cooked, remove the bacon and baste the bird well. 5 minutes later baste again, dredge with flour, baste, and return to the oven. This is termed "frothing."
3. Serve the bird on a croûte of fried bread (unless the bird is a large one), and garnish with watercress.
4. Serve the Bread Sauce, gravy, fried crumbs, chipped potatoes, and green salad, dressed with French salad dressing, separately.

FRIED CRUMBS. 2 oz. white breadcrumbs. 2 tablespoonfuls clarified butter.

Stir over gentle heat until the crumbs have absorbed the fat quite evenly. Brown them slowly, stirring the crumbs very frequently and giving them constant attention.

ENTREMETS DE LÉGUMES

(Dressed Vegetables and Potatoes)

THE attractive service of vegetables has increased in popularity of recent years. They are not now regarded as merely a necessary accompaniment to a meat dish, but are definitely of interest in themselves. Vegetables less well known in England, such as aubergines, corn cobs, and sweet peppers, are becoming popular, and can be served on a variety of occasions. To serve a dressed vegetable as a separate course in a luncheon or dinner menu is fashionable in a smart meal.

CHARACTERISTICS OF DRESSED VEGETABLES

1. Choose a vegetable that is in season and at its best, or something really uncommon. e.g. fresh peas   carrots etc.

2. See that it is not the characteristic ingredient of any other dish in the menu.

3. As a rule the dish is somewhat elaborate, but choice green peas, asparagus, or similar vegetables may be perfectly cooked and served with oiled butter (beurre fondu).

4. Popular methods of serving dressed vegetables are as beignets or soufflés, or they may be served au gratin, farcis, cold, braised, or accompanied by a rich sauce.

5. Good sauces are largely used in the preparation of vegetable entremets, some of the favourites being Espagnole, Béchamel, Hollandaise, Piquante.

THE PREPARATION OF VEGETABLES

Vegetables are often prepared in a most haphazard way, with no particular trouble taken to consider accurate timing for cooking. Serve them as quickly as possible after they are cooked, because they spoil very quickly on being kept warm. Cook them in small quantities in relays, if the meal is spread over any length of time as in a hotel.

1. Use vegetables in great variety, both in the choice of the food itself and in the method of preparation.

2. Do not wash root vegetables until required for use. The accumulation of soil acts as a preservative.

3. Trim all vegetables well, but economically.

4. Avoid over-soaking vegetables after preparation and before cooking.

5. Blanch strong-flavoured vegetables first, or cook them in plenty of water.

6. Avoid over-cooking vegetables, a more frequent fault than under-cooking them.

7. For most made vegetable dishes, a certain amount of pre-liminary cooking is necessary.

8. Drain vegetables very thoroughly. Many varieties are better if they are well rinsed in cold water as soon as they are cooked (refreshed) and then reheated in butter.

ARTICHAUTS (GLOBE ARTICHOKES)

Globe Artichokes are obtainable most of the year round, if those imported from foreign markets are used as well as the English ones. They are rather scarce in November and December.

This vegetable has three parts—

(*a*) The leaves—of delicate flavour.

(*b*) The fond, or bottom, the firm and fleshy part.

(Both of these are edible.)

(*c*) The choke, which is the fibrous part, and always removed.

Artichokes should be young, fresh, and green looking; unless very large, one is allowed per person.

Artichokes are frequently boiled plainly and served with a suit-able sauce, such as Hollandaise, Tomato, Piquante, or Italienne. The fonds are cooked in different ways, and are often served cold as part of an hors d'œuvre.

To Prepare Artichokes—

Cut off the stalk even with the leaves. Remove the outer leaves near the bottom, and trim the tips of the remainder with a pair of scissors. Rub with cut lemon to preserve the colour. Drop the artichokes into boiling salted water for 10 minutes. Refresh in cold water, then remove all the fibre from the centre.

ASPERGES (ASPARAGUS)

French asparagus is larger and rather stronger in flavour than the English green variety, and also comes into season somewhat earlier. Lauris asparagus is a very choice early French variety, that of Argenteuil following later. Sprew is a very small kind of green asparagus, most useful for garnishes.

In choosing asparagus make sure that it is fresh. Note the cut stalks as well as the tips; they should be fresh and moist, not dry. The tips should be firm: flabbiness is a sure sign of staleness.

To Prepare Asparagus—

Cut the stalks of even length, scrape each lightly without breaking, and dip in water occasionally. Tie into bundles with tape, about 10 or 12 in each, grading the asparagus if it varies in thickness of stalk. Lay in cold water until required for cooking.

AUBERGINES (EGG PLANT)

The delicate flavour of this accommodating vegetable (in reality a fruit, as are also cucumber, tomatoes, and vegetable marrows) lends itself to variety in cooking, and is equally suitable for serving as a dressed vegetable or a simple accompaniment.

Aubergines are in season in the late Summer and Autumn, and are of two varieties—those having glossy skins of deep purplish green and the white aubergine, which is smaller, less attractive, and more egg-like. One medium-sized aubergine will serve two people.

CÉLERI-RAVE (CELERIAC)✓ *Season Nov–Aps.*

Celeriac is a large turnip-shaped variety of celery, cultivation being concentrated on the root. It is more popular in continental markets than in our own.

It has the same flavour as celery, and is really preferable for cooking, as it is less stringy. It has a very delicate flavour; when boiled and served with a suitable sauce, it forms a good accompanying vegetable for boiled turkey or fowl.

Celeriac may also be served raw, when it is usually shredded into fine julienne strips and served in hors d'œuvre, or in salad, mixed with mayonnaise. Also it may be cooked first, cut into dice or shreds, and served cold with mayonnaise.

CHAMPIGNONS (MUSHROOMS)

Cultivated mushrooms, which have a pale fawn colour underneath the caps, are most suitable for cookery, but the fresh English field mushroom has a very fine flavour. Meadow mushrooms are in season in late Summer and in very early Autumn before the frosts come; cultivated mushrooms are in season most of the year and may also be obtained from France.

Mushrooms should be firm and dry, the flesh white and brittle; they should smell fresh and peel easily. See that they come from a reliable source. When soddened and black they are no longer fit for food.

Preparation of Mushrooms—

Trim off the earthy ends of the stems, scrape them, and use for flavouring sauces, etc. Peel the caps, and if it appears to be necessary wash them quickly in salted water, drying well.

CHICORÉE (ENDIVE)

Curled Chicory, or Chicorée frisée, is incorrectly called endive in this country, and is treated as a green salad plant. The other variety, Belgian chicory, is a cultivated form of chicory grown in its natural state in the open air (Flemish chicory).

In cooking Belgian chicory, take care to keep the colour, and remove excess of bitter flavour by parboiling for 7–8 minutes, then refresh in abundant cold water and finish cooking in boiling salted water.

CHOUX DE MER, OR CHOUX MARIN (SEA-KALE)

Sea-kale is a blanched stem, and belongs to the same family as asparagus. Like celery, it is banked up with earth to keep it white, and the effect of light is to make it taste strong and bitter.

It is important to use sea-kale as soon as possible after it is cut, and while white and crisp. When limp and discoloured it is not worth cooking.

It is delicate in flavour, easy of digestion, and stimulating to the appetite.

To Prepare Sea-kale—

Separate the stalks and brush lightly in salted water. Tie in small bundles with tape, as for asparagus, or cut in pieces about 1½ in. long.

COURGES OR COURGETTES (SMALL PUMPKINS)

Very small vegetable marrows can take the place of pumpkins, which are not now much grown in this country. They make most delicious dishes. Unfortunately marrows do not find their way into our markets until they are large and flavourless, but those who grow their own and can cut them when about the length of a small melon will find them delicious.

ÉPINARD (SPINACH)

A particularly wholesome vegetable, rich in iron. It is useful as a component of fish and meat entrées and luncheon dishes, and also as a dressed vegetable. Its greatest drawback is the length of time required for preparing it, because it grows so near the soil that it is usually very gritty, and requires thorough cleansing.

To Prepare Spinach— *served most usually with egg or ham.*

(a) Pick over the leaves, and remove the stalks.

(b) Wash in several waters—usually 5 or 6 are needed to ensure that the last water is perfectly clear.

(c) Put the wet leaves into the saucepan, adding no extra water for cooking.

FLAGEOLETS (SMALL HARICOT BEANS) ✓

Flageolets are beans similar to Haricots, but delicately green in colour and slightly longer and narrower in proportion. They can be obtained fresh in the late Summer, and then cook very quickly. For the remainder of the year recourse can be made to the dried variety, or they may be obtained in tins. Dried Flageolets are soaked overnight in cold water after washing, and cooked like Haricots; but as their skins are less tough, bicarbonate of soda is unnecessary, and a shorter time is required for cooking.

Flageolets can be used as a garnish if tossed in a little butter with pepper and salt after cooking, or made into a delicate purée. *⟨handwritten annotation⟩*

HARICOTS VERTS (RUNNER BEANS)

To ensure serving these in perfection it is essential to use only those which are very young, and to promote a brilliant green colour in cooking. For the latter: soak them in icy cold water after slicing and before boiling, drain them quickly, and plunge them into a large pan of fast-boiling water, then boil rapidly until *just* cooked. Drain and refresh with abundant cold water until absolutely cold. Re-heat in butter and serve.

MAÏS (AMERICAN SWEET CORN OR CORN ON THE COB) ✓

Sweet corn can be obtained fresh from August to November, and is then suitable for serving "on the cob," plainly boiled, and with oiled butter handed separately. The tinned variety can be obtained for use in made dishes all the year round—Corn Fritters, Cream of Corn Soup, Corn Scallops or Soufflés, etc., are simply prepared and very appetizing, and Sweet Corn also forms a good stuffing for tomatoes.

To Prepare and Boil Corn—

Trim the corn and pull out the silky threads from the stem end. Tie into shape if necessary, place in boiling salted water with a little milk added, and boil 25–40 minutes according to size and age, until the grain is soft. Drain very well, and serve on a folded napkin, pulling back the leaves that surround it, and exposing the bared cob.

If fresh Sweet Corn is to be served as an accompaniment or for made dishes, scrape the grains from the stalk, and for the former use toss it in a little butter or cream with seasoning.

MARRONS (CHESTNUTS)

Chestnuts are very cheap and plentiful, and their possibilities in cookery are often not realized in this country—numerous dishes which are nourishing and appetizing are made from them in Spain, Italy, France, and Switzerland. There are several varieties of edible chestnuts, but the Spanish or Italian are most suitable for culinary purposes, as they are larger and of better flavour.

In Italy, chestnuts are ground to a meal which is used for thickening soups and also for making bread; but in this country they are used mostly in the form of a purée, as soup, as an accompanying garnish for meat, as stuffing, or as a sweet.

To Skin Chestnuts—

Make a slit across the point of each nut, place them in a pan of boiling water, and boil for 10 minutes. Drain, and remove the outer husk and the inner skin with a small knife, breaking the nuts as little as possible. Or, after slitting, place them in a moderate oven on a tin containing a little water, and bake for 8–10 minutes.

OSEILLE (SORREL)

A very pungent vegetable, which may be used as a substitute in practically any recipe containing spinach. It is particularly good in omelettes or as an accompaniment to veal, but should be served in definitely small portions.

To Prepare and Cook Sorrel—

Pick over and remove any pieces of violet colour on the stalks. Wash thoroughly and cut the leaves into shreds, unless the vegetable is to be sieved afterwards. Cook gently in a little butter, or a suspicion of water, when the sorrel appears to melt down and soften. Drain and finish as for spinach.

POIVRONS DOUX (SWEET PEPPERS, OR PIMENTOS)

These large Capsicums are quite mild in flavour, and must not be confused with the strong burning variety from which the various kinds of pepper are manufactured.

These larger Capsicums can be green, yellow, or red in colour, and can be served as a dressed vegetable (the green ones being somewhat the better variety to use for this purpose), and the red ones are used largely as a garnish.

If they are large and somewhat old, grill them, or drop them into boiling water first to remove the skins. For use as a garnish, braise them after peeling, and cut in rings or as desired.

Red capsicums may also be procured in tins for garnish or for use in made dishes.

Prepare green pimentos as on p. 116.

TOPINAMBOURS (JERUSALEM ARTICHOKES)

Jerusalem artichokes are the tubers of the Girasole plant, a variety of sunflower, and the vegetable has no connection with Palestine at all.

The delicate flavour of this vegetable makes it a very suitable accompaniment, although its somewhat smoky taste causes it to be an acquired flavour to some people.

Preparing and Cooking Jerusalem Artichokes—

In preparing and cooking, aim specially to keep the white colour. In order to do this scrub the tubers, then peel them in water acidulated with lemon juice or white malt vinegar. Keep them in fresh water similarly prepared until ready to boil—about 35–45 minutes (until tender) in salted and acidulated water. Drain and coat at once with sauce; or lay a folded cloth closely on top, to keep them from contact with the air until the sauce is quite ready.

ASPERGES AU BEURRE FONDU
(Asparagus, oiled butter)

1 bundle asparagus.	Beurre Fondu (see p. 12).
Salt and a lump of sugar.	

1. Prepare the asparagus as on p. 102.
2. Cook in boiling salted water, to which the lump of sugar is added, putting in first the bundles with the thicker stems.
3. Boil gently until tender, remove, and drain well.
4. Serve in a hot vegetable dish with a little Beurre Fondu poured over the tips, and the remainder served separately in a hot sauce-boat.

Note. Other sauces suitable for serving with asparagus are: Béchamel, Velouté, Hollandaise, Béarnaise, Mayonnaise, Remoularde, and Tartare Sauces. French Salad Dressing may be served with asparagus when cold.

AUBERGINES FRITES

2 aubergines.	Fried parsley.
Milk.	Tomato Sauce (see p. 252).
Seasoned flour.	

1. Peel the aubergines, and cut in thin slices on the slant. Pass in milk, then in seasoned flour.
2. Fry in deep fat, being very careful to keep the slices separate.
3. Serve overlapping on a gratin dish, with fried parsley in the centre.
4. Hand tomato sauce separately.

Note. If the aubergines seem rather watery, express some of the liquid by piling the slices on a plate and sprinkling them with salt. Place another plate on top with a weight on it, and leave for an hour.

Slightly thicker slices may be coated with egg and breadcrumbs before frying.

AUBERGINES GRILLÉES

Peel, slice, and extract water as above. Dip each slice in salad oil and grill until tender and golden-coloured.

Either of these methods is excellent for preparing aubergines to serve with veal.

AUBERGINES AU GRATIN

2 aubergines.	Dried crumbs.
Frying fat.	Shavings of butter.
Farce, as for Courgette Farcie (see p. 114).	Tomato or Piquante Sauce (see pp. 252, 249).

1. Cut the aubergines in half lengthwise. Cut criss-cross over the surface lightly to ensure even cooking.

2. Cook in smoking fat until brown.

3. Take out part of the inside, chop and mix with the farce. Refill the case, sprinkle with breadcrumbs, and put small shavings of butter on top.

4. Place on a greased tin to cook in a moderate oven, and serve with Tomato or Piquante Sauce poured round.

A Simple Stuffing—

Melt 2 oz. butter in a small saucepan and fry ½ tablespoonful finely chopped onion in it. Add 2 oz. cooked minced lean ham, the chopped pulp of the aubergines, and 2 oz. fresh breadcrumbs. Season, and heat all well to bind. Cool somewhat, add 1 oz. grated cheese, and mix well. Proceed as above.

AUBERGINES AUX TOMATES

2 medium-sized aubergines.	½ tablespoonful finely chopped parsley.
¼ lb. tomatoes.	
½ tablespoonful finely chopped onion.	Salt and pepper.
	Shavings of butter.

1. Peel and slice the aubergines thinly. Cook the slices in boiling salted water for 10 minutes.

2. Drain well, and place in layers in a buttered fireproof dish with slices of skinned tomatoes, and a sprinkling of chopped onion and parsley, salt, and pepper, alternately.

3. Put shavings of butter on the top layer, which should be

formed of aubergine slices, put on the lid, and cook gently in the oven for 1 hour.

Alternatively. Add 2–3 tablespoonfuls stock to the dish; cover the top with breadcrumbs, grated cheese, and butter shavings. Omit the lid, and, after baking as above, brown under a griller for a few minutes, and serve at once.

CAROTTES À LA BRUXELLOISE
(Carrots with a cream sauce)

½ bunch of young spring carrots.
1 oz. butter.
1 gill white stock.
2 yolks of eggs.

½ gill cream.
Seasoning.
1 teaspoonful finely chopped parsley.

1. Wash and scrape the carrots, trim, and leave whole if very tiny, or cut lengthways into halves and quarters.
2. Blanch them in slightly salted water.
3. Drain and dry the carrots, and toss them over the fire in the butter, without browning.
4. Add the white stock, season, and cook gently until the carrots are tender, time according to size.
5. Beat the yolks with the cream, remove the carrots, and blend the liaison with the stock.
6. Add carrots to reheat, and also the finely chopped parsley.
7. Serve in a hot dish.

Note. If old carrots are used take 3 or 4 of medium size. Cut in half lengthways after peeling thinly, place cut side on a board, and slice thinly. Cut out the yellow part with a small round cutter of about the size of a shilling, leaving a semi-circular space.

CAROTTES GLACÉES

Carrots.
Butter.
Sugar.

Salt.
Parsley.

1. Cut the carrots into 1¼ in. lengths, and then into sections. "Turn" the pieces of carrot in barrel shapes.
2. Place the carrots in a saucepan, add a pinch of salt, a large pinch of sugar, and a small piece of butter. Cover with cold water and bring to boil, covered with the lid.
3. Allow to cook rapidly until tender, then remove the lid, and continue the rapid boiling until all water is evaporated.
4. Toss the carrots over heat to glaze them.
5. Dish neatly, piled in a vegetable dish, and sprinkled with chopped parsley, or use as garnish.

Note. Small young carrots may be left whole.

CELERIAC BOUILLI

1 large celeriac.
Boiling water.
Lemon juice.

½ pint of Egg, Parsley, or Cheese Sauce.

1. Wash and brush the celeriac; peel off the outside brown skin, and remove any brown parts.

2. Cut the vegetable into small cubes and soak in cold water for ½ hour.

3. Drain off the soaking water. Cook in boiling water, to which the juice of half a lemon has been added, from ½–¾ of an hour, until quite tender when pierced with a fork.

4. Drain well, and put the celeriac into a hot serving-dish.

5. Coat with sauce which has been made partly with the liquid in which the vegetable has been cooked.

CELERIAC EN COQUILLES

1 large celeriac.
½–¾ pint coating sauce.
Dried white breadcrumbs.

Oiled butter.
Coralline pepper.
Sprigs of parsley.

1. Boil the celeriac as above.

2. Put a little of the sauce into 5 greased scallop shells, and arrange the cubes in a mound in each.

3. Coat with the sauce, sprinkle with dried white breadcrumbs and the oiled butter. Brown under a griller.

4. Sprinkle with the coralline pepper and serve, garnished with sprigs of parsley.

CHAMPIGNONS FARCIS

8 small flap mushrooms.
1 dessertspoonful chopped cooked ham.
1 tablespoonful breadcrumbs.
1 teaspoonful finely chopped onion.
1 teaspoonful chopped parsley.

½ oz. butter.
Pepper and salt.
1 tablespoonful brown or white sauce.
4 croûtes of fried bread.
Coralline pepper.

1. Wash the mushrooms in salted water; remove the skins and stalks.

2. Stamp into equal-sized rounds with a cutter.

3. Chop the trimmings finely.

4. Fry the onion and chopped mushrooms in the butter for 10 minutes.

5. Add the other ingredients, with sufficient sauce to bind.

6. Pile the mixture on the underside of the prepared mushrooms.

7. Put on a greased tin, cover with greased paper, and bake until soft in a moderate oven about 20 minutes.

8. Dish on the fried croûtes, and decorate with coralline pepper.

CHICORÉE À LA CRÈME

4–5 heads of chicory.
1 oz. butter.
1 tablespoonful cream.
Salt, pepper, and nutmeg.

1½ gills Béchamel Sauce (see p. 244).
Lemon juice.
Croûtons of fried bread.

1. Wash and pick over the chicory thoroughly. Remove the outside leaves, trim the ends, and examine the inside of the leaves carefully.

2. When it is drained, cook in boiling salted water until tender, and drain again.

3. Rinse in cold water, press well to extract all the water, and cut the chicory into even-sized pieces.

4. Place the chicory in a casserole with the butter, salt, pepper, and nutmeg. Stir over heat with a wooden spoon, and add a tablespoonful of thick cream.

5. Dish up, and pour over the Béchamel Sauce, acidulated with lemon juice, and garnish with croûtons of fried bread.

Note. Do not allow any metal to touch the chicory while cooking, as this causes it to lose its colour.

Chicory may also be served "en coquilles" as for celeriac (see p. 110).

BEIGNETS DE CHOU-FLEUR

1 medium-sized cauliflower.
½ pint thick white sauce.
Paprika pepper.
Fried parsley.
Tomato Sauce (see p. 252).
Batter—
 2 oz. flour.

½ oz. butter (oiled).
1 yolk of egg.
1 tablespoonful cream.
½ gill lukewarm water.
2 whipped whites of eggs.
Salt.

1. Boil the cauliflower in the usual way, removing it when barely cooked.

2. Divide it into sprigs, and dip them when cold into the hot sauce. Allow them to become set and quite cold.

3. Dip in coating batter and fry in deep fat.

4. Drain, and pile in a gratin dish, sprinkled with paprika pepper, and garnished with fried parsley.

5. Hand the Tomato Sauce separately.

Note. Take GREAT CARE that the cauliflower does not become overcooked.

CRÈME AU CHOU-FLEUR

½ gill cauliflower purée.
¾ gill cream.
¾ gill Béchamel Sauce (see p. 244).
¼ gill stock.
Salt and pepper.
¼ oz. gelatine.
¼ gill water.

Decoration—
  Liquid aspic jelly.
  Truffle.
  Balls of cooked carrots.
For the Garnish—
  Chopped aspic.
  Small cress.

1. Line a mould with liquid aspic, and decorate with the truffle and carrot. Mask again, and set the decoration with jelly.

2. Prepare the purée from cooked cauliflower. Half whip the cream, and mix it with the sauce, stock, purée, and seasoning.

3. Dissolve the gelatine in a little water, and add it.

4. When the mixture is setting creamily, pour it into the prepared mould and allow to set.

5. Unmould, and garnish with chopped aspic and bunches of small cress.

Notes. (*a*) A purée of almost any kind of vegetable may be used—spinach, green peas, and Jerusalem artichokes being specially suitable.

(*b*) A more economical cream may be made by omitting the cream and doubling the white sauce.

CHOU-FLEUR POLONAISE

1 medium-sized cauliflower.
3 oz. butter.
1 teacupful white breadcrumbs.

1 hard-boiled egg.
1 tablespoonful chopped parsley.

1. Plainly boil the cauliflower in the usual way, taking it up when *barely* cooked, and dividing it into sprigs. Drain these on a cloth.

2. Place the sprigs on a buttered tin, with a few tiny shavings of butter on top. Season, and dry them off in the oven.

3. Arrange the sprigs dome-shaped in a vegetable dish.

4. Fry the breadcrumbs in the remaining butter until golden brown. Mask them over the surface of the cauliflower.

5. Sprinkle the surface with sieved hard-boiled egg yolk and chopped parsley Arrange chopped white at each end.

6. Pour a little nut-brown butter carefully into the dish.

CHOU DE MER

1 bundle sea-kale.
  (about 1 lb.).
Boiling salted water.
Juice of half a lemon.

1 tablespoonful flour.
Slice of toast.
Hollandaise or other suitable Sauce.

1. Separate the stalks of the kale, and brush lightly in cold water, cutting off the roots, and being careful not to brush off the buds.

2. Tie the pieces in small bundles with tape, as for Asparagus (or cut into small pieces, about 1½ in. long).

3. Have ready a saucepan of boiling water (sufficient to cover the sea-kale) to which has been added the lemon juice and the flour slaked with a little water.

4. Cook until tender, ¾–1 hour, boiling gently meanwhile. Drain thoroughly. Some of the liquid may be reserved to make the sauce, if desired.

5. Serve neatly on a piece of toast, to complete the draining, with Hollandaise or similar good sauce poured over.

Note. Sea-kale may also be served cold with Vinaigrette or Mayonnaise.

CASSOLETTES DE CONCOMBRE

1 long, straight cucumber.	Croûtes of fried bread.
1 oz. cooked minced chicken.	Strips of chilli skin or small
1 oz. cooked minced ham or tongue.	rounds of pimento.
2 anchovy fillets, minced.	Garnish—
Salt and pepper.	Small cress or watercress.
Mayonnaise to mix.	½ pint aspic.

1. Cut the cucumber into blocks about 1 in. long, and stamp out cassolette cases with a fluted cutter for the outside and a plain one for the inside.

2. Cook the cases in boiling salted water for about 7 minutes, being very careful to preserve their shape.

3. Mix the chicken, ham, and anchovies with mayonnaise to hold all together, adding the seasoning.

4. Mount each cassolette when cold on a croûton of fried bread, and fill it with the mayonnaise mixture, piling it slightly at the top.

5. Place cross strips of chilli skin or a small round of pimento on each. Baste with liquid aspic.

6. Dish in a circle on a round dish, with chopped aspic in the centre.

7. Garnish with the prepared cress between each cassolette, and serve iced if possible.

CONCOMBRE ÉTUVÉ

1 large, straight cucumber.	Pepper, nutmeg, and lemon
½ teaspoonful sugar.	juice.
Salt.	1 yolk of egg.
1 oz. butter.	1 dessertspoonful finely chopped
1 dessertspoonful flour.	parsley.

1. Trim a small piece off each end of the cucumber. Peel it, and cut in ½ in. slices.

2. Stamp out the seeds in the centre with a small plain cutter to form rings.

3. Place these in a fireproof casserole with the sugar, salt, and just sufficient boiling water or white stock to cover.

4. Put on the lid and simmer until the cucumber is tender but not broken.

5. Drain and arrange the cucumber neatly in a hot dish; reserve the liquid to make sauce.

6. Melt the butter in the casserole, blend it with the flour, and complete the sauce.

7. Season with pepper. nutmeg, and lemon juice, remove from heat, and stir in the yolk and parsley.

8. Cook carefully until thickened, and pour the sauce over the cucumber; see that it is not too thick to show the shapes of the rings.

Note. This dish is particularly suitable to serve with veal because of its delicate flavour.

COURGETTE FARCIE

1 very small pumpkin or marrow.
Mirepoix (see p. 14).
½ pint thickened brown gravy.
Stuffing—
  1 small onion.

2 tomatoes.
1 oz. butter.
2 oz. cooked meat (minced or chopped).
1 oz. braised rice (see p. 201).
Seasoning.

1. Cut the stalk of the pumpkin or marrow with a small piece of the fruit left on it. Peel the fruit chosen, and scoop out the seeds with a vegetable scoop. Reject any seeds and chop up any of the pulp finely.

2. Plunge the case into boiling water for 2 minutes and then into cold water.

3. THE STUFFING. Fry the chopped onion in the butter, and add the concassed tomatoes (see p. 281). Simmer for a further 10 minutes. Add the meat and rice, season well, and mix thoroughly.

4. Fill the case with the stuffing, knocking it occasionally to ensure even packing.

5. Prepare a mirepoix in a Yorkshire pudding tin and place the case on this, replacing the stalk to act as lid.

6. Cover with a greased paper. Cook on top of the stove until the stock used in making the mirepoix boils, then place in the oven until tender, at least 1 hour, in moderate heat.

7. Serve in a hot gratin dish with the gravy poured round.

ÉPINARDS À LA CRÈME

2 lb. spinach.
1½ oz. butter.
½ oz. flour.
Pepper, salt, and nutmeg.

½ gill cream or Béchamel Sauce (see p. 244).
Triangular croûtons of fried bread.

1. Wash the spinach thoroughly in five or six waters and put the leaves into a saucepan while still very wet.
2. Add a little salt and cook without additional water until tender.
3. Refresh the spinach under running water until quite cold. Strain in a colander, and squeeze into small balls in the hand.
4. Pass the spinach through a fine wire sieve. Melt 1 oz. butter in a saucepan. When smoking hot and nut coloured put in the spinach and dry it off, adding Beurre Manié (made from the remaining butter and the flour) in small pieces to bind.
5. Correct the seasoning, and stir in sufficient cream or boiling Béchamel Sauce to form a creamy texture.
6. Serve mounded in a hot vegetable dish, neatly marked with a knife. Garnish with triangular croûtons.

Triangular Croûtons of Fried Bread—

Cut slices of ¼ in. thickness from a sandwich loaf. Cut into squares, and again into triangles. Bevel the edges with a small sharp knife, and fry golden brown in clarified butter.
Note. Hard-boiled egg—sliced or having yolk sieved and white coarsely chopped separately—might be used as an alternative garnish.

FLAGEOLETS MAÎTRE D'HÔTEL

½ pint dried flageolets.
½ pint Béchamel Sauce (see p. 244).

2 teaspoonfuls finely chopped parsley.
Lemon juice.
Seasoning.

1. Soak and cook the flageolets as on p. 105.
2. Prepare the Béchamel Sauce (flowing consistency); add the well-drained flageolets, the chopped parsley, lemon juice, and seasoning.
3. Toss all lightly together and heat well. Serve in a hot dish.
Note. Allow twice the amount of fresh or tinned flageolets.

POIVRONS DOUX AU GRATIN

(Stuffed Green Peppers)

6 even-sized small green peppers.	Alternative Stuffings—
White stock.	Duchesse Potatoes (see p. 119).
Dried crumbs.	Minced veal in white sauce
Shavings of butter.	(see p. 171).
6 croûtons of fried bread or toast.	Cooked sweet corn in white sauce (see p. 105).
Suitable Sauces—	Veal stuffing, to which a
Demi-glace.	little chopped cooked ham
Tomato.	is added (see p. 17).
Jus lié.	Braised rice (see p. 201).

1. Wipe the peppers—there is no need to skin them if they are young.

2. Cut off the stem ends, and reserve them. Slit the peppers down one side; remove the seeds and white pith with a teaspoon.

3. Parboil the peppers in water boiling gently, 5–10 minutes, according to their age and size.

4. Stuff the peppers as desired. Almost any stuffing may be used at discretion, but it is essential to choose one of delicate flavour, which will not mask the flavour of the pepper itself. Replace the stems, fastening them in position with game skewers.

5. Place the peppers in a greased fireproof dish, and add white stock to come half way up the peppers. Sprinkle with dried crumbs and butter shavings, and bake gently for 20–25 minutes.

6. Serve each pepper on a strip of fried bread or toast, and hand a suitable sauce separately.

SALSIFIS AU BÉCHAMEL

1–1¼ lb. salsify.	½ pint Béchamel Sauce (see p. 244).
2 teaspoonfuls lemon juice or white malt vinegar.	Coralline pepper.

1. Wash the salsify, and scrape it thoroughly, using a teaspoonful of lemon juice or white malt vinegar to acidulate the water.

2. Tie in bundles and boil gently in water acidulated as foregoing. Cook for about ½ hour.

3. Drain well, and coat at once with the Béchamel Sauce. Sprinkle with the coralline pepper and serve.

TOMATES POCHÉES

9 small even-sized tomatoes.	Greaseproof paper.
2 oz. butter.	Chopped parsley.

1. Select firm tomatoes; carefully remove the skins.

2. Fold a piece of buttered seasoned paper round each, holding it in place with a small rubber band. Place the tomatoes on a buttered tin with a small piece of butter on top of each.

3. Lay a greased paper over and cook in the bottom of a moderate oven until quite tender.

4. Remove paper and serve with chopped parsley on top.

TOPINAMBOURS FRITS

1 lb. Jerusalem artichokes.	1 egg. Coating crumbs.
Lemon juice. Salt.	Fried parsley.
1 gill milk.	1 gill Tomato Sauce (see p. 252).

1. Peel the artichokes, putting them at once into water containing lemon juice or vinegar.

2. Cook in about 1 quart of boiling salted water, to which the juice of half a lemon and 1 gill of milk have been added.

3. When the artichokes are barely cooked, drain, and fold them in a teacloth until cold.

4. Coat each with egg and breadcrumbs, fry in deep fat, and drain well.

5. Prepare the tomato sauce, using some of the liquid in which the artichokes were cooked, and hand this separately.

6. Garnish the artichokes with fried parsley and serve.

POMMES DE TERRE

POMMES ALLUMETTES

1. Cut potatoes into slices, then into the size and shape of a large match.

2. Wash, soak, and drain in the usual way. Place the potatoes into fat which is barely smoking to poach. When cooked, remove the potatoes and place them aside.

3. Reheat the fat until smoking, and cook the potatoes a second time until golden in colour.

4. Serve them as soon as they are ready, as they do not keep crisp, dishing them on a paper on a hot dish, and sprinkling with fine salt.

Note. This method may also be used for larger strips of potatoes, which are often quite wrongly called "chips."

POMMES DE TERRE ANNA

About 1½ lb. potatoes.	2–3 oz. butter.
1½ oz. dripping	Chopped parsley.

1. Melt the dripping in a small sauté pan or shallow cake tin, and with this well grease the mould chosen.

2. Peel the potatoes, cut them in even slices of the thickness of a shilling. Dry them well or they will stick.

3. Heat the dripping until smoking in the tin, and range the slices of potato in the form of a circle, slightly overlapping, in the prepared tin. Sprinkle each layer with oiled butter and seasoning.

4. Continue to the depth of $1\frac{1}{2}$ in.–2 in. See that the potatoes are closely packed and press well. Cook the potatoes as soon as they are packed or they are liable to blacken.

5. Put the tin into a fairly hot oven (380° F.) and cook until somewhat brown. Turn over the cake of potatoes with the aid of a flat saucepan lid. Slide it back into the tin, and return it to the oven to cook until both sides are the same colour.

6. The time for cooking varies according to thickness, but the above quantity will take $\frac{3}{4}$–1 hour.

7. Invert on to a hot silver dish, put a little butter on the top and some chopped parsley.

Note. The potatoes should turn out like a cake, which should be soft inside and crisp without.

POMMES CHÂTEAU

1–$1\frac{1}{2}$ lb. potatoes.	Salt and parsley.
Clarified butter and dripping.	

1. Cut some medium-sized potatoes in quarters, shaping them into large olives. Blanch in salted water, and drain at once.

2. Place sufficient dripping and butter in a meat tin to cover the bottom when melted. When it is smoking hot, drain the potatoes in a cloth and put them into the fat.

3. Allow the potatoes to colour all over quickly, cover with a baking tin, place in a moderate oven, and cook steadily until the potatoes are tender.

4. Season lightly with salt during cooking. Strain off the fat and drain the potatoes well.

5. Serve piled neatly in a hot vegetable dish, sprinkled with a little fine salt and chopped parsley.

POMMES CHIPPES

1. Choose large potatoes and cut them in half lengthways.

2. Trim off the ends if they are at all pointed, and slice them thinly down on to a chopping-board.

3. Soak them in plenty of very cold water, separating the slices to prevent them from matting together.

4. Drain in a colander, then leave wrapped in a cloth for 20 minutes, again separating the slices.

5. Fry the potatoes in a frying-basket a few at a time in fat

which is just smoking, and remove them when the bubbling subsides.

6. Two or three batches may be put together for the second frying in smoking hot fat. Turn them loose into the pan as soon as there is no danger of the fat bubbling over, and keep them well separated with a wire frying-spoon.

7. When evenly golden brown, remove with the wire spoon, drain, and pile on a plain dish paper on a hot dish. Sprinkle with salt. Do not cover with a lid.

Note. If the potatoes are small take whole slices across. These potatoes are often colloquially called "game potatoes," as they are served with roast game or poultry.

POMMES CROQUETTES

6–8 oz. cooked potatoes.
1 yolk of egg.
½ oz. butter.
½ teaspoonful chopped parsley.

Salt, pepper, and nutmeg.
Egg and coating crumbs.
Fried parsley.

1. Boil ¾ lb. even-sized potatoes. Drain, dry off, and press through a wire sieve or potato masher.

2. Return the potato to the saucepan, and add the yolk of egg, butter, chopped parsley, salt, pepper, and nutmeg.

3. Beat over gentle heat, until all is blended thoroughly.

4. Spread evenly on a floured plate, and mark into 8 portions.

5. When cold, form each portion into a ball, using a dredging of flour to prevent sticking.

6. Coat twice with egg and breadcrumb, pressing on the crumbs firmly.

7. Fry in deep fat until golden brown. Serve piled on a hot dish garnished with fried parsley.

Note. Potato Croquettes are liable to burst when cooking. To prevent this—

(*a*) Coat *twice* with egg and breadcrumbs.

(*b*) Make sure that there is sufficient fat completely to immerse the Croquettes at once.

(*c*) See that the fat is smoking over the whole surface.

(*d*) Do not lift the Croquettes out of the fat until they are likely to be completely cooked.

POMMES DUCHESSE I

8–10 oz. cooked potatoes.
1 yolk of egg.
1 tablespoonful cream.
Salt, pepper, and nutmeg.

½ oz. butter.
Beaten egg to brush over.
Coralline or Paprika pepper.

1. Boil 1 lb. of even-sized potatoes. Drain, dry off, and press through a wire sieve or potato masher.

2. Return the potato to the saucepan, and add the egg yolk, cream, salt, pepper, nutmeg, and butter. Beat well over heat until the mixture is light.

3. Put the mixture into a forcing bag, fitted with a large rosette forcer (12 cuts). Pipe in rosettes on a greased baking tin, and brush lightly with beaten egg.

4. Bake in a hot oven (420° F.) until golden brown.

5. Pile in a hot gratin dish, and sprinkle with coralline or Paprika pepper.

POMMES DUCHESSE II

1. Prepare Duchesse potato mixture as foregoing, making sure that it is well steamed and dry; do not add any milk or cream.

2. Turn this potato pastry out on a floured board, and roll it into an oblong or square. Cut it into 8 pieces.

3. Score across with the back of a knife diagonally.

4. Brush with beaten egg and bake until golden brown on top.

5. Dish leaning one against the other in a slanting line on a fireproof dish.

6. Sprinkle with Paprika and serve.

Note. Each portion may be shaped to a flat round cake and scored lattice fashion, if preferred.

POMMES FRISÉES

3 medium-sized potatoes. | **Frying fat.**

1. Cut the potatoes into slices, ¾ in. thick. Trim off any projecting points, and peel each slice round and round, sufficiently thinly for the grey colour of the knife to show through. Make the ribbons as long as possible.

2. Soak the ribbons in cold water for 20 minutes; drain, and leave them wrapped lightly in a cloth for a further 20 minutes.

3. Plunge the potatoes into smoking fat, and when the bubbling has subsided turn them loose into it, and fry golden brown.

4. Remove, drain, and serve sprinkled with a little fine salt.

POMMES ITALIENNE
(Potatoes with Bacon)

About 1 lb. cooked potatoes.	**A nut of butter.**
2–3 thin rashers streaky bacon.	**Browned crumbs.**
1 level tablespoonful grated cheese.	**Paprika pepper.**
	½ pint Velouté Sauce (see p. 251).

1. Slice the plain boiled potatoes and place a layer of them in a greased fireproof dish.

2. Sprinkle with dice of the lightly fried bacon.

3. Season, and pour the Velouté or any rich white sauce over. Repeat.

4. The top layer should be of potato, but cut in neat rounds and arranged in rows overlapping alternate ways.

5. Place in the oven to become thoroughly hot and brown on top.

Note. The surface may be sprinkled with grated cheese, if liked.

POMMES MACAIRE
(Baked Potato Cakes)

$1\frac{1}{2}$–2 lb. large potatoes, baked in their skins.
Salt and pepper.
1–$1\frac{1}{2}$ oz. butter.
1 unbeaten egg white, or a little beaten whole egg.

Oil and butter for frying.
2 teaspoonfuls finely chopped parsley.
Small sprigs of parsley.

1. Cook the potatoes (pricked) gently in the oven.

2. Break them open, and empty the pulp into a saucepan. Add to it a little seasoning, the butter, and egg as above.

3. Mix all well with a wooden spoon, and form into 5 or 6 flat cakes, using a little flour for shaping.

4. Fry in a sauté- or frying-pan on both sides in butter and oil, until golden coloured and set. Slide a palette knife under for turning, and also to lift out the cakes for draining.

5. Serve on a paper on a hot oval fireproof dish in a slanting line, sprinkled with the chopped parsley, and with sprigs of parsley at the side.

Note. The mixture may be made into 1 flat cake of 1 in. thickness if preferred, and browned in a small omelette pan. Brush the top with a little oiled butter just before serving.

POMMES MARQUISE
(For 6 portions)

1 lb. potatoes.
1 oz. butter.
Nutmeg.
Salt and pepper.
2 yolks.

$\frac{1}{2}$ gill tomato purée.
1 large firm tomato.
A nut of butter.
Finely chopped parsley.

1. Plainly boil the potatoes; drain and steam them very well over heat. Pass through a wire sieve. Place in a saucepan with the butter, nutmeg, salt, and pepper.

2. Beat well over gentle heat until the mixture leaves the sides of the pan.

3. Add the yolks and tomato purée, and cook again.

4. Shape with a bag and coarse vegetable rose pipe on a greased floured baking-sheet, leaving a hole in the centre.

5. Place in a hot oven to colour.

6. Fill the centre hole with concassé tomatoes (see p. 281) tossed in a little butter.

7. Sprinkle with parsley, and serve flat on a dish on a dish paper.

POMMES MOUSSELINE

(For 6 portions)

1 lb. potatoes.	1½ oz. butter.
Salt and pepper.	Beaten egg to brush over.
1 egg.	Sprigs of parsley.

1. Plainly boil the potatoes, and dry them well in the saucepan.

2. Season with salt and pepper, add a beaten egg (reserving a little for brushing over) and the butter. Beat and heat all well together.

3. Use two tablespoons to make them into Quennelle shape, and put them on a greased floured baking sheet. The spoon used to scoop out the mixture from the first spoon is dipped into hot water first to facilitate shaping.

4. Decorate in small ridges over the top of the Quennelle with the point of the spoon. Drip some beaten egg over each, guiding the flow with the point of the brush.

5. Bake in a brisk oven until golden colour.

6. Dish in a circle on a paper on a round dish, with points to the centre, and garnish with parsley.

POMMES PAILLES

(Straw potatoes)

1. Choose large potatoes. Peel, trim square-cornered, cut in slices, and then into straws lengthways.

2. Wash the potatoes thoroughly, and soak to avoid matting.

3. Drain and dry in a cloth for 10 minutes.

4. Place the straws in a frying-basket, then into smoking fat. When the bubbling abates, turn out the potatoes into the fat itself, shaking them with a wire frying spoon all the time.

5. Drain on soft crumpled paper, and dish on a hot dish with a dish paper, as high as possible, and like a straw stack.

Note. When fried, the potatoes should be dry and golden coloured, and not at all greasy. Thorough soaking and a large pan with abundant frying fat or oil helps to effect this.

POMMES À LA PARISIENNE

| 1 lb. potatoes. | Fine salt. |
| Clarified butter and oil. | Chopped parsley. |

1. Scoop out the peeled potatoes with a vegetable cutter into small balls of the size of marbles.

2. Blanch the balls briskly in salted water and drain them.

3. Heat sufficient oil and butter to cover the bottom of a Yorkshire pudding tin to the depth of $\frac{1}{2}$ in.; put in the potatoes and toss them over heat for a few minutes.

4. Bake in a fairly hot oven (350° Fahr.) for about 10 minutes until golden coloured.

5. Drain, and serve sprinkled with a little fine salt and chopped parsley.

POMMES AU PERSIL

$\frac{1}{2}$ lb. cooked potatoes.	$\frac{1}{2}$ level tablespoonful finely
$\frac{1}{2}$ oz. butter.	chopped parsley.
1 tablespoonful milk or cream.	Seasoning.

1. Press the potatoes through a wire masher as soon as they are drained.

2. Heat the butter, seasoning, and milk in a saucepan, add the potatoes, and heat and beat until light. Add half of the chopped parsley.

3. Place the mixture in a bag fitted with a large rose pipe, force out into rosettes on a greased tin.

4. Bake in a brisk oven until golden brown.

5. Serve on a hot dish sprinkled with the remaining chopped parsley.

POMMES PURÉE

1 lb. potatoes (even size).	Salt, pepper, and nutmeg.
A nut of butter.	Coralline pepper or chopped
2 tablespoonfuls boiling milk.	parsley.
2 tablespoonfuls cream (optional).	

1. Plainly boil the potatoes until tender. Strain, dry them off, and press them through a potato masher or wire sieve.

2. Return to pan; add a little butter and sufficient boiling milk (and the cream, if desired) to make a light creamy texture.

3. Beat well over heat, and serve mounded in a hot vegetable dish, marked neatly with a knife, and sprinkled with coralline pepper or chopped parsley.

POMMES RISSOLÉES

1. Cut the potatoes into large allumettes (see p. 117). Blanch them, strain immediately, and drain well.

2. Put some butter and oil in a sauté- or frying-pan; when it is smoking put in the potatoes all at once, shake and toss them well over brisk heat.

3. Leave them for a few minutes, then scoop them over lightly with a slice. Toss them occasionally, then cover with a lid.

4. Cook for about half an hour, folding them over lightly with a slice occasionally. Drain, but the fat should be practically absorbed.

5. Sprinkle with chopped parsley and serve.

POMMES SAUTÉES

(Sauté Potatoes)

1–1¼ lb. cooked potatoes.	Seasoning.
Butter and oil for frying.	Chopped parsley.

1. Cut the potatoes (which should be firm) into slices ¼ in. thick, and season them.

2. Heat the butter and oil until just smoking, and fry golden brown on either side.

3. Drain, sprinkle with the salt, and serve with the slices leaning one against the other on a hot dish.

4. Sprinkle with the parsley.

POMMES SOUFFLÉES

(Soufflé Potatoes)

1. Scrub the potatoes (which should be of large size), and put them aside for at least a day to dry.

2. Peel, but do not put them in water; wipe them very dry on a cloth, and *very evenly* cut them in slices lengthways of the thickness of half-a-crown; again pat them dry in a cloth.

3. Have ready two baths of fat, one which is heated but well below smoking-point, and the other smoking hot.

4. Place the pieces a few at a time in the cool fat.

5. Lift them into the bath of smoking fat, and they should soufflé. Press them down into the fat with a wire frying spoon, and cook until they are quite dry.

6. Drain the potatoes well, and pile them on a dish paper in a hot dish, sprinkled with salt.

ENTREMETS SUCRÉS

(Sweets)

THE SWEET COURSE

THIS Section includes both hot and cold sweets. Actually in practice an iced sweet is outstandingly popular at the present time, and as a general rule any second sweet which is on the menu receives scant attention.

RULES FOR THE SERVICE OF ENTREMETS SUCRÉS

1. The sweets for a Luncheon or Dinner are usually light in character, because the most substantial part of the menu has been already served.

2. It is usual to serve at least two sweets—one hot and one cold or iced.

3. In selecting two or more Sweets to serve in the same meal, consider the composition, colour, and flavour of the dishes, to avoid similarity.

4. The hot sweet is placed first on the menu, followed by the cold and then the iced one.

5. Large iced puddings, soufflés, bombes, etc., are always served as part of this course, but small ices may be served with the dessert.

6. Sweets may be served in one whole, but it is more usual now to prepare them in individual portions, as appearance is thus improved and service is simplified.

7. Hot Sweets cannot be so smartly decorated as cold ones, but their dishing can be smart, neat, and effective.

VARIETIES OF SWEETS

Recipes for Sweet Entremets are legion, but for the most part will fall automatically into one or other of the following main divisions.

I. HOT

1. Various light mixtures, steamed or baked and served usually with a suitable sweet sauce.

2. Soufflés, baked or steamed.

3. Custards and Caramels.

4. Fritters of fruit or custard mixtures, and pancakes.

5. Yeast mixtures—Babas and Savarin.

6. Omelettes.

125

I. Hot (*Contd.*)

  7. Charlottes.
  8. Hot Fruit Sweets.
  9. Various Pies, Fancy Tarts, and Tartlets.

II. Cold.

  1. Flans and Tartlets.
  2. Puff Pastries and Vol-au-Vents.
  3. Génoise and Choux Pastries.
  4. Creams and Jellies.
  5. Bavarois.
  6. Meringues.
  7. Charlottes.
  8. Cold Fruit Sweets.
  9. Cold Soufflés and Mousses.
  10. Iced Puddings.

JELLIES AND CREAMS

JELLIES

Brilliantly clear jelly is a most important factor in the making of artistic cold dishes, both savoury and sweet.

CLASSIFICATION

  1. Cleared Jellies, e.g. lemon, wine, aspic.
  2. Uncleared Jellies, e.g. port wine, orange, egg, milk (*note* Port is not a clear wine, and so cannot be used for making clear wine jelly; oranges lose much flavour when made into clear jelly).
  3. Packet Jellies, Jelly Crystals, etc.
  All jellies may be sub-divided into—
  (*a*) Sweet Jellies.
  (*b*) Savoury Jellies.

FOOD VALUE

Gelatine has no flesh-forming properties of itself. It is an albuminoid, and a "protein sparer," aiding the flow of the digestive juices. It thus admits of very easy digestion, and nourishing food, such as eggs and milk, and in some cases stimulating material, can be conveyed agreeably and in small quantities.

GELATINE

This is a most important ingredient of jellies of this kind, as few people nowadays would care for the trouble involved in boiling down calves' feet each time gelatine is required.

Kinds of Gelatine. Commercial Gelatine is obtained from the tendons, connective tissue, cartilage, bones, and even from the

horns and hoofs of animals, purified in the process of preparation.
It is of various kinds—

1. French leaf gelatine.
2. Powdered gelatine, such as Cox's.
3. Strip gelatine, which requires to be soaked.

OTHER STIFFENING MATERIALS—

1. Isinglass, prepared from the swimming bladder of the
sturgeon. It is the purest form of gelatine, has great stiffening
power, and is tasteless. It is, however, more expensive than
gelatine.

2. Gelatine obtained from boiling calves' feet in water. This is
very pure and delicate in flavour, and on that account is used
largely for invalids.

Either of these forms of stiffening has the same dietetic value
as gelatine.

3. Agar-agar is prepared from seaweed. Its stiffening properties
are greater than those of gelatine, and it can be used in vegetarian
cookery, as it is of purely vegetable origin.

AMOUNT OF STIFFENING TO BE USED

A jelly should be only just stiff enough to support its own
weight when turned out of the mould. Aspic jelly should always
be slightly stiffer than the sweet varieties; and also in hot weather
or for large moulded jellies a trifle more gelatine may be added.

Average Proportions of Stiffening—

French Leaf Gelatine—1¾–2 oz. to set 1 quart of liquid.
Powdered Gelatine—1¾–2 oz. to set 1 quart of liquid.
Strip Gelatine—1½ oz. to set 1 quart of liquid.
Isinglass—1 oz. to set 1 quart of liquid.
Agar-agar—½ oz. to set 1 quart of liquid.

RULES FOR JELLY MAKING

1. Use good gelatine in the correct proportions.
2. Have the white of egg perfectly fresh, and free from all yolk.
The use of too much egg white impoverishes the flavour of the
jelly.

3. Loaf sugar is preferable for jelly making, as it is less adul-
terated, and so produces a more brilliant jelly.

4. Have scrupulous cleanliness of all utensils and materials,
and use a deep saucepan in which to whisk the jelly.

5. Whisk and strain carefully, according to the directions on
p. 136.

6. Place a small jug or measure of boiling water gently on the
suspended cloth, cover with a blanket or thick folded cloth, and

avoid draughts. In this way very little jelly should remain on the cloth.

1. Keep the cloth only for straining purposes.
2. Choose an even-threaded linen tea-towelling, not too fine, and scald it with boiling water just before use.
3. After use, scrape the cloth, soak, wash, and boil it in plain water. It follows that a well-kept jelly cloth is always a bad colour, but the least suspicion of soap or soda left in the cloth clouds the jelly.

CREAMS

A Cream mixture may be prepared and set in a jelly-lined decorated mould, or it may be poured into coupe glasses, covered with a thin layer of jelly, and decorated. A variety of attractive cold sweets can be made from these mixtures, which can also be used for filling small meringue cases, or moulded in a tin lined with sponge finger biscuits, as for Charlotte Russe.

VARIETIES

1. The richest mixtures are made entirely from cream, and are often flavoured with a liqueur.
2. Creams can also be composed of custard and cream—usually in equal quantities. Flavouring is added, and if desired pieces of fresh or glacé fruits, nuts, etc.
3. Fruit creams, made with fruit purée and cream, or more economically with fruit purée and partly custard and cream. *Note.* All these mixtures are stiffened by the addition of gelatine, carefully melted in a little water or wine.

RULES FOR MAKING CREAMS

1. Use pure fresh cream, half whipping it to give the correct sponge-like texture to the mixture.
2. Use gelatine in the correct proportions—$\frac{1}{4}$ oz. powdered gelatine will set $\frac{3}{4}$ pint cream mixture, this quantity including the water in which the gelatine is dissolved.
3. Avoid overheating the gelatine, when dissolving it, as this spoils the texture of the cream. Add it through a heated strainer, so that the gelatine does not set before it is lightly mixed, and see that all the gelatine passes through.
4. Make the cream, custard, and purée of the same consistency as far as possible; but if there is any difference in them, add the thinner ingredients to the thicker.
5. Stir the cream mixture gently until it is thickened creamily and has no sensible warmth, then use it as required.

6. If it is moulded, turn out the cream when set, and arrange chopped jelly lightly around it.

RECIPES FOR HOT SWEETS
ABRICOTS COLBERT

16 halves of tinned apricots.
Rice Filling—
    1 gill milk.
    Scant 1 oz. ground rice.
    A nut of butter.
    $\frac{1}{2}$ tablespoonful castor sugar.
    $\frac{1}{2}$ yolk of egg.
Icing sugar to dredge.
8 glacé cherries.
Flour to dredge.

Coating—
    1 beaten egg.
    Dried white crumbs.
Sauce—
    $\frac{1}{4}$ pint apricot juice and water.
    1 oz. lump sugar.
    1 large tablespoonful apricot jam.
    1 teaspoonful arrowroot.

  1. Lift out the apricot halves on to a sieve to drain.

  2. *For the Rice Filling.* Mix the ground rice smoothly with a little milk, heat the remainder, and pour it over. Boil well, until thick and well cooked, adding the sugar. Add the butter and yolk. Recook carefully, and spread on a plate to become set and cold.

  3. Put a teaspoonful of rice filling on an apricot half, then add a glacé cherry, and a little more of the rice on top. Cover with a second half over all.

  4. Flour the fingers, press the rice into shape, and roll the whole lightly in flour. Repeat until 8 apricot balls are formed.

  5. Coat the apricots with beaten egg and dried white crumbs. Fry lightly in smoking hot fat, until pale golden coloured.

  6. Drain, and dredge with icing sugar.

  7. *For the Sauce.* Dissolve the sugar in the syrup and water, and boil for 5 minutes. Add the apricot jam, and when it is dissolved add the arrowroot mixed smoothly with a little water. Stir, and boil well 6–7 minutes, until the arrowroot is quite clear.

  8. Pour out the sauce on a round silver dish, and arrange the apricots on it. *Serve hot.*

BEIGNETS DE POMMES PRINCESSE
(Apple Fritters)

3 medium even sized apples.
1 tablespoonful castor sugar.
The grated rind of half a lemon.
1 tablespoonful rum or liqueur.
2 stale sponge cakes.
Apricot Syrup and Sauce—
    2 gills water.

12 lumps sugar.
  2 tablespoonfuls apricot jam.
Frying Batter (see p. 12).
Water Icing—
    2 oz. icing sugar.
    1 dessertspoonful water.
    $\frac{1}{2}$ teaspoonful vanilla essence.

1. Core and peel the apples, and cut them in ¼ in. slices.

2. Lay these slices in a dish, and sprinkle with the sugar, lemon rind, and rum or liqueur. Turn them over from time to time.

3. Drain the slices, and dip in the hot apricot syrup. Coat with sponge-cake crumbs.

4. Pass the prepared apple rings through the coating batter, and fry golden brown in deep fat.

5. Drain the fritters well, and place them on a hot greased tin.

6. Brush the top of each fritter with the water icing, and place in a hot oven ½–1 minute to glaze.

7. Serve at once, very hot, handing the apricot sauce separately.

Note. Any apricot syrup left over after dipping may be thickened with a little arrowroot, flavoured with lemon juice, and served as sauce.

BISCUIT AUX FRUITS

Genoese pastry, baked in a 6 in. cake tin, 1½ in.–2 in. in depth.	A piece of angelica.
2–3 tablespoonfuls apricot marmalade.	Meringue—
	1 egg white.
	2 oz. castor sugar.
3 tablespoonfuls chopped browned almonds.	1 tablespoonful glacé cherries.
Small tin of fruit salad.	Apricot Sauce to pour round.

1. Have the Genoese pastry a day old, cut it in half transversely as far as half way across, and take out the section.

2. Brush the sides of the cake with hot apricot marmalade, and dip in chopped browned nuts. Brush the upstanding top piece, and sprinkle with nuts separately, also top and sides of the separate piece.

3. Heat the fruit in its syrup, after cutting it in small pieces, and cut diamonds from a small piece of angelica, soaked in water. Place the cake on the serving-dish.

4. Arrange the fruit salad on the lower half of the cake, piling it up, and put on the lid slanting.

5. Make a meringue, and pipe it along the join and around the side. Dredge with icing sugar, and put in the oven to brown lightly. Arrange the glacé cherries cut in halves along the join, with a diamond of angelica between when the meringue is half set.

6. Return to oven to finish browning the meringue, pour the sauce round, and serve hot.

Alternatively—(a) Cut the top section right off, arrange fruit over top of cake, and cut the lid in half, raising both sections.

(b) Serve the sweet cold, piping Crème Chantilly in place of meringue.

GÂTEAU MERINGUÉ AUX FRAISES
(Meringued Cake with Strawberries)

1 shallow Genoese cake, baked in a 6 in. cake tin.	Meringue— Whites of 2 eggs.
3 tablespoonfuls fruit syrup.	4 oz. castor sugar.
1 tablespoonful sherry or Maraschino.	½–1 lb. strawberries. Icing sugar to dredge.

1. Soak the cake on a fireproof dish with the syrup and wine or liqueur, and coat it with meringue (see p. 224).
2. Cover the surface with ½ of the halved strawberries.
3. Dredge with icing sugar, cover with a further thin layer of meringue.
4. Lay on about ½ of the remaining strawberries, reserving the remainder for decoration.
5. Coat the whole with meringue, and dredge with icing sugar.
6. Place in a fairly hot oven to brown lightly, and decorate with strawberries.

Note. If the sweet is to be served cold, Crème Chantilly may be used in place of the meringue. This sweet is also known as Fraises en Surprise.

PAINS PERDUS
(Bread Fritters)

4 slices stale bread, cut ½ in. thick.	1 beaten egg.
1 gill milk.	2–3 oz. fresh butter.
1 tablespoonful granulated sugar.	Castor sugar.
A few drops of vanilla essence, or 1 tablespoonful Marsala or sherry.	A little powdered cinnamon (optional). 2 tablespoonfuls jam.

1. Remove the crust from the bread, and cut it into equal shapes—finger, square, triangular, round, or oval.
2. Heat the milk sufficiently to dissolve the sugar in it, and add the essence or wine. Leave to cool.
3. Arrange the pieces of bread in a large pie dish or soup plate, and pour over them the prepared milk. Leave to soak for 10 minutes.
4. Remove each slice carefully, and drain on a folded cloth. Beat the egg in the pie dish or soup plate, and dip each piece of bread in it carefully.
5. Melt the butter in the frying-pan; when it is just beginning

to smoke, place the pieces of bread side by side in it, but not close enough to touch.

6. When browned on one side, turn to the other carefully, and brown again.

7. Sift a little sugar and cinnamon on each slice as it is removed from the pan.

8. Dish in a circle on a round hot dish, one piece overlapping the other, and fill in the centre with the hot jam.

POUDING À L'ANANAS

(Pineapple Pudding)

2 small eggs.	Decoration—
Their weight in: butter; castor sugar; flour.	Pieces of pineapple.
	Pieces of angelica.
A pinch of baking powder.	10–12 glacé cherries.
1 tablespoonful chopped tinned pineapple.	1 tablespoonful sherry.
	Sauce à l'ananas (see p. 253).
1 tablespoonful pineapple syrup.	

1. Grease a ¾ pint plain oval charlotte mould. Fit a disk of greased paper, cut exactly to fit at the bottom. Decorate with small rounds of pineapple, joined by thin strips of angelica. Sprinkle the glacé cherries with the sherry, and leave to marinade.

2. Prepare the mixture, as for Pouding d'Oranges (see p. 135), omitting the orange rind and substituting pineapple syrup for orange juice.

3. Place the mixture carefully in the prepared tin, and steam for 1¼ hours until quite set.

4. Unmould and pour the sauce round. Place the drained heated cherries in a pile at each end of the dish. Any sherry remaining may be strained and added to the sauce.

POUDING BRUN

(Brown Bread Pudding)

2 oz. brown bread (with crust and crumb).	1 small whole egg.
	Grated rind of half a lemon.
½ pint milk.	½ oz. cornflour.
2 oz. butter.	2 whisked whites of eggs.
2 oz. castor sugar.	2 oz. mixed dried fruits.
2 yolks of eggs.	Apricot Sauce (see p. 253).

1. Cut the bread into dice, and soak it in the milk. Prepare a bread panada by placing these in a saucepan over heat. Stir until the mixture boils, and dry off until the panada leaves the sides of the pan.

2. Cream the butter, add the sugar, and cream again. Beat in the yolks one at a time, and the whole egg. Add the grated lemon rind, and then the panada.

3. Sprinkle in the cornflour, and fold in the stiffly whisked whites, together with the prepared fruit.

4. Divide into 5 dariole moulds of ¾ gill capacity, prepared by buttering and sugaring.

5. Place the moulds in a Yorkshire pudding tin with water to come half way up the sides. Allow the puddings to rise to the top of the moulds with the tin placed over heat, then poach the puddings in the oven about 15 minutes.

6. Unmould on to a hot dish, and pour Apricot Sauce round.

POUDINGS DE CABINET AU RHUM

2 oz. sponge fingers.
Scant 1 oz. currants and glacé cherries mixed.
1 small tablespoonful rum.

1 gill milk.
1½ oz. castor sugar.
1 egg, and 2 yolks.
Sauce Sabayon (see p. 255).

1. Prepare individual moulds of ¾ gill capacity (darioles) by buttering and sugaring.

2. Cut the sponge fingers into dice, and soak the currants and cherries, cut up small, in the rum.

3. Beat the egg and yolks, pour on the hot milk, and pass through a strainer.

4. Arrange the sponge fingers in the darioles in alternate layers with the sugar and soaked fruits. Pour any remaining rum into the custard.

5. Fill up the moulds with the custard, a little at a time, using a spoon or ladle, so that the cake mixture does not rise.

6. Stand the moulds in a large baking tin with water to come about half way up the sides of the moulds.

7. Stand the tin on top of the oven until the puddings rise, then poach them in the oven until firm.

8. Run a knife carefully round each; unmould on to a hot dish with a lace paper on it. Hand the sauce separately.

POUDINGS AU CHOCOLAT
(Chocolate Puddings)

2 oz. plain chocolate.
1 gill milk.
3½ oz. stale cake crumbs.
1½ oz. butter.
1½ oz. castor sugar.
2 eggs.

Few drops vanilla essence.
Crème à la Chantilly (see p. 14), or Sauce au Chocolat (see p. 254) or Sauce Sabayon (see p. 255).

1. Prepare 5–6 dariole moulds of $\frac{3}{4}$ gill capacity. Scrape the chocolate with a knife, dissolve it in the milk, and boil up, stirring well.

2. Pour this on to the stale cake crumbs, and mix thoroughly. Cover with a plate, and leave to soak for $\frac{1}{2}$ hour.

3. Cream the butter, add the sugar, and cream again. Beat in the yolks one at a time.

4. Add soaked crumbs and vanilla essence. Fold in the stiffly whisked whites, and divide into the prepared moulds.

5. Twist a greased paper over each and steam until set, about 50 minutes.

6. Unmould carefully, sprinkle the tops of the puddings with a little castor sugar, and serve hot on a lace paper doily. Hand Crème à la Chantilly separately.

Note. If these puddings are served with either of the other two sauces mentioned above, unmould on to a hot dish and pour the sauce chosen round.

POUDING MELBA CHAUD

(Hot Melba Pudding)

3 fresh peaches.
$\frac{1}{4}$ lb. loaf sugar.
$\frac{1}{2}$ pint water.   **or** $\frac{1}{8}$ tin sliced peaches.
Vanilla essence.   2 tablespoonfuls peach syrup.

$\frac{1}{2}$ pint milk.
2 oz. fresh breadcrumbs.   2 tablespoonfuls raspberry con-
1 tablespoonful castor sugar.   serve or sieved raspberry
The yolks of two eggs.   jam.
Vanilla essence.   Meringue—
                                                   Whites of 2 eggs.
                                                   4 oz. castor sugar.

1. If fresh peaches are used, poach them in vanilla-flavoured syrup, and slice them when cold. Reduce the syrup.

2. Place the prepared fruit at the bottom of a china soufflé case of 6 in. diameter with a little of the syrup.

3. Heat the milk, stir in the crumbs, and cook for a minute or two. Turn out into a basin, cover, and leave $\frac{1}{2}$ hour to soak, adding the sugar while hot.

4. Beat in the yolks, flavour with vanilla essence, and pour the mixture into the soufflé case. Cook in a moderate oven until set.

5. Spread the surface with raspberry conserve.

6. Pile the meringue on top, dredge with castor sugar, and return to a cool oven to cook until the meringue is pale biscuit colour and crisp.

POUDINGS D'ORANGES

(Orange Puddings)

2 small eggs.
Their weight in—
  Butter.
  Castor sugar.
  Flour.

A pinch of baking-powder.
The grated rind of a large orange.
1 tablespoonful orange juice.
Angelica to decorate.
Sauce Marmelade (see p. 255).

1. Prepare 5–6 dariole moulds, of ¾ gill capacity (or one ¾ pint plain charlotte mould), and place a small round of angelica in the bottom of each.

2. Cream the butter and grated orange rind, add the sugar, and cream again. Add the well-whisked eggs by degrees, beating well.

3. Add the flour sieved with the baking-powder, and the orange juice.

4. Place the mixture in the prepared moulds or large mould. Twist a greased paper over each, and steam 45–50 minutes for small puddings, or 1¼–1½ hours for a large one.

5. Unmould on to a hot dish, and pour the sauce around.

POUDING SAXON

(Saxon Pudding)

1 gill milk.
3 penny sponge cakes.
4 almond macaroons.
1 dozen ratafias.
2 small eggs.
Scant ½ gill cream.
¼ gill sherry.

½ teaspoonful vanilla essence.
Decoration—
  1 oz. almonds (blanched, shredded, and baked).
  1 oz. glacé cherries.
  A few pieces of angelica.

1. Grease a plain charlotte mould, and place a disk of greased paper cut exactly to fit at the bottom.

2. Decorate with halves of cherries and the pieces of angelica, and sprinkle the sides thickly with the prepared almonds.

3. Heat the milk, and pour it on the sponge cakes and biscuits (cut up). Leave to soak for ½ hour.

4. Add the eggs well beaten, cream, sherry, essence, and any trimmings from the decoration, other than angelica.

5. Mix all thoroughly, and pour gently into the prepared mould.

6. Cover with a greased paper, and steam for 1½ hours.

7. Unmould on to a hot dish on a lace paper doily, and hand hard sauce (Sauce Dur, p. 254) separately.

ZAMBAIONE

(A Venetian Sweet)

Yolks of 3 new-laid eggs.	1 tablespoonful Marsala or sherry.
Scant 1 oz. castor sugar.	Thin slices of sponge cake.

1. Beat together the yolks, sugar, and wine in a small basin; then place it over a saucepan containing hot water, and whisk until the mixture thickens and rises.

2. Serve immediately in tall glasses well warmed.

3. Dry and crisp thin slices of the sponge cake in the oven, and hand these separately.

RECIPES FOR COLD SWEETS

GELÉE AU CITRON

(Lemon Jelly)

1½ pints cold water.	2 cloves.
¼ pint lemon juice.	6 oz. loaf sugar.
The thinly peeled rinds of two lemons.	1¾ oz. gelatine.
	Shells and whites of 2 eggs.
1 in. cinnamon stick.	1 gill sherry.

1. Scald a large pan, and place all the ingredients in it, except the shells and whites of the eggs, and the sherry.

2. Dissolve the sugar and gelatine over very gentle heat, stirring with the whisk. Do not allow the mixture to become hot, and withdraw the pan from the heat immediately these two ingredients are dissolved.

3. Slightly whisk the whites of eggs. Wash the shells inside and outside, crush, and add to the pan with the whites.

4. Return to brisk heat, and whisk steadily until boiling-point is almost reached.

5. Allow the jelly to boil to the top of the pan quite undisturbed, then draw it aside, and allow the contents to sink.

6. Slide the pan back over heat, and boil up for a second time, then a third.

7. Leave the jelly to settle for 5 minutes, then pour through a scalded jelly cloth, scraping out the pan well. Remove the basin of jelly which has passed through the cloth, and put another basin in its place.

8. Pour the first jelly which has passed through the cloth again very slowly through the filter, together with the sherry.

9. Cover with a blanket, and leave in a warm place free from draughts until all the jelly has run through.

10. Use the jelly when quite cold for moulding, lining moulds, etc.

Note. In hot weather, or if the jelly is required to set quickly, use 2 oz. gelatine.

For Gelée au Vin Blanc increase the sherry to ½ pint and decrease the water to 1¼ pints. For Gelée au Vin Rouge the proportions are similar, substituting claret or burgundy for sherry, and adding ½ teaspoonful carmine with the first ingredients.

BAVAROIS AU RHUM

Custard—
 1 egg, and 1 yolk.
 2 teaspoonfuls castor sugar.
 1½ gills milk.
 The rind of an orange.
Decoration—
 Liquid lemon jelly.
 Shreds of browned almonds.
 Shreds of pistachios.
Cream Lining—
 3 tablespoonfuls lemon jelly.
 1½ tablespoonfuls cream.

1 teaspoonful rum.
Carmine.
Filling—
 ¾ gill cream.
 1 level tablespoonful castor sugar.
 1 tablespoonful rum.
 Juice of half an orange.
 Scant ½ oz. gelatine.
 Scant ½ gill water.
Garnish—
 Chopped lemon jelly.

1. Make the custard, infusing the thinly chipped rind of the orange in the milk. Leave it to cool.

2. Mask a fancy mould with jelly, decorate, and set the strips of nuts in the jelly.

3. Line the mould thickly with the cream lining, so that an opaque coating is formed.

4. Add the half-whipped cream to the custard, with the sugar, rum, orange juice, and dissolved gelatine.

5. When the mixture is thickening creamily, pour it into the prepared mould, and allow to set.

6. Unmould, and encircle lightly with the chopped jelly.

BAVAROIS RUBANÉ À TROIS PARFUMS

2 yolks of eggs.
½ tablespoonful castor sugar.
½ pint milk.
Scant ½ oz. gelatine.
Scant ½ gill water.
¾ gill cream or evaporated milk.
Coffee essence.

Vanilla essence.
Green colouring.
A few drops of rum.
1 large tablespoonful whipped cream.
½ teaspoonful sugar.
A few drops of vanilla essence.

1. Put the yolks and sugar in a basin, and work them well with a little whisk.

2. Heat the milk, and prepare the custard in the usual way.

3. Dissolve the gelatine in the water, strain it into the mixture, and leave to cool.

4. Divide into 3 portions, whisk the cream slightly, and add one-third of it to each portion.

5. Add a little coffee essence to the first portion, pour it into an enamelled mould, and allow to set.

6. Flavour the second portion with the vanilla essence, and pour it into the mould when the first portion is set.

7. Flavour the third portion by adding a few drops of rum, and colour green. Pour on top when the second portion is set.

8. When the whole is set, unmould, and decorate around the base with roses of whipped cream, sweetened and flavoured.

CHARLOTTE À LA NAPOLÉON

Genoese Pastry, made 6 in. diameter × 2 in. depth—3 eggs, etc. (see p. 220).
1–2 tablespoonfuls sherry, or liqueur syrup.
About 1 teacupful Royal icing.
1 tablespoonful strawberry jam.

1–1½ doz. Savoy finger biscuits, or wafers.
2 bananas or a similar bulk of drained fruit.
Sugar to dredge.
1½ gills lemon or wine jelly.
½ gill Crème Chantilly (see p. 14).

1. Prepare the Genoese pastry, and when cold cut in half transversely, and sandwich with the jam. Sprinkle with the sherry or liqueur.

2. Prepare the icing, and trim the biscuits along the sides until they will fit evenly together.

3. Spread the sides of the cake with icing, and place it on the dish on which it is to be served.

4. Press the biscuits upright around the cake, or wafers may be placed overlapping. Tie a narrow tape around the biscuits to hold them in place.

5. Arrange the fruit, cut up and dredged with the sugar, in the case.

6. Pile chopped jelly over the fruit, and pipe the edge with roses of Crème Chantilly.

7. Replace the piece of tape with a ribbon, and serve.

CHARLOTTE RUSSE À LA ST. JOSÉ

Lemon jelly.
A few cubes glacé pineapple.
1 sheet silver leaf.
6–8 sponge finger biscuits.
Filling—
  1 gill custard.
  1 gill cream.
  1 oz. castor sugar.
  ½ gill pineapple syrup.
  Scant ½ oz. powdered gelatine.

Scant ½ gill water.
2 oz. chopped pineapple (tinned).
Decoration—
  2 tablespoonfuls whipped cream.
  A few drops pineapple essence.
  2 heaped tablespoonfuls chopped jelly.

1. Pour a thin layer of lemon jelly into a plain charlotte mould. When it is set, decorate with slices of glacé pineapple cut in triangles, and run a little silver leaf into the centre.

2. Pour in jelly to the depth of ½ in., and leave to set.

3. Separate the sponge fingers; trim and arrange them closely around the tin so that there are no spaces.

4. *Filling.* Make the custard, and leave it to cool; half whip the cream, add the sugar and pineapple syrup. Dissolve the gelatine in the water. Add the custard to the other ingredients, and the well-drained chopped pineapple. Add the strained gelatine last.

5. Stir the mixture gently until it is setting creamily, then pour it quickly into the prepared mould. (If poured in when too thin it will ooze between the biscuits.)

6. When it is set, trim the biscuits to the level of the cream mixture.

7. Dip the bottom of the mould in hot water, when the pudding is quite set, and turn it out.

8. Decorate the joins of the biscuits with piped whipped cream, and encircle lightly with chopped jelly.

CHARTREUSE DE BANANES

1¼ pints lemon or wine jelly.	2–3 bananas.
1 teaspoonful finely chopped pistachios.	¾ gill Crème Chantilly.

1. Line a border mould with clear jelly. Mix together the chopped pistachios with a large tablespoonful of the jelly, and run it into the mould. Put aside ¼ pint of the jelly to become set.

2. When set, add clear jelly to the depth of ½ in. and allow to set.

3. Peel a banana and slice it evenly. Dip each piece separately in jelly, and arrange the slices overlapping in a circle (or oval) in the mould.

4. Add liquid cold jelly to come ½ in. above the top of the bananas.

5. Repeat the layers until the mould is full, finishing with jelly.

6. Put aside until set.

7. Unmould, and pipe the Crème Chantilly into the centre, raising it well; encircle lightly with chopped jelly.

Note. Other fruit may be used in place of the bananas—strawberries are very attractive, with little pieces of angelica placed to represent the hulls. Or mixed fruits may be used, in which case the sweet is known as Macedoine des Fruits en Gelée.

COMPOTE DE CERISES

1 gill cherry syrup and water (stewed or tinned).
1 oz. loaf or granulated sugar.
1 piled teaspoonful red currant jelly or jam.

Carmine.
¼ lb. stoned cherries.
1 small tablespoonful Kirsch.
A few drops lemon juice.

1. Make a syrup with the sugar and water, skimming it to make it clear. Add the jelly or jam and the carmine, and boil up.
2. Strain the syrup on to the cherries, add the Kirsch, and leave all to chill in a cold place.
3. Serve in coupe glasses as cold as possible, handing Hungarian Nut Biscuits separately.

Note. If desired, the compote may be decorated with whipped sweetened Kirsch-flavoured cream; or the compote may also be used as a garnish.

CRÈME D'ABRICOTS

(Apricot Cream)

1 gill apricot purée.
½ gill apricot syrup.
1 gill cream.
About 1 oz. castor sugar, to taste.
½ teaspoonful lemon juice.

Scant ½ oz. gelatine.
½ gill water.
Decoration—
 Pistachio nuts.
 Small pieces of apricots.
 Lemon jelly.

1. Mask a mould with jelly, and decorate with strips of pistachio nuts and pieces of apricots. Set the decoration in sufficient jelly to cover.
2. Sieve the apricots through a hair sieve, after draining them to obtain the purée.
3. Half whip the cream; add the purée, syrup, sugar, and lemon juice.
4. Dissolve the gelatine in the water, and add it to the cream mixture.
5. Stir gently until thickening creamily, then pour at once into the prepared mould.
6. When it is set, unmould; and encircle with lightly chopped jelly.

Note. Other fruits (e.g. fresh fruit such as strawberries) may be treated similarly and the cream named accordingly.

CRÈME DE CERISES

Decoration—
Liquid jelly to line the mould.
A few unstoned cherries.
Filling—
1 gill cream.
1 gill cherry purée.
½ gill cherry syrup.

1 teaspoonful Kirsch.
1 tablespoonful castor sugar.
Carmine.
Scant ½ oz. gelatine.
Scant ½ gill water.
Garnish—
Compote de cerises (see p. 140).

1. Mask a mould with lemon jelly, decorate with cherries (unstoned, so that they are of good shape), and set them in the jelly.
2. Prepare and mould the mixture as for Crème d'Abricots.
3. When it is set, unmould, and serve, with the compote of cherries around—arranging the cherries at the ends, with the syrup flowing around the mould.

CRÈME NAPOLITAINE

(Neapolitan Cream)

Red wine jelly (see p. 137).
1 gill custard.
1 gill cream.
1 oz. castor sugar.
½ oz. gelatine (divided into four ⅛ oz.).

2 tablespoonfuls water.
Decoration—
1 sheet of silver leaf.
Scant ½ gill Crème Chantilly (see p. 14).

1st Portion. Leave white, and flavour with **vanilla essence.**

2nd Portion. Colour green, and flavour with **maraschino, rum, or ratafia essence.**

3rd Portion. Add **coffee essence.**

4th Portion. Colour pink, and flavour with **strawberry essence.**

1. Line a plain charlotte mould of ¾ pint capacity with the red wine jelly. Set the sheet of silver leaf in jelly, near the surface, then pour in more jelly to the depth of ½ in.
2. When the custard is cold, mix it with the sugar and slightly whisked cream, and divide into 4 equal portions to be coloured and flavoured separately as above.
3. Melt one portion of the gelatine, and add to each portion of the cream mixture, as ready.
4. Pour in the white portion first, leave to set; when ready add the green portion, which must be perfectly cold, but not set. Colour and flavour the 3rd portion with the coffee essence, and add when ready; pour in the pink portion last.
5. Place aside to set. Unmould, and serve either cold, decorated with whipped cream, or cut in pieces like Neapolitan ices.

CRÈME AU VANILLE

(Vanilla Cream)

1 gill custard.
1½ gills cream.
About 1 oz. castor sugar to taste.
Small teaspoonful vanilla essence.

Scant ½ oz. gelatine.
½ gill water.
Decoration—
    Pieces of glacé cherries.
    Strips of browned nuts.
    Lemon or wine jelly.

1. Mask a mould with jelly, and decorate with pieces of the glacé cherries and the strips of browned almonds. Set the decoration in sufficient jelly to cover.

2. Prepare the custard, and leave to become cold.

3. Half whip the cream; add the custard, sugar, and vanilla essence.

4–6. As for Crème d'Abricots (see p. 140).

CRÈMES À L'ESPAGNOLE

(Spanish Creams)

5 ratafia biscuits.
Orange jelly.
1 gill custard.
1 gill cream.
¼ oz. gelatine.

2 tablespoonfuls water.
Sherry to flavour.
Decoration—
    ½ gill cream.
    1 teaspoonful castor sugar.

1. At the bottom of each of 5 coupe glasses place a ratafia, and cover it to the depth of about ½ in. with orange jelly. Leave to set.

2. Prepare the custard, and when cold mix it with the half-whipped cream.

3. Sweeten, and flavour with sherry to taste.

4. Dissolve the gelatine in the water, add to the custard mixture, and, when just setting creamily, pour it into the coupes to within ½ in. of the top.

5. When it is set, pipe a rose of sweetened sherry-flavoured cream on each coupe, and scatter a pinch of chopped pistachio over.

6. Stand the coupes on a small silver tray, and serve as cold as possible.

"DAY DREAMS"

6 apricot halves.
1 gill lemon jelly.
Rum Cream—
    ½ gill custard.
    ½ gill cream.
    ½ oz. castor sugar.
    1 tablespoonful milk.

1 teaspoonful rum.
¼ oz. powdered gelatine.
Scant ½ gill water.
Scant ½ gill Crème Chantilly.
Carmine.
Chopped pistachios.

1. Drain the apricots thoroughly, cut them in small pieces, and place at the bottom of some coupe glasses.

2. Cover with lemon jelly, and allow to set.

3. Pour on a layer of Rum Cream (made as Vanilla Cream).

4. Tinge the Crème Chantilly faintly pink with the carmine, and pipe a rose of it in the centre of each.

5. Sprinkle lightly with chopped pistachios.

Note. This quantity makes 5 portions.

FRUITS RAFRAÎCHIS AU KIRSCH

3-4 oz. loaf sugar.	1 large tablespoonful Kirsch.
½ pint water.	A few drops vanilla essence.
¾ pint fresh fruits cut in small pieces.	Juice of half a lemon.

1. Make a syrup with the sugar and water, and boil gently for 7 minutes.

2. Have the fruits in a bowl, marinaded in the Kirsch. The bowl may, with advantage, be packed round with ice.

3. Add the vanilla essence and lemon juice to the syrup, and pour this mixture over the fruit while very hot.

4. Stir up well, and cover with a plate, piled up with ice if possible.

5. Stir again from time to time, adding a little more Kirsch, if necessary.

6. Serve in coupe glasses or small individual earthenware cocottes.

GÂTEAU D'ANANAS

(Pineapple Cake)

Genoese pastry, made with three eggs, etc. (see p. 220).	Butter Icing—
	1½ oz. butter.
Pineapple Jelly—	3 oz. icing sugar.
½ pint jelly square.	Pineapple essence.
Juice from tinned pineapple.	Orange colouring.
¼ oz. gelatine.	¼ small tin of pineapple cubes.
Scant ½ gill sherry.	1½ oz. almonds.
1 drop of carmine.	A few cubes of preserved pineapple.

1. Make the Genoese pastry, bake it in a 6 in. cake tin, and leave for 24 hours.

2. Heat the necessary amount of pineapple juice, and dissolve the jelly in it. Dissolve the gelatine in the wine, and add it to the jelly. Add the 1 drop of carmine to warm the colour. Allow to set poured into a shallow tin, so that the depth of the jelly is ½ in.

3. Split the cake transversely, and spread each side lightly with the butter icing. Place a layer of well-drained finely chopped pineapple between, and fix together firmly.

4. Blanch the almonds, split them transversely, and brown them to a biscuit shade in the oven.

5. Spread the outside of the cake evenly with the butter icing, and press the almonds around the sides.

6. Cut a round from the firm jelly with a pastry cutter of 3 in.–3½ in. diameter, and place it in the centre.

7. Decorate with triangles cut from preserved pineapple, arranged at the edge and pointing to the centre.

8. Decorate also with roses of the butter icing tinted a little deeper.

9. Serve on a glass or silver dish with the chopped trimmings of jelly around.

GÂTEAU DE RIZ
(French rice cream)

Scant 1 pint milk.
The thinly chipped rind of a lemon.
½ in. cinnamon stick.
2 oz. Carolina rice.
1 oz. castor sugar.

½ oz. gelatine.
Scant ½ gill water.
1 gill cream.
Lemon jelly.
Compote de Cerises (see p. 140).

1. Boil the milk, with the lemon rind and cinnamon, stir in the rice, and cook gently until quite soft (this is best carried out in a double saucepan, or in a pie dish in the oven).

2. When it is ready, turn the mixture out into a basin, remove the rind and cinnamon, and when nearly cold add the sugar, the gelatine dissolved in a little water, and the half-whipped cream.

3. Line a plain round charlotte mould with the lemon jelly, and set ½ in. of plain jelly in the bottom.

4. When it is thickening creamily, pour in the mixture, and leave to set.

5. Unmould on to a fancy dish, and arrange Compote de Cerises around.

GELÉE À LA MADELEINE

Fresh fruits, such as cherries, grapes, or strawberries.
1 pint clear lemon or wine jelly.
Vanilla Cream—
½ gill milk and 1 yolk of egg for the custard.

½ gill cream or evaporated milk.
1 tablespoonful fresh milk.
½ teaspoonful vanilla essence.
1 teaspoonful castor sugar.
⅛ oz. powdered gelatine.
1 tablespoonful water.

1. Prepare the jelly, and divide it in half.
2. Line a mould, and set a layer of fruit in jelly at the bottom.
3. Add the remainder of the first half of the jelly.
4. When it is quite set, pour in the layer of vanilla cream, and allow to set.
5. Fill up with the remainder of the jelly.
6. Unmould, and serve with a little chopped jelly round.

Note. If preferred, the second portion of jelly may be slightly tinted with carmine and flavoured with liqueur.

For the Vanilla Cream

Make the custard, and when cold mix it with the cream, fresh milk, vanilla essence, and a teaspoonful of castor sugar. Dissolve the gelatine in water, strain it into the mixture, and when it is thickening creamily use as required.

HUNGARIAN NUT BISCUITS

4 oz. ground almonds.
4 oz. castor sugar.
4 oz. unsalted butter.

A pinch of bicarbonate of soda or baking powder.
4 oz. flour.

1. Mix all the ingredients thoroughly, until they will hold together.
2. Place on a lightly floured board, flatten, and press out with a rolling-pin.
3. Shape into small rounds with a cutter.
4. Bake for a few minutes in a slow oven, until slightly brown.

Note. Do not add more flour when rolling out the mixture.

PETITES CAISSES À LA PRINCESSE

Custard—
1½ gills milk.
Thinly peeled rind half a lemon.
2 yolks.
1 oz. castor sugar.
⅛ oz. gelatine.

½ teaspoonful vanilla essence.
1 tablespoonful thick cream.
1 stiffly whisked white of egg.
Fresh strawberries or bright red cherries.
Fine sugar.

1. Flavour the milk with the lemon rind, and make a custard with the milk, sugar, and yolks.
2. Dissolve the gelatine in a little water, and add.
3. Cool slightly, then add the cream, vanilla essence, and the stiffly whisked white.
4. Fill 5 glass coupes three parts full with the mixture, and leave until set.

5. Arrange the strawberries, or cherries as a substitute, in pyramids on the top of the mixture in each coupe.

6. Serve as *cold* as possible. Crushed ice may be placed on the dish around the glasses.

POIRES AU VIN ROUGE

1 gill claret.	A strip of lemon rind.
1 gill water.	1 heaped teaspoonful powdered
5 small fresh pears.	arrowroot.
4 oz. loaf sugar.	1 oz. finely shredded almonds.
1 in. cinnamon stick.	

1. Mix the claret and water in a casserole, add the loaf sugar, and dissolve it. Add the cinnamon and strip of lemon rind. Boil up these ingredients to form a syrup.

2. Peel the pears, leaving on the stalks but removing the eye from the bottom of each pear. Drop them into the boiling syrup.

3. Place a piece of paper with a hole in the centre on top to keep the pears under the syrup.

4. Poach the pears in the oven until quite tender. Remove the pears, strain the syrup, and reduce it somewhat.

5. Mix the arrowroot smoothly with a little water, add it to the syrup, and boil well while stirring for about 7 minutes, until perfectly clear.

6. Arrange the pears, with the stalks upward, in a fancy dish, and coat them with the syrup when it has cooled.

7. Sprinkle the fruit with the almonds, finely shredded and lightly browned in the oven.

8. Serve as *cold* as possible, with whipped cream as an accompaniment if desired.

POUDING CREME AU CARAMEL

Caramel—	½ pint milk.
3 oz. loaf sugar.	1 oz. castor sugar.
¾ gill water.	½ teaspoonful vanilla essence.
2 yolks and 2 whole eggs.	

For the Caramel

Dissolve the loaf sugar in the water, apply slow heat to caramelize it to rich brown colour.

For the Pudding

1. Pour the caramel at once into a ¾ pint plain charlotte mould, which is dry and hot. Coat the mould all over and leave until quite cold and set.

2. Beat the eggs, and pour on the milk, heated with the sugar. Add the vanilla essence.

3. Strain the custard mixture into the prepared mould, twist a greased paper over, and stand the mould in a Yorkshire pudding tin, half filled with water.

4. Cook in a very moderate oven 1–1½ hours.

5. Allow to stand for 5 minutes, then unmould on to a fancy dish, and leave until cold.

Note. This pudding may also be served hot.

PRUNES EN SURPRISE
(Prunes masked with cream)

4 oz. large prunes.	Small thin rounds of sponge cake.
1 gill water.	
1 oz. sugar.	¾ gill cream.
1 Jordan almond for each prune.	1 tablespoonful stiffly whisked egg white.
2 tablespoonfuls sherry.	
Icing sugar to dredge.	Ratafia crumbs.

1. Wash the prunes thoroughly, and soak them overnight.

2. Simmer gently with the water and sugar until soft enough for removal of the stones. Drain from the syrup.

3. Stone the prunes, and put a blanched almond in each. Sprinkle with the sherry, and leave for an hour or two.

4. Again drain the prunes, and dredge them with icing sugar.

5. Cut the rounds of sponge cake just large enough to support two prunes, and arrange them in a fancy dish.

6. Soak the pieces of cake with a little prune juice mixed with the sherry drained from the prunes. Arrange two prunes on each.

7. Whisk the cream until it will just hang from the whisk, and fold the stiffly whisked egg white into it lightly.

8. Cover each portion of fruit and cake completely with the cream mixture, and sprinkle the ratafia crumbs on top.

ENTREMETS SAVOUREUX

(*Savouries*)

MANY Hors d'Œuvres are suitable as Savouries, and vice versa. The Savoury is the last item to be served before the dessert.

Serving a Savoury is an English custom, and this tasty bonne-bouche serves to clear the palate—the popularity of the Savoury has much increased in recent years.

There is ample choice for selection, and it is a good plan as far as possible to use any scraps which are left over that are suitable—these can often be utilized to make perfectly adequate Savouries without anything being bought specially for the purpose.

PREPARATION AND SERVING OF SAVOURIES

1. Have them very small, as they come at the end of the meal, making them as far as possible in small portions, one of which would be sufficient for one guest.

2. In flavour, see that they are well seasoned, piquant, and pleasant, and in appearance smart, dainty, and attractive.

3. In small dinners, avoid a fish savoury if fish has already appeared on the menu as an hors d'œuvre and in the fish course.

4. Also, in small dinners, avoid serving a cheese savoury if cheese has been used in the preparation of the dressed vegetable.

5. Savouries may be served hot or cold, according to the materials used and the blending of them. Usually a hot savoury is the more popular.

6. It is not suitable to serve substantial materials as savouries, and omelettes and farinaceous products are usually banned. Oysters are very popular when in season, and caviare is also used, but both of these are expensive. Scraps of lobster, smoked fish, roes, ham, and cheese are also popular substances for serving in a variety of ways.

AMANDES SALÉES FARCIES

1 oz. Valencia almonds.
2 tablespoonfuls salad oil.
Fine salt.
A few grains of cayenne.
A small cream cheese.

Small cheese biscuits or croûtons.
Coralline pepper.
Small cress or shreds of lettuce.

1. Blanch and skin the almonds, and rub them in a cloth.
2. Heat the oil in a small frying-pan, and fry the almonds golden brown in it.

148

3. Partially drain on crumpled paper, and while still warm sprinkle with the salt by means of a salt dredger, and dust with a very few grains of cayenne.

4. Shape some little balls of cream cheese with the butter hands, and when the almonds are quite cold press one on each side of each ball.

5. Dish each cheese-ball on a small biscuit or croûton, and sprinkle with the coralline pepper. Arrange small cress around.

BEIGNETS DE GRUYÈRE

2–3 oz. Gruyère cheese (new).	Paprika pepper, if white crumbs
¾–1 gill thick white sauce.	are used.
Beaten egg and panurette or	Sprigs of Parsley.
coating crumbs.	

1. Cut the cheese into small neat blocks of even size.

2. Coat each piece with the white sauce, and place on a wire tray to set.

3. Dip each block in the beaten egg and roll in the panurette.

4. Fry in a basket in deep fat, drain, dish up, and sprinkle with Paprika pepper if necessary.

5. Serve very quickly, garnished with sprigs of parsley.

BISCUITS DE FROMAGE À LA CRÈME

Small biscuits of cheese pastry.	Seasoning.
Cream—	Garnish—
½ gill cream.	Watercress.
2 teaspoonfuls grated Par-mesan.	A few radishes or coralline pepper.

1. Make the pastry, prick it well, and cut in rounds with a cutter 1½ in. diameter.

2. Bake the biscuits a delicate brown colour, and allow them to cool.

3. Select 6 of the biscuits, and store the remainder in a small tin for future use.

4. Whisk the cream carefully, and stir in the Parmesan cheese and seasoning lightly.

5. Pipe a full upstanding rosette on each biscuit, using a large vegetable forcer.

6. Stick thinly cut slices of radish into the cream, or sprinkle with coralline pepper.

7. Dish in a circle, garnished with watercress in the centre, and serve as *cold* as possible.

BISCUITS À LA ROSEBERY

Cheese pastry, 1 oz. flour, etc.
(see p. 217).
Scant ½ gill whipped cream.
1 teaspoonful anchovy essence.

8–9 olives.
Steamed egg white.
A few capers.
Small cress.

1. Prepare the cheese pastry. Cut it into diamond-shaped croûtons, and bake on greased paper on a tin. Leave to cool.
2. Whisk the cream, adding the anchovy essence. Put it into a paper bag fitted with a fine rosette icing-pipe.
3. Pipe the cream to cover 8–9 biscuits, and pipe a little into each olive.
4. Put an olive in the middle of each biscuit, with a tiny diamond, cut from a slice of egg white, leaning against it at each end, and a caper on each point of the diamond of cheese pastry.
5. Pipe a small rose of cream on the top of each olive, and place a tiny spray of cress on top.
6. Dish in a circle, points of diamonds to the centre, and garnish with small cress.

BONNES BOUCHES AUX PRUNEAUX

5 large French Plums.
5 stoned olives.
2–3 anchovy fillets.
10 capers.
Anchovy essence.

5 small thin pieces of streaky bacon.
5 small squares of hot buttered toast.
Coralline pepper.
Watercress to garnish.

1. Soak the French plums overnight. Remove the stones, and fill the cavity with a stoned olive which has been farced with a piece of anchovy fillet wrapped round a couple of capers.
2. Wrap each prepared plum in a thin piece of bacon, and tie round with coarse thread.
3. Bake in a fairly quick oven for about 10 minutes.
4. Remove the thread, and dish each on a small square of hot buttered toast, sprinkled with the anchovy essence.
5. Dredge lightly with coralline pepper, and serve at once *very hot*, garnished with watercress.

Note. Allow one French plum to each person. This dish may be served as a savoury or a hot hors d'œuvre.

CROÛTES DE FOIE DE VOLAILLE

5 small oblong croûtes of fried bread or buttered toast.
2 chickens' livers.
5 small thin slices of bacon.
Seasoning.

Fried parsley.
Glaze.
Mustard butter to decorate (see p. 151).

1. Wash and dry the livers, and sauté them lightly in butter.

2. Divide on to the thin slices of bacon, season well, and roll up.

3. Thread the savouries on a skewer, and bake for a few minutes in a hot oven until cooked and crisp. Brush with the glaze.

4. Have the croûtes hot, spread a little mustard butter on each, and lay one of the small rolls on top.

5. Pipe a little mustard butter on each roll, garnish with the fried parsley, and serve at once.

CROÛTES DE JAMBON

5 small round croûtes of brown bread.
1–2 cold cooked potatoes.
1 oz. chopped lean ham.
Small cress to garnish.

Mustard Butter—
$\frac{1}{2}$ yolk of hard-boiled egg.
$\frac{1}{2}$ teaspoonful of mixed mustard.
$1\frac{1}{2}$ oz. of butter.
Salt and pepper.

1. Cut out the croûtes, and spread each with the mustard butter. For the latter mix all the ingredients, and pass them through a hair sieve.

2. Cut rounds of the potatoes with a cutter of the next size smaller, and mount one on each croûton.

3. Pipe around the edges with the mustard butter, and fill in the centre with the chopped ham.

4. Serve on a plain paper on a gratin dish, garnished with small cress.

DIABLOTINES AU PARMESAN

(Devilled Cheese Savoury)

Scraps of rich pastry.
Anchovy paste.
Coralline pepper.
Filling—
$\frac{1}{2}$ oz. butter.

1 teaspoonful cornflour.
$\frac{1}{2}$ gill milk.
1 egg.
1 oz. grated Parmesan cheese.
Salt and cayenne.

1. Line 1 dozen tiny patty tins with the pastry rolled out thinly, and put a suspicion of anchovy paste in the middle of each.

2. Make a sauce with the butter, cornflour, and milk. Beat in the egg yolk, and add the Parmesan cheese, reserving a little for dishing. Season with salt and cayenne and fold in the stiffly whisked egg white.

3. Fill the prepared tins $\frac{3}{4}$ full with the mixture.

4. Bake in a moderately hot oven, until set and golden brown.

5. Pile quickly in a hot gratin dish on a plain dish paper, and sprinkle with grated cheese and coralline pepper. Serve at once, *very hot.*

FILETS DE LAX DIABLÉ

Fingers of toasted brown bread.
¼ tin of Lax.
½ a yolk of hard-boiled egg.
1 teaspoonful butter.
A saltspoonful curry powder.

A few grains cayenne.
Small cress.
1 tablespoonful finely chopped parsley.
Paprika pepper.

1. Mix the butter, curry powder, and sieved egg yolk.

2. Prepare the toast, and spread with the above.

3. Drain the Lax and wipe it very dry. Arrange in small pieces slightly overlapping on the prepared fingers.

4. Heat in the oven about 10 minutes.

5. Garnish half with chopped parsley, and half with Paprika pepper.

6. Arrange star fashion on a hot dish, with cress in the centre.

7. Serve at once, *very hot.*

JAMBON À LA DIABLE

10 rounds of cooked ham, 1½ in. diameter.
Devil Mixture—
  ½ teaspoonful French mustard
  ½ teaspoonful English mustard.
  1 teaspoonful sieved chutney.

Salt.
A few drops of lemon juice.
Salad oil.
5 preserved champignons.
5 rounds of hot buttered toast.
Watercress to garnish.
Coralline pepper.

1. Cut the rounds of ham, and sandwich each two together with a little of the devil mixture, prepared by blending the ingredients.

2. Brush the tops with salad oil, and put the remainder of the devil mixture into the cups of the champignons, from which the stalks have been removed.

3. Put the champignons in a small tin in a moderate oven to heat them through.

4. Grill the ham 2–3 minutes, and place each round on a round of freshly made hot buttered toast, cut exactly to fit.

5. Place a champignon (filled side uppermost) on each round of ham and toast, and serve at once, *very hot*, with a few sprigs of watercress in the centre, and coralline pepper sprinkled on each champignon.

PETITES CRÈMES JOSEPHINE

(Savoury Haddock Creams)

2 tablespoonfuls cooked, flaked smoked haddock.
1 oz. butter.
1 egg.

1 small tablespoonful cream.
Salt and pepper.
Extra beaten egg and panurette for coating.

1. Butter 8 or 10 small boat-shaped moulds.
2. Remove all skin and bones from the haddock, and chop it well. Add the fish to the oiled butter, with the well beaten egg, cream, salt, and pepper.
3. Fill the moulds, making them quite level, and stand them in a Yorkshire pudding tin with a little water in it.
4. Cook 10–15 minutes in a moderate oven until set.
5. Unmould on to a folded tea-cloth to cool.
6. Dredge with flour, then coat with egg and panurette.
7. Fry in deep fat; drain and serve *hot* on a round gratin dish in the form of a star, with fried parsley in the centre.

PETITS BATEAUX DE MERLUCHE

Short pastry—2–3 oz. flour, etc. (see p. 216).
Devil Mixture—
1 small teaspoonful chutney.
1 small teaspoonful French mustard.
1 small teaspoonful dry mustard.
Pepper and salt.

Haddock Mixture—
2 oz. cooked dried haddock.
2 small anchovy fillets.
½ oz. butter.
Seasoning.
Garnish—
Shreds of gherkin and chilli skin.

1. Make the pastry, and line 5 or 6 boat-shaped moulds with it neatly.
2. Mix all ingredients for the devil mixture, and put a suspicion at the bottom of each pastry case.
3. *For the Haddock Mixture—*
(a) Remove the skin and bone from the fish, and chop it finely.
(b) Chop the anchovy fillets.
(c) Oil the butter, add the prepared fish, and season well.
4. Fill each case with the haddock mixture, arranging it quite level on the top.
5. Cover with a greased paper, and cook in the oven for 15–20 minutes. Garnish with the shreds of gherkin and chilli skin.

PETITS CHOUX PIQUANTS

Choux Pastry, half quantity (see p. 221).
1 hard-boiled yolk of egg.
1 oz. butter.
2 teaspoonfuls chutney.

2 teaspoonfuls cream.
½ teaspoonful anchovy paste.
¼ teaspoonful made mustard.
A few grains cayenne.
Sprigs of parsley to garnish.

1. Make the Choux pastry, and season it with a little pepper and salt.
2. Put it into a bag, fitted with a ¾ in. plain pipe, and force it into 5 balls on a greased baking-sheet.

3. Brush with egg, and bake in a hot oven 25–30 minutes. Reduce the heat, and cook until quite crisp.

4. When they are cooked remove from the baking-sheet. Make a short cut of ½–1 in. in the side of each to allow escape of steam, and leave until cold.

5. Mix all the ingredients for the *Savoury Butter*, and pass through a hair sieve. Leave in a cool place until required for use.

6. Put the Savoury Butter into a bag, fitted with a coarse rosette icing-pipe, and pipe a little of the butter inside each case. Further, pipe 4 or 5 upstanding spikes of the butter on each case as decoration.

7. Dish in a circle on a round dish, on a dish paper, with sprigs of parsley between.

RAMAQUINS DE FROMAGE

1 gill cream.
½ gill aspic.
1 oz. grated Parmesan.
Cayenne.
Made mustard.

1 tablespoonful whipped seasoned cream.
1 tablespoonful chopped aspic.
Paprika pepper.

1. Prepare 5 small ramekin cases by fastening a small band of stiff paper with a rubber band round the outside of each.

2. Half whip the cream, have the jelly melted but quite cold, and stir the cheese and seasoning into it.

3. Add all these ingredients to the cream, stirring in lightly and carefully.

4. When it is almost setting, pour into the prepared ramekin cases to come just above the edge.

5. Place aside to set.

6. Remove the paper, and pipe roses of seasoned cream at the edge, and pipe a little chopped aspic into the centre of each.

7. Decorate with Paprika pepper.

SARDINES À LA PIÉMONTAISE

Finger-shaped croûtes.
A little clarified butter.
5 small sardines.
Coralline pepper.
Finely chopped parsley.
Sprigs of watercress or parsley.

Coating Sauce—
 2 yolks of eggs.
 ¼ oz. butter.
 ½ teaspoonful tarragon vinegar.
 ½ teaspoonful white malt vinegar.
 ¼ teaspoonful made mustard.
 Salt.

1. Cut thin croûtes of oblong shape of the same size as the sardines. Fry them in clarified butter, and keep hot.

2. Remove the skins and tails from the sardines. Place the

fish in a small buttered tin, covered with a buttered paper, and heat them gently in a warm oven.

3. *For the Sauce.* Whisk the yolks, add the remaining ingredients, and whisk in a small basin over steam from hot water, until a thick coating consistency is obtained.

4. Put the sardines on the croûtes, and coat the whole with the sauce.

5. Decorate half the savouries with a line of coralline pepper down the centre, and the remainder with a line of finely chopped parsley.

6. Dish on a heated round gratin dish in a star, with sprigs of the watercress or parsley in the centre.

Note. This savoury may be served as Hors d'Œuvre if preferred. Omit the croûtes, and arrange 9–10 small sardines (skinned) in a small hors d'œuvre dish. Coat with sauce, and decorate with straight lines of coralline pepper and chopped parsley. Place a few sprigs of parsley or watercress at one end.

TALMOUSES DE MERLUCHE FUMÉE

Cheese pastry, made with 1 oz. flour, etc. (see p. 217).	1 yolk of egg.
½ oz. butter.	½ oz. grated cheese.
1 tablespoonful cooked flaked smoked haddock.	Salt, pepper, and cayenne.
	Beaten egg.
	Coralline pepper.

1. Make the pastry, roll it out thinly, and cut it in rounds, 1¾–2 in. diameter. Brush the edges with beaten egg.

2. Melt the butter, and stir in the prepared fish, yolk, cheese, and seasoning.

3. Spread out the mixture to cool, then place a ball of it in the middle of each round of pastry.

4. Fold up the triangular shape, pinching each of the three corners to keep them in shape. Brush over with the beaten egg.

5. Bake in a moderately hot oven, 10–15 minutes, until set and golden brown.

6. Sprinkle with coralline pepper, and pile upon a small hot gratin dish, with a dish paper on it, and serve at once *very hot*.

DESSERT

THIS course includes fresh fruits, as well as those preserved and candied, nuts, and frequently various bon-bons, petits fours, tiny biscuits, and small ices.

Bon-bons, petits fours, etc., may be arranged artistically on tiny fancy dishes, and form part of the table decorations if desired, and as a general rule English fruit calls for no special treatment before service.

There are, however, many tropical fruits now served as dessert, since increasingly rapid transport and electric refrigeration have "put a girdle round the earth," and bring many things at moderate prices which were not obtainable some years ago. They arrive in autumn and winter mainly, and so add variety to our English fruits.

Very interesting fruits come from Madeira, the nearest tropical island to this country, but there is also a wide choice from the Empire, especially from South Africa.

The following is a selection which can be served *au naturel* for dessert so that their full flavour can be enjoyed. It is possible to obtain many of these in tins, bottled, or made into jelly.

AVOCADO PEARS

The Avocado pear is sometimes called an "alligator" pear, but it is only like a pear in shape—its size varies considerably and it has a very smooth, clear skin of bright green. It has a large central seed, which must be removed, together with its membraneous cover.

The Avocado pear is a favourite West Indian and South American fruit, and is the product of a tropical tree, although it is now grown in large quantities in Madeira, and is also grown in California, where it is called a calavo. When ready for eating it should yield to gentle pressure, be slightly resilient. Like the banana it is gathered for transport before it is ripe, and allowed to ripen afterwards.

To serve it simply as dessert, halve the fruit lengthways, remove the seed, and beat the yellow pulp smooth with a small spoon—the pulp is luscious when the fruit is ripe, and resembles that of Cantaloup melon, with a slightly nutty flavour. Sprinkle the pulp with castor sugar and a suspicion of cinnamon, and serve, allowing one half of a sizeable fruit for each person.

This versatile fruit makes an equally good hors d'œuvre. Prepare as above, substituting French salad dressing for the sugar and cinnamon. It is invaluable in salads, blending well with lettuce and pineapple, and can be used for making ices. No cooking is needed, and the Avocado is easily digested by children and invalids.

Custard Apples

Custard apples have a white juicy pulp somewhat of the consistency and flavour of custard when they are quite ripe, and are best eaten in their natural state. If large, serve half an apple as a portion, or if of medium size cut off the top. In either case stand the fruit on a few leaves on individual plates, and place a grape-fruit spoon for eating it. The black pips are discarded and castor sugar is handed with the fruit.

Lychées

Fresh Lychées come mainly from South Africa. They have interesting looking thin shells, which can be broken and peeled off quite cleanly—there is a large centre kernel. Their flavour and texture resemble those of the Muscat Grape.

Mangoes

Mangoes are not considered a luxury by the Hindus, who eat them quite freely as a food. When not quite ripe they may be boiled and made into chutney or sweetmeats, and also they may be dried. A Mango resembles a very large pale-coloured plum, and is obtained plentifully from Madeira. It is peeled, and the pulp which surrounds the stone is somewhat of the same consistency as a plum.

Paw-paws

In their fresh state Paw-paws are rather more scarce in this country because of the difficulty in ripening them. They are essentially a tropical fruit, and bottled paw-paws are sent from Jamaica. When ripe the pulp is soft and yellow, resembling melon, and for dessert the fruit is usually cut in half, the seeds being removed, and served with a little sugar and lemon juice. In Bengal, where they are plentiful, paw-paws are used in the making of curry, chutneys, and pickles, and their digestibility is a byword.

Paw-paws have the great advantage of making tough meat tender, even when very fresh—a great advantage in tropical climates. It is sufficient to wrap the meat in the rinds of the fruit.

When ripe, paw-paws may also be served as hors d'œuvre with salt, pepper, or ginger.

PASSION FRUIT

Passion fruit is the edible fruit of the Passion Flower vine, and is exported from Australia both fresh and in tins. The Granadilla is its twin, but comes from Madeira.

When ripe, the passion fruit is delicious to eat raw, with the addition of a dash of lemon juice or maraschino, and a little sugar. It is an egg-shaped fruit, and looks well if served in brightly coloured stemless egg-cups—the top may be cut off, and the fruit eaten just as a boiled egg.

The seeds are inclined to be troublesome, although actually they contain a great deal of the flavour of the fruit, and may be masticated slowly. The pulp of the fresh or tinned variety may be passed through a sieve and added to fruit salad, or used for making an open tart (thickened with cornflour), or for making water ices.

PERSIMMONS

Persimmons are eaten in large quantities in China and Japan; and as they grow there prolifically, the trees look very beautiful when laden with the fruit, which is of red gold colour, of the size of a tangerine orange, but with the smooth skin of a tomato or plum.

When unripe, Persimmons have a very rough flavour, which often causes a dislike of the fruit. It should not be eaten until the colour becomes a deep glowing red all over, and the skin is slightly crinkled. Persimmons grow very freely and travel well—they are very largely exported from Madeira.

GLACES

(*Ices*)

ICED preparations have become much more popular during the last few years, and are no longer regarded as luxuries which are served occasionally, but form a favourite type of pudding or refreshment, which is served frequently or even regularly in many households.

CLASSIFICATION OF ICES

1. CREAM ICES

(*a*) Custard plus cream—usually in equal quantities—plus flavouring or flavouring additions.

(*b*) Fruit purée plus an equal quantity of cream and custard together, or cream only, or, more rarely, custard only.

II. WATER ICES

III. COMPOUND ICES

These are more elaborate, and include Iced Soufflés and Mousses, Bombes, Poudings Glacés, and Sorbets.

NECESSARY APPLIANCES

An Ice-cream Freezer is essential for making Ices, and can be obtained in great variety of size, but moulds and an ice cave are only necessary in special cases. There is a very widespread idea that a refrigerator is necessary for making ices, and although it is helpful (because all materials used in making the Ices can be chilled so easily, and in the modern refrigerators a large proportion at least of the ice required can be made) the only essentials in making ices are the freezer itself and satisfactory media for freezing.

ICE-CREAM FREEZER

The most satisfactory freezing mixture consists of ice and coarse salt; though if the former is not easily obtainable, a chemical freezing compound (consisting usually of ammonium nitrate and washing soda) can be used.

The disadvantages of the chemical freezing compound are that it is more expensive, and that it is more difficult to maintain the steady low even temperature which is required for satisfactory freezing. It must also be used in a freezer of special shape.

(a) *A Rotary Freezer* consisting of a wooden tub, a container made of pure tin or pewter, which fits at its base on to a socket in the tub, and a crank and handle working on the centre dasher, gives the best and most creamy results when making ices. It has, however, the disadvantage that it is rather hard work turning the handle unless an electric attachment is available.

A steady, even turning movement is desirable for good results. In most modern types of crank freezer, the dasher moves in the opposite direction to the freezing pot, so that all freezing mixture which congeals round the sides of the container is detached.

(b) *A Vacuum Freezer* is less effective in producing an iced preparation of smooth creamy texture unless it is constantly scraped from the sides and beaten up during the process of freezing. It has, however, the great advantage that no turning is necessary, and it is also very useful for storing an ice-cream mixture after it is frozen.

ICE MOULDS

These are best made from heavy pewter, and usually open easily into two parts, being hinged at one side and closely bolted at the other so that no salt water can possibly enter the mould. Ice pudding moulds of large size may have a separate piece at the bottom, and are made in large, imposing shapes which are more elaborate. Small sizes can be obtained suitable for individual portions. A bombe mould is a very favourite smart shape—it consists of a plain bomb-shaped container with a screw at the top (convenient to release when the pudding is being turned out) and a closely fitting cover with a ring attached in the centre.

ICE CAVE

An Ice Cave is useful for the preparation of Ice Soufflés and similar sweets, but is not necessary for Ice Puddings. It is in appearance like a small cupboard, but has a space between the outside and the inner lining which can be filled or "charged" with finely crushed ice and salt.

After filling, cover with a double thickness of woollen material, and open the door as seldom as possible. Occasionally draw off melted ice water by means of a plug which is placed at the bottom and re-charge with more ice and salt as required. Dishes when prepared are placed in the ice cave and left for at least two hours to freeze.

A substitute for an ice cave consists of a tin biscuit box large enough to contain the sweet, packed round with ice and salt.

MAKING THE ICES

Preparation of Mixture to be Frozen

1. Have the mixture perfectly cold before placing it in the freezing pot.

2. Make sure that the mixture to be frozen is just comfortably sweet to the taste. If made too sweet it will not freeze (the juice of half a lemon added will often correct this); and if it is not sufficiently sweet it will freeze hard and rough.

3. Be careful that no freezing salt enters the mixture. Just one grain is sufficient to spoil it completely.

Preparation of Freezer

1. Have the freezer perfectly clean and the can scalded.

2. If a rotary freezer is used, adjust the can on the pivot, fix all parts in position, and see that the freezer is working smoothly before packing round with ice and salt.

3. Pack round with chipped ice and salt in layers, allowing one part of freezing salt to six parts of ice. If the ice is crushed too small it wastes rapidly; but on the other hand if it is left too large the temperature will not be so low in the can, and the salt tends to fall through the layers of ice to the bottom of the tub.

4. Fill the tub three-quarters of the way up the freezing can, and always have the last layer of ice, and not of salt. These precautions lessen the likelihood of salt entering the can. Also wipe the lid of the can before removing it.

5. Do not fill the can more than two-thirds full of mixture to be frozen, because the beating of this mixture during the process of freezing causes it to become lighter and to expand.

Rules for Freezing

1. Cover the bucket with a double piece of woollen material or a clean old sack to exclude warm air—damp it if the weather is hot.

2. Stand the freezer in a cool place while working.

3. Once the mixture is placed in a rotary freezer, continue turning the handle steadily until mixture is frozen.

4. If solid pieces of fruit find a place in the recipe, add them when the mixture is half frozen.

5. As the ice melts, drain the ice water away, and repack with ice and salt.

6. When the mixture is thick, stop turning, remove the centre dasher, and press all the mixture together.

7. Place a piece of greaseproof paper under the lid, replace firmly, and repack with ice and salt if necessary.

8. Re-cover with the sack or woollen material, and stand aside in a cool place to mellow for an hour if possible.

Rules for Moulding Ices

1. Fit the mould together, and note that all is in order. Scald it, and keep on ice until it is required.

2. Have all the requisites at hand before beginning work— to ensure success no delay must occur.

3. Have sheets of greaseproof paper and lard in readiness.

4. Have the mixture firmly frozen, and fill the mould very full, pressing it with a small wooden spoon into every part of the mould, and occasionally knocking the mould on the table to settle the mixture.

5. Secure the mould, and scrape away any excess of mixture which exudes. Seal all joints thickly with the lard.

6. Wrap the whole mould in a large sheet of thickly larded greaseproof paper, folding in the edges of the paper securely, to prevent any melted ice water from entering the mould.

7. Place the wrapped mould back into the tub, which has been drained and partially emptied, taking care that there is a thick layer of firm chipped ice and salt at the bottom. Pack round the sides similarly, and cover completely with a thick layer of ice and salt. A large deep enamelled bowl can be substituted if the wooden tub is needed again for immediate use.

8. Cover with the sack or woollen material and leave for two to four hours, according to the size of the mould.

9. Drain and recharge the tub or basin if necessary. Excellent results are easily obtainable if it is possible to stand the tub in the bottom of a refrigerator, but in any case stand it in as cold a place as possible.

To Unmould Ices

1. Take out the mould, remove the paper, and hold the mould under a running cold-water tap for a sufficient time for the water to run over the whole of it. Cold water acts on an ice mould in the same way that hot water acts on a jelly mould, i.e. it gives a slight shock which causes the material to be loosened in the mould.

2. Cut off the lard quickly with a knife; and if the mould has a separate bottom piece, remove that first, then the top and sides.

3. If the mixture appears to stick in any particular spot, wring a cloth quickly out from hot water, and apply it to the outside of the mould where needed.

4. Have a chilled glass or silver dish in readiness for unmould-ing, and decorate rapidly with fruits, Crème Chantilly, Spun Sugar, etc., as desired.

SORBETS AND PUNCHES

These are semi-frozen Ices, served in small goblets or sherry glasses before the roast, to clear the palate, and to serve as a refreshing digestive for the remaining dishes of the dinner. They approximate to iced drinks, and are frozen barely stiffly enough to pile up in the glass, and must be of drinkable consistency.

The general characteristic of a Sorbet is that of a water ice made from fruit juices, and flavoured with wine, spirit, or liqueur.

Sorbets are, as a rule, served only at elaborate dinners, and it is not correct to note them on the menu card.

SUMMER AND PARTY BEVERAGES

1. Freshly made tea is an ingredient very largely used. The tea must be of good quality, and poured off at the end of three minutes for Indian or five minutes for China tea.

2. Sugar is always better when added to drinks in the form of a syrup—it makes a better blended product, and is more economical ($\frac{1}{2}$ lb. sugar, $\frac{1}{2}$ pint water, dissolve, and boil for 10 minutes). The syrup will keep well if poured into a jar or bottle and lightly covered.

3. Two or three kinds of fruit syrup will help to lend variety and these can be supplemented by home-made kinds, or simple juice from fresh fruit. Lemon juice is indispensable, and when rightly used will help to bring out the flavour of delicate fruits.

4. Ginger ale or cider may be combined with freshly made tea poured quickly on to a lump of ice, to make a refreshing drink.

5. Ice should be pure and clean, and should be broken in pieces which are not too large for the glasses. Do not put ice into wine cups.

6. Fresh fruit drinks, especially those made from citrous fruit, are of great value in hot weather, and well-made barley water is appreciated in this case too.

SERVING

1. Much of the attractiveness depends on the way the beverage is served—see that the tumblers or "long drink" glasses are well polished.

2. Float a slice of lemon on the top of iced tea, and, like iced coffee, this is served in small pony glasses.

3. To iced coffee add a spoonful of whipped cream to float on the top, and hand powdered sugar separately.

4. A bright red cherry or strawberry hidden among the ice gives colour to a fruit drink.

FOUNDATION ICE-CREAM MIXTURES
CHOCOLATE CREAM ICE

2 oz. plain chocolate.
Scant 1 gill milk.
1½ gills custard.

1½ gills cream.
1 teaspoonful vanilla essence.
Extra sugar as required.

1. Scrape the chocolate with a knife, add it to the milk, dissolve and boil until smooth.

2. When it is cold, add to the prepared custard, then add the half-whipped cream.

3. Flavour with vanilla essence, add sugar as necessary, and freeze.

FRUIT CREAM ICE

1 pint fruit purée.
Sugar according to acidity of fruit.

½ pint custard.
½ pint cream.

1. Prepare the custard as for vanilla ice-cream mixture (see p. 165).

2. Blend all the ingredients, and freeze in the usual way.

GINGER CREAM ICE

1½ gills custard.
1½ gills cream.
1½ oz. preserved ginger.

½ teaspoonful ginger essence, or 1 tablespoonful syrup from jar ginger.
½–1 oz. castor sugar.

1. Mix together the custard and half-whipped cream, add the sugar as required, and the ginger essence or syrup.

2. Add the chopped preserved ginger when the mixture is beginning to thicken by freezing.

3. Freeze until firm, and use.

PISTACHIO CREAM ICE

½ pint custard (see p. 165).
¼ pint cream.
Scant ½ oz. castor sugar.

¼ oz. shredded pistachios.
Green colouring.
Rum or maraschino to flavour.

Blend all these ingredients when cold, colour and flavour to taste. Freeze in the usual way, adding the pistachios when the mixture begins to thicken.

PRALINÉE CREAM ICE

½ pint custard.
¼ pint cream.

3 oz. praline (see p. 255).
A little coffee essence.

Blend the ingredients, reserving the praline to be added when the mixture begins to thicken. Freeze in the usual way.

VANILLA CREAM ICE

1 pint milk.
2½ oz. castor sugar.
2 whole eggs and 2 yolks.

1 pint cream or evaporated milk.
Vanilla essence to taste—about
1 tablespoonful.

1. Heat the milk and sugar until almost boiling.
2. Beat eggs and yolks thoroughly, and pour the milk on slowly, whisking briskly meanwhile. It is not necessary to cook the eggs further, as the mixture will froth up better and will be lighter if this is not done.
3. Strain the custard and allow it to cool.
4. Add the vanilla essence and the cream, slightly whisked, or evaporated milk.
5. When cold, freeze until stiff enough to serve.

FRUIT WATER ICE

1 pint sugar syrup (see below).
1 pint fruit purée or fruit juice
(other than lemon).

The stiffly beaten whites of 2
eggs.
Colouring if necessary.

1. Prepare the syrup, and leave it to become quite cold.
2. Pass the fruit through a hair sieve, or prepare the juice, and add it to the syrup.
3. Freeze partially, then add the stiffly whisked whites.
4. Continue freezing until firm.

LEMON WATER ICE

1 pint water.
6 oz. loaf sugar.
The zest of two lemons.

Juice of 3 lemons (¾ gill).
Stiffly beaten whites of 2 eggs.

1. Place the water and the sugar, which has been rubbed on the lemons to remove the zest, into a saucepan.
2. When the sugar is dissolved, boil just steadily for 10 minutes (220° Fahr.).
3. When it is quite cold add the strained lemon juice, and when partially frozen add the stiffly whisked whites of eggs.
4. Continue freezing until firm.

SYRUP FOR WATER ICES

½ lb. loaf or granulated sugar. | 1 pint water.

1. Dissolve the sugar in the water completely before allowing the liquid to boil.
2. Boil just steadily for 10 minutes (220° Fahr.).

RECIPES FOR ICED SWEETS
BOMBE À L'ABOUKIR

Pistachio Cream Ice (see p. 164). | Garnish—
Pralinée Cream Ice (see p. 164). | Glacé fruits or pieces of ice
                                        wafer.
                                    $\frac{1}{2}$ gill Crème Chantilly.

1. Scald a bombe mould, and keep on ice until required.
2. Prepare and freeze each portion of ice-cream separately.
3. Arrange a lining of pistachio cream ice around the sides of the mould $\frac{1}{2}$ in. thick, fill in the centre with the pralinée ice-cream, and cover the top with pistachio ice.
4. Put on the lid of the mould, lard the joints, wrap in larded paper, and freeze for 4 hours.
5. Unmould the pudding (see p. 162) on to a lace paper doily, pipe large roses of Crème Chantilly around the base, and decorate with glacé fruits or pieces of ice wafer.

OMELETTE SOUFFLÉ EN SURPRISE

A thin sheet of Genoese pastry. | 1 yolk.
Well frozen ice-cream. | 3 oz. castor sugar.
For the Soufflé— | Vanilla essence.
   3 whites of eggs. | Chopped pistachios.

1. Cut the cake to fit into a fireproof dish.
2. Cream the yolk and 2 oz. of the sugar. Flavour with the vanilla essence.
3. Whip the whites very stiffly, and fold in 1 oz. of sugar gradually. Fold these into the yolk and sugar.
4. Pile well-frozen ice on the cake (or this may be frozen in a neapolitan ice mould first) and cover as quickly as possible with the soufflé mixture.
5. Dredge with the castor sugar, and place the dish in a Yorkshire pudding tin with a little water in the bottom.
6. Place in a very hot oven for 1–2 minutes to brown the soufflé mixture, and serve instantly.

POUDING GLACÉ AUX FRUITS

$\frac{1}{4}$ oz. of pistachio nuts. | 1–2 tablespoonfuls maraschino
2 oz. preserved Metz fruits (in | or sherry.
   variety of colour). | $\frac{1}{2}$ pint custard.
1 tablespoonful brandy. | $\frac{1}{4}$ pint cream.

1. Blanch the pistachios and cut into chips. Cut the fruits small, and soak both nuts and fruit in the brandy and maraschino.
2. Mix all the ingredients together, half whipping the cream.

3. Freeze and mould in the usual way.

4. Bury the prepared mould in crushed ice and salt for 3–4 hours according to size.

COUPES GLACÉES ARC-EN-CIEL

(Rainbow Ices)

Frozen ice-cream mixtures of various colours. | Fresh, preserved, or glacé fruits.

1. Pipe the frozen ice mixtures into small china or paper ramekin cases or coupe glasses, using a bag fitted with a large rose vegetable pipe.

2. Decorate with pieces of preserved or fresh fruit, or fruits dipped in hard glaze.

COUPES GLACÉES CAPRICE

For each coupe glass allow—

Half a small banana sliced.
1 scoopful vanilla cream ice.
2 teaspoonfuls strawberry jam. | 1 teaspoonful whipped cream, or marshmallow.

1. Place the banana at the bottom of the chilled coupe glass, with the portion of vanilla cream ice on top.

2. Cover with the strawberry jam, and finish with the whipped cream or marshmallow.

COUPES GLACÉES AUX MARRONS

Vanilla Cream Ice.
Allow 1 Marron Glacé for each coupe glass, and 1 teaspoonful rum to each. | Crème Chantilly.
1 crystallized violet to each coupe glass.

1. Chop each marron coarsely, and place it in a coupe glass with the rum. Leave covered for one hour.

2. Place a scoopful of the vanilla cream ice on top of each.

3. Garnish with a piped rose of Crème Chantilly, and top with a crystallized violet.

COUPES GLACÉES ROSE-MARIE

For each coupe glass allow—

1 tablespoonful fruit salad, cut in small pieces.
1 scoopful strawberry cream ice. | 1 tablespoonful half-whipped cream, tinted to a delicate shell pink colour.
A crystallized rose petal.

1. Place the fruit salad in the chilled coupe glass, and the strawberry cream ice on top.

2. Coat with the prepared cream, and lay a rose petal on top.

COUPES GLACÉES TUTTI-FRUTTI

1 orange.	1 dessert apple.
2 bananas.	Cream Ice mixtures of two
Stock syrup (see p. 165).	colours (see p. 164).
Small bunch of grapes.	Metz fruits to garnish.

1. Cut up the orange and the bananas. Pour a little of the sugar syrup over. Stone the grapes, slice and cut the apple in small pieces. Add to the salad.

2. Put a spoonful of the fruit salad at the bottom of 5 coupe glasses, and two small portions of cream ice (one of each colour, side by side).

3. Decorate each portion with pieces of Metz fruits, and serve.

COUPES GLACÉES SAINT JACQUES

Compote of Fruit—	1 gill syrup from fruits.
Sliced peaches, fresh or tinned.	2 oz. loaf sugar.
Skinned pipped grapes.	Kirsch to flavour.
Fresh fruit, such as pears and cherries or strawberries.	Vanilla Cream Ice (see p. 165).
	Crème Chantilly—$\frac{3}{4}$-1 gill for each 5 coupes.

1. Prepare the compote of fruit, flavoured with the kirsch; allow to become quite cold, and keep on ice until required.

2. Place a portion of frozen cream ice mixture into each tall stemmed glass (chilled), and a spoonful of the prepared compote over.

3. Top with a rose of whipped cream, and serve at once.

FRAMBOISES EN SURPRISE

Vanilla cream-ice mixture.	Crème Chantilly (see p. 14).
Firm, whole raspberries.	Crystallized rose petals.

1. Press some firm vanilla cream ice into a coupe glass.

2. Arrange firm raspberries on this and cover with another layer of cream ice.

3. Pipe a rose of Crème Chantilly in the centre, using a coarse rose forcer.

4. Sprinkle with crushed crystallized rose petals, and serve with an ice wafer at the side.

MAPLE NUT SUNDAES

For each sundae glass allow—

1 scoopful vanilla cream ice.
1 large tablespoonful maple syrup.

2 or 3 kiln-dried walnut halves, broken in pieces.

1. Place the vanilla ice-cream in the chilled glass.
2. Pour over the maple syrup, and scatter the coarsely chopped walnuts over.

VANILLA SUNDAES

For each Sundae plate allow—
$\frac{1}{2}$ tablespoonful Maraschino Cherries, cut in halves.
1 scoopful Vanilla Cream Ice (see p. 165).

$\frac{1}{2}$ tablespoonful half-whipped Crème Chantilly (see p. 14).
$\frac{1}{2}$ tablespoonful grated vanilla chocolate.

1. Put the prepared cherries in the middle of the plate, with a little of the syrup, and arrange the vanilla cream ice on the top.
2. Coat lightly with the cream, scatter the chocolate over thickly, and serve at once.

LUNCHEON ENTRÉES AND GRILLS

THERE is great variety of light meat dishes, as well as grilled foods, which are very suitable for serving at smart luncheons, yet which would be out of place in a dinner menu.

For recipes for omelettes, egg and farinaceous dishes, and pies, which are also popular, and for specimen menus, see pp. 203, 190, 193, 225 and 271 respectively.

BOUCHÉES ALEXANDRA

Puff or Rough Puff pastry, made with 6 oz. flour, etc.

Salpicon—
$\frac{3}{4}$ gill thick white coating sauce.
1 tablespoonful cream or evaporated milk.

2 oz. chopped cooked chicken.
1 oz. chopped cooked ham.
1 tablespoonful chopped truffles or champignons can be added at discretion.

1. Make the sauce, season it highly, and add the chopped chicken, and the cream or evaporated milk.
2. Add the chopped ham, and truffles or mushrooms (if used).
3. Spread the mixture out to cool.
4. Roll out the pastry thinly, and cut in rounds of 2 in.–2$\frac{1}{2}$ in. diameter with a fluted cutter.
5. Brush half of the rounds with slightly whisked egg white, and divide the salpicon between these.
6. Cover with the remainder of the rounds, pressing well to shape.
7. Mark with a plain cutter to raise the edge.
8. Bake in a hot oven at first until the pastry is well risen and brown. Continue cooking 25–30 minutes in all.
9. About 5 minutes before the Bouchées are cooked brush them with egg yolk, and put back into oven to dry.
10. Arrange overlapping in a circle on a dish, filling in the centre with fresh-picked parsley sprigs.

Note. The Bouchées may be served *hot* as a light entrée, handing a suitable sauce separately in a tureen. If served *cold,* they are suitable as Buffet refreshments.

CROQUETTES DE JAMBON
(Ham Croquettes)

¼ lb. cooked ham.
2 oz. fresh breadcrumbs.
1 tablespoonful mashed potato.
2 tablespoonfuls white sauce.
Half a beaten egg.

Seasoning and Paprika pepper.
Beaten egg and breadcrumbs
for coating.
Tomato or Hollandaise Sauce
(see pp. 252 and 246).

1. Mix together the minced ham, fresh breadcrumbs, and potato.
2. Place these ingredients in a small saucepan, and bind with the beaten egg and white sauce over gentle heat.
3. Season well, spread on a plate, divide into equal portions, and allow to cool.
4. Shape the portions into rolls, coat with egg and breadcrumbs, and fry golden brown in deep fat.
5. Drain, dish up, scatter Paprika pepper over, and garnish with fried parsley.
6. Hand the sauce chosen, separately in a sauce-boat.

ÉMINCÉ DE VEAU EN PETITES CAISSES
(Minced Veal in Ramekins)

½ lb. lean cooked veal.
2 oz. cooked ham.
¼ teaspoonful grated lemon rind.
Cayenne and salt.

½ pint Velouté Sauce (see p. 251).
The sieved yolk of a hard-boiled
egg.
5 stoned olives.

1. Mince the veal and ham, or cut it into dice. Add the lemon rind, cayenne, and salt.
2. Prepare the sauce, add the meat, and heat all thoroughly together in a casserole, without reboiling.
3. Divide the mixture into small fireproof cases of the size for individual portions.
4. Decorate the top of each with the sieved yolk of the hard-boiled egg, and place a stoned olive (heated in stock) on top.
Alternatively, the mince may be sprinkled with breadcrumbs, grated cheese, and butter shavings, and browned lightly under a griller. In this case sprinkle with coralline or Paprika pepper.

ÉMINCÉ DE VOLAILLE DUCHESSE

Remains of cooked fowl—about ½ lb. (or ½ lb. cooked veal).
Duchesse potato mixture (see p. 119).
½ pint coating white, or Béchamel Sauce.

½ doz. champignons.
1-2 oz. fresh grated cheese.
A few browned crumbs.
A few shavings of butter.

1. Remove the chicken from the bones, and cut it into small neat pieces.

2. Prepare the Duchesse potato mixture, and heat it well.

3. Pipe the potato in a twisted cable round the sides of a round buttered gratin dish.

4. Drip a little beaten egg from a brush over this, and bake light golden brown in a hot oven.

5. Put a layer of well-seasoned sauce in the centre of the dish, with a little fresh-grated cheese.

6. Arrange a layer of chicken pieces over, and chopped mushrooms, then repeat with sauce, cheese, meat, and mushrooms.

7. Finish with sauce, coating it over very lightly.

8. Sprinkle with cheese, breadcrumbs, and a few shavings of butter.

9. Put into the oven to heat through, and brown lightly under a griller.

FRIANDINES DE VOLAILLE

Trimmings of puff pastry.
Salpicon—
  3 tablespoonfuls chopped cooked chicken and ham.
  1 tablespoonful thick white sauce.
  1 tablespoonful cream or evaporated milk.
  Seasoning.

1 teaspoonful chopped truffle and 1 teaspoonful chopped champignon (both optional).
Beaten egg.
Coating crumbs.
Sprigs of fried parsley.
Tomato, Piquante, or Espagnole Sauce (see pp. 252, 249, and 246).

1. Roll out the pastry as thinly as possible, and cut in rounds with a 2 in. fluted cutter.

2. Mix together the ingredients for the Salpicon, and put a small teaspoonful in the centre of half of the rounds, previously brushed lightly with white of egg.

3. Press a second round on the top of each very firmly.

4. Coat with egg and breadcrumbs, and fry in deep fat which is just smoking, 8–10 minutes.

5. Dish in a circle, leaning one against the other, and garnish with the fried parsley in the centre.

6. Hand a tureen of suitable sauce separately.

Note. Friandines may also be made from Game or Foie Gras, and named accordingly.

FRITTO MISTO

4 small scallops of pork, veal, sweetbread, liver, kidneys.
4 chipolata sausages.
Flour, egg, and breadcrumbs.
Butter and oil for frying.
A few sprigs of cooked cauliflower.

French beans.
Quarters of tomatoes.
Coating batter (see p. 12).
1–2 oz. nut brown butter.
2 slices crimped lemon.

1. Prepare the scallops, and bat them out thinly with a wet rolling pin. Prick the sausages.

2. Pass the scallops through flour, then egg and breadcrumbs.

3. Fry in the butter and oil, frying the liver last.

4. Dip the vegetables separately into the coating batter, and fry in deep fat.

5. Arrange on a fireproof dish, and sprinkle nut brown butter over.

GALANTINE DE BŒUF

(Beef Galantine)

½ lb. lean beef.
¼ lb. pork sausages.
¼ lb. streaky bacon.
3 oz. fresh breadcrumbs.
½ gill strong stock.
1 egg.
Salt, pepper, nutmeg.
A pinch of mixed herbs.

Meat glaze or mock glaze.
Garnish—
Croûtons cut from aspic jelly.
1 oz. creamed savoury butter (see p. 13).
Small cress.

1. Pass the meat through the mincer.

2. Add the sausage meat, crumbs, and seasoning.

3. Remove the rind and rust from the bacon, and cut the rashers across in fine shreds.

4. Beat the egg, add the stock, and mix all the ingredients thoroughly, adding the salt, pepper, nutmeg, and herbs.

5. Form into a roll, and tie tightly in a dry pudding cloth.

6. Boil for 2 hours, in stock if possible.

7. Remove the cloth, and again tie the galantine tightly in a fresh dry one.

8. Press between two plates for 12 hours.

9. Remove the cloth, brush the galantine with glaze, and cut a thin slice from each end.

10. Pipe the top with the savoury butter. Encircle with the prepared cress. Arrange croûtons of aspic around the edge of the dish.

LANGUE DE BŒUF ROULÉE À LA GELÉE
(Rolled Ox Tongue, with Savoury Jelly)

1 ox tongue, lightly pickled.	Celery or leek, in season.
Bouquet garni.	Decoration and Garnish—
2–3 carrots and turnips, cut in large pieces.	Meat glaze.
	Aspic jelly.
2 onions, each stuck with a clove.	Green salad or sprigs of parsley.

Choice—

1. Select a tongue which has a smooth skin, as a rough skin is a sign of age.

2. A tongue fresh from pickle need not be soaked, unless it has been very much salted—then an hour or two of soaking in cold water is advisable.

3. A tongue which has been smoked may need at least 12 hours soaking, and the water should be changed once or twice during the time.

Cooking—

1. Place a tongue fresh from pickle into lukewarm water, and a smoked tongue into cold water. Bring slowly to boil, skim well, and add the herbs and prepared vegetables for flavouring.

2. Reduce the heat, and allow the tongue to simmer gently until tender. The time required will depend on the size of the tongue, and also whether it has been smoked or not. Time required for a—

> small unsmoked tongue $2\frac{1}{2}$–3 hours.
> large   ,,   ,,   3 –4 ,,
> small smoked   ,,   3   ,,
> large   ,,   ,,   4 –5 ,,

3. Carry out the cooking very slowly, skimming constantly a necessary.

4. When the tongue is ready, the tip of it can be pierced easily with a metal skewer.

5. When the tongue is cooked plunge it into cold water, so that the skin can be removed easily.

Rolling and Dishing the Tongue—

1. After skinning, trim the root of the tongue, reserving pieces of tender edible meat, either to put in the middle of the tongue when rolled, or for flavouring another dish.

2. Roll the tongue round, and put it either in a press or in a small cake tin, completely to fill it. Put any small pieces in the centre.

3. Place a board or dish on top, and a heavy weight. Leave 24 hours.

4. Unmould the tongue carefully, place it on an icing rack, and brush it with glaze or baste it with mock glaze.

5. Baste finally with the liquid aspic.

6. Dish with chopped aspic and a little salad round, and arrange croûtons cut from aspic on the tongue and round the dish.

MIXED GRILL

2 sheeps' kidneys.
2 small lamb cutlets.
4 rashers bacon.
2 small beef fillets.
4 chipolata sausages.
2 pieces liver.
4 tomatoes.

4 mushrooms.
1 tablespoonful olive oil.
2 teaspoonfuls Maître d'Hôtel butter (see p. 13).
2 large potatoes.
Watercress to garnish.

Preparation—

1. Skin, core, and cut open each kidney, without cutting it right through. Place a small skewer to keep it open.

2. Trim the cutlets neatly, leaving only a narrow rim of fat.

3. Remove the rind and rusty part of the bacon, and form into rolls if streaky bacon is used.

4. Cut the tomatoes transversely in half.

5. Skin the mushrooms, soak in salted water for 1–2 minutes, then dry well.

6. Prepare the Maître d'Hôtel butter.

7. Heat and grease the gridiron.

8. Brush each piece to be grilled with olive oil.

9. Cut and soak the potato ribbons (see p. 120). Pick the watercress into sprigs, cleanse, and soak it.

Grilling—

1. Have the deflector red hot, and grill 2–3 pieces at a time, turning each several times.

2. The cutlets, sausages, and fillets of beef take the longest time, and should have 7–9 minutes.

3. The bacon and tomatoes take the shortest time, and need only about 4 minutes.

Dishing—

1. Pile the grilled food slantwise across the centre of a large fireproof dish.

2. Arrange fried ribbon potatoes at one end, and watercress at the other.

3. Place Maître d'Hôtel butter in small pieces over the top of the grilled food.

Note. The above quantity provides sufficient for 4 people, allowing choice of kidney or liver, and cutlet or beef fillet. Four small joints of chicken may be added if desired.

POUDING DE PERDREAUX
(Partridge Pudding)

2 breasts of tender young partridges.	2–3 streaky bacon rashers, blanched.
Salt, pepper, and a few grains of cayenne.	6 small flap mushrooms.
	1 hard-boiled egg.
A few strips of tender steak.	Suet Pastry, made with ½-lb. flour, etc. (see p. 219).

1. Remove the breasts of the partridges, and make some strong stock, adding the bones of the carcasses. Use the legs for another dish.

2. Season the game, cutting it in pieces, together with the strips of steak.

3. Cut the bacon across the rashers in thin strips, and cut the egg in quarters. Cleanse and cut up the mushrooms.

4. Make the suet pastry, and line a greased pudding basin.

5. Arrange half the game and steak in the bottom, then half the bacon and mushrooms, with the pieces of egg in the middle. Repeat the bacon and mushrooms, and the remainder of the game and steak. Pour in a little of the stock.

6. Put on the lid of pastry, cover with a scalded pudding cloth, and boil for 4 hours.

7. Serve hot in the basin, with a folded table-napkin pinned round.

8. Hand the remainder of the stock, well skimmed and seasoned, in a sauce-boat separately.

Note. This English dish should correctly be called by its English name.

POULET BOUILLI AU BÉCHAMEL
(Boiled Fowl, Béchamel Sauce)

1 boiling fowl.	1 hard-boiled egg.
1 carrot, turnip, and onion.	Chopped parsley.
1 pint coating Béchamel Sauce.	

Preparation—

1. Singe the bird, cut the skin round the hock joints, and draw out the sinews. Cut off the legs.

2. Draw the bird, and wipe inside and outside with a damp cloth.

3. Place the first two fingers inside the bird, break through the flesh just below the leg joint, loosen the skin around the legs, place the thumb against the knee joint. Push the leg upward until it slips inside the bird. Repeat with the other leg. This is called "pocketing" the legs, and is done to make the bird of better shape for coating with the sauce.

4. Draw the skin smoothly over the bird to give it a plump even appearance, and truss with needle and string as for roast fowl.

To Boil the Fowl—

1. Rub the breast with lemon juice to whiten it.

2. Put breast downward in boiling water. Boil for 3 minutes, and skim well. The bird may be wrapped first in a clean old table-napkin, like a roly-poly, if it is desired to keep it specially white.

3. Add the prepared vegetables, and salt.

4. Simmer gently until tender. Allow 50–60 minutes for a tender young fowl. 2 or even 3 hours is necessary for an old bird.

5. Remove the string, and allow the bird to remain on a hot dish to drain for a few minutes.

6. Press the bird with pieces of soft kitchen paper to dry it, remove to the serving dish, and coat with the prepared sauce.

7. Garnish the breast with sieved yolk of hard-boiled egg, and arrange the two halves of white of egg, filled with sieved yolk, at one end of the dish.

8. Sprinkle a little chopped parsley on the sauce around the dish, and serve.

ROGNONS SAUTÉS TURBIGO

4 sheeps' kidneys.
4 flap mushrooms.
1 oz. butter.
$1\frac{1}{2}$ oz. dripping.
$\frac{1}{4}$ lb. chipolata sausages.

4 small slices of bread.
Chopped parsley.
A little white wine.
$\frac{1}{2}$ pint brown sauce.

1. Cut the kidneys in half, and remove the skin. Peel the mushrooms, wash, and cut in halves, removing any surplus black part. Cook them in butter with a little water and salt.

2. Put sufficient dripping in a sauté pan to cover the bottom, and when it is smoking put in the kidneys, cut side down to stop the blood from running out. When they are set, fit the sausages in position, and complete the frying.

3. Arrange the kidneys on toast croûtons in two lines along the dish, with the sausages down the middle. Arrange the mushrooms on top, and sprinkle a little chopped parsley to finish.

4. Pour off the fat from the pan, add the wine and evaporate it, pour in the brown sauce. Reheat all well together, and pour around the kidneys.

SAUCISSES ST. GERMAIN

½ pint cooked green peas.	Salt and pepper.
½ pint Béchamel Sauce (see p. 244).	6 oz. Paris sausages.
	Crescents of fried bread.

1. Cook the peas, and drain them very well. If tinned peas are used, rinse them thoroughly, then scald, and drain very well.

2. Make the Béchamel sauce.

3. Add the peas to the sauce, season well with the salt and pepper, and reheat all, mixing lightly not to break the peas.

4. Grill the sausages, and cut out the crescents from slices of bread with a ½ in. cutter. Fry in a little butter, and drain on paper.

5. Place the Béchamel mixture in a hot round gratin dish, and arrange the sausages, radiating from the centre.

6. Place the crescents of fried bread between, and serve *very hot*.

SPATCHCOCK OF CHICKEN

1 tender young chicken.	Garnish—
Salt, pepper, and lemon juice.	Watercress and cut lemon.
Dripping for basting.	Accompaniments—
1 tablespoonful olive oil or oiled butter.	Tomato sauce.
1 tablespoonful browned crumbs.	Potato chips.

1. Pluck, draw, and singe the chicken, and split it right through the centre backbone.

2. Flatten the bird well, and wipe it with a damp cloth.

3. Cut off the feet and the points of the wings, and fix the bird quite flat with two strong skewers.

4. Sprinkle both sides with salt, pepper, and lemon juice. Unless the bird is very small, cook it for 30–35 minutes in a hot oven, basting well. Dry off the last basting.

5. Brush with oil, and grill the bird on alternate sides for 20 minutes in all, turning it frequently, and sprinkling occasionally with a little oil.

6. Brush with oil, sprinkle with crumbs, brown lightly under griller, then remove the skewers, and serve at once, *very hot*, garnished with lemon and watercress.

7. Serve tomato sauce and potato chips separately.

SALADS AND MAYONNAISE

SALADS add colour to meals and make them attractive, as well as providing the vitamins and salts necessary from a health point of view.

There is perhaps no dish so elastic in scope as a Salad. It may consist of one salad plant only; but if this is of good quality, correctly prepared, and daintily dished and finished, it can be a smart and most refreshing dish. Or a salad can be equally attractive when it consists of many blended flavours with elaborate dishing.

CLASSIFICATION

Salads may be divided into seven groups—

1. Those which are prepared with green salad plants.

2. Those prepared from vegetables, e.g. cooked artichokes, asparagus, beetroot, cauliflower, salsify, peas, potatoes, runner beans, cooked carrots, raw grated carrots, radishes, tomatoes, etc.

Note. Further additions may be made to either of the above, to make attractive Luncheon or Supper salads by the thrifty utilization of small, savoury left-over portions—such as tongue, ham, sausage, cheese, or such fruits as apples, bananas, oranges, grape-fruit, and pineapple. There is much scope for novelty and originality in this direction.

3. Fish Salads. Fish having firm flesh are best for use, such as salmon, halibut, or turbot, and oven-steamed cod is quite suitable for the purpose. Flake the fish or divide it into neat pieces, removing skin and bones. Shell-fish, such as lobsters, crabs, and prawns, can be used, and fish salads are usually garnished with anchovy fillets, strips of herring fillets, prawns or lobster feelers.

4. Poultry, Game, or Meat Salads. Small scraps of any of these may be utilized when roasted, or the birds may be carved into neat small joints, and the meats sliced. If the latter is cooked specially for the purpose, it is best to braise it; also smoked or salted meats are suitable.

5. Fruit Salads. The use of fruit is not now limited to sweet salads, and there are many fruits which are excellent when served with fresh salad dressing and garnished with lettuce or watercress. Grape-fruit, oranges, pears, melon, pineapple, grapes, apples, and Avocado pears are examples, and nuts, such as walnut kernels and Brazils, are frequently added.

6. Jellied Salads. Savoury Jelly, such as aspic, is frequently used in connection with cooked vegetables, as in a moulded Salade à la Russe, and Tomato jelly, set in small moulds or in a border mould, is a colourful addition.

7. Miscellaneous salads—prepared with cheese, eggs, rice, macaroni, etc., as characteristic ingredients.

SALADS IN THE MENU

1. *As an accompaniment to hot roast meat or poultry.* In this case green salad plants are used almost entirely, and a French salad dressing is used—a separate plate must always be laid for it at table.

2. *As an accompaniment to cold meat.* Those made from green salad plants, cooked vegetables, or fruits are most suitable. French salad dressing, mayonnaise, or salad cream can be used for dressing these salads.

3. *As a Luncheon or Supper dish.* Salads with a distinctive ingredient—lobster, cheese, fish, meat, poultry, or a salad using small savoury scraps—are most suitable.

4. *As a Hors d'Œuvre.*

HEALTH VALUE

Green salads have excellent dietetic value, because much of the saline matter which is extracted by even the most careful cooking of vegetables is retained in the plants. Green salads contain comparatively little nourishment of a heat-giving and flesh-forming character.

The cellulose which forms the framework of the plant gives the bulk which is necessary to digestion, and the oil used in a salad dressing has excellent food value, and aids in the digestion of the salad itself.

SALAD DRESSINGS

It is important to use good oil in making salad dressings, and the best olive oil is Huile de Provence, which should be stored in a dark cool (although not cold) place. Purchase in small quantities, as oil quickly becomes rancid. Cream, sour cream, and condensed milk can sometimes be substituted, if oil is disliked.

White malt vinegar or French wine vinegar are more delicate in flavour than the ordinary malt variety.

1. French Salad Dressing, or Vinaigrette, consisting of two-thirds oil and one-third vinegar, salt and pepper. A little mustard may be added, if desired. (See p. 252.)

2. Mayonnaise—the richest and best type of salad dressing (see further notes on pp. 182 and 248).

3. Home-made Salad Creams, Mock Mayonnaise, etc.

MAKING A SALAD

Rules for Preparing Green Salad Plants

1. Use young salad plants, and remove all coarse discoloured parts.

2. Wash the plants thoroughly, and leave them lying in fresh very cold water for a time.

Note. If the plants are gritty or grub-eaten, wash them quickly in salted water, but do not leave them lying in it, or they become slimy. Always give watercress this quick washing in salted water, to remove a microscopic fungus which may sometimes be present.

3. Drain thoroughly, first in a colander, then by swinging the plants gently to and fro in a salad basket or a cloth held by the corners. Hang them up in a draught for 10–15 minutes to crisp the plants well.

4. Tear salad plants apart with the fingers. Cos lettuce may be shredded with a knife if preferred, but avoid the use of a steel knife as far as possible.

5. Have cooked vegetables most carefully prepared, avoiding over-cooking, which would prevent cutting into neat dice or slices.

Essentials of a Successful Salad

1. Careful preparation of ingredients used—it is imperative that salad greens are crisp, clean, and dry.

2. The choice of a suitable salad dressing for the type of salad—the dressing being sufficient but not over-abundant.

3. Dressing the salad only a short while before serving, to avoid loss of crispness.

4. Attractive dishing and garnishing. Dress a salad high in the bowl if one large salad is served, but attractive individual portions are now popular. In the case of a mixed salad, have a good colour scheme. Daring in this direction is now fashionable, but avoid the proximity of similar colours which clash.

Garnishes for Salads

Strips of pimento; hard-boiled egg white; anchovy or herring fillets.

Olives stoned and cut in rings; rings of red or green peppers.

Powdered egg yolk; chopped parsley; lobster coral. Or a mixed powder, consisting of chopped egg white and powdered yolk, lobster coral, and chopped parsley.

Curled celery; radish roses; gherkin tassels; dice or balls of cooked vegetables. Pickled cabbage and pickled Spanish onion shreds.

Capers; chopped gherkins; chopped pickles; chopped jelly; and flavouring butters.

SEASONINGS AND FLAVOURINGS

Pepper, salt, fines herbes (see p. 14), flavoured vinegars, such as Tarragon or Chilli, chopped pickles and capers are frequently used.

If a slight onion flavour is required, either blend a little chopped shallot with the ingredients, or rub the bowl with a cut onion or shallot, or put in the bottom of the bowl a small crust of bread on which is spread one clove of crushed garlic.

MAYONNAISE

To Make Mayonnaise—

1. Use pure fresh ingredients—good oil and new laid eggs are essential (for proportions see p. 248).

2. Drain the yolks *thoroughly* from all whites.

3. Keep the ingredients cool during the process of mixing.

4. Cream the salt, pepper, and dry mustard thoroughly with the yolks before beginning to add any oil.

5. Add the oil quite literally drop by drop at the beginning. Later, when some of the vinegar has been added, the oil may be added more quickly.

6. If a large quantity of mayonnaise is made a whisk may be employed for the mixing, but for a small quantity a wooden spoon is preferable.

7. Take great care not to allow the mayonnaise to become too thick. This may be remedied by adding vinegar when required.

Note. Failure to observe any of the above rules is liable to cause curdling.

To Remedy Curdling

(*a*) Add a little cold water.

(*b*) Add the curdled mixture, drop by drop, to a fresh yolk.

SAUCES PREPARED FROM A FOUNDATION OF MAYONNAISE—

(*a*) Tartare Sauce. This consists of mayonnaise, to which chopped gherkins, tarragon, chervil, and capers are added.

(*b*) Green mayonnaise—coloured by the addition of a purée of parsley, tarragon, spinach, etc.

(*c*) Mayonnaise à la Cardinal—made with the addition of lobster coral.

(*d*) Caper mayonnaise—made with the addition of capers.

(*e*) Truffled mayonnaise—made with the addition of chopped truffles.

SALADE À L'AMÉRICAINE
(Savoury Fruit Salad)

4 cabbage lettuces.
Filling—
  2 dessert apples.
  3 small firm bananas.
24 grapes.

Dressing—
  1 tablespoonful castor sugar.
  3 dessertspoonfuls oil.
  1 dessertspoonful vinegar.
  Salt and pepper.
  1 large tablespoonful cream.
  The juice of $\frac{1}{2}$–1 lemon.

1. Remove the hearts from the lettuces, cleanse them thoroughly, and crisp them in cold water, then drain well.

2. Mix together the diced apples, bananas cut in $\frac{1}{4}$ in. rings, and the grapes skinned and stoned.

3. *Prepare the dressing.* Place the sugar in a small basin, and mix it smoothly with the oil, vinegar, salt, and pepper. Add the cream, and beat well. Add the juice of the lemon just before pouring over the salad.

4. Place a tablespoonful of the prepared fruits in each lettuce heart, and the remainder of the fruits in the bottom of the salad bowl, mixed with some of the dressing.

5. Arrange the lettuce hearts in the bowl, place a small spoonful of dressing in each, and serve at once. Any dressing remaining may be handed separately.

SALADE D'ANANAS
(Savoury Pineapple Salad)

4 rings of pineapple.
4 even-sized leaves of cabbage
  lettuce.
About 2 in. of cucumber.

$\frac{1}{2}$ gill mayonnaise (see p. 248).
Half a pimento.
Young nasturtium leaves or
  sprigs of watercress.

1. Lay each slice of pineapple on a lettuce leaf on an individual plate. Cut the pineapple in sections, and place together again.

2. Fill the centre of each round of pineapple with finely diced cucumber, moistened with the mayonnaise.

3. Cross two narrow strips of pimento on top, and garnish each at one side with a nasturtium leaf in season, or a sprig of watercress.

SALADE AUX BANANES
(Savoury Banana Salad)

3 bananas—not too ripe.
1 small cabbage lettuce.

1 tablespoonful mayonnaise or
  salad dressing (see pp. 248
  and 250).
2 small firm tomatoes, skinned.

1. Prepare the lettuce, and make a border of it in the salad bowl.
2. Peel the bananas, and cut them in slices. Mix with the well-seasoned salad dressing.
3. Pile the banana mixture in the centre of the salad bowl, and decorate with slices of tomato round.

SALADE DE BETTERAVE AU CÉLERI

1 small beetroot.
2 tablespoonfuls French wine vinegar.
3 or 4 sticks of white celery.

1 small shallot or a slice of onion.
Pepper and salt.
2 tablespoonfuls Vinaigrette dressing (see p. 252).
1 hard-boiled egg.

1. Cut the beetroot in thin slices, and marinade in a little vinegar for an hour or two.
2. Scrub the celery, cut a stick in thin slices crossways, and curl the remainder for decoration.
3. Drain the beetroot, and stamp out in fancy shapes with a cutter.
4. Chop the shallot, or onion, very finely, and mix it with the chopped beetroot trimmings, pepper, and salt, the chopped white of hard-boiled egg, half of the yolk, and the celery slices.
5. Pile the mixture in the centre of a salad bowl. Arrange the fancifully cut pieces of beetroot to cover, and scatter with the remaining half of the hard-boiled egg, passed through a coarse strainer.
6. Encircle with the curled celery (see p. 13), and serve.

SALADE DE CONCOMBRES

(Cucumber Salad)

1 small cucumber.   Vinaigrette dressing.

1. Peel the cucumber, and cut in thin slices in the ordinary way.
2. Season with the vinaigrette dressing, and serve with boiled salmon, etc.

SALADE DES GOURMETS

¼ lb. cooked ham, tongue, salt beef, game, or poultry.
An equal volume of cooked diced vegetables.
Salt and pepper.
Garnish—
    3–4 gherkins

Sliced beetroot, fancifully cut.
1 small cabbage lettuce.
Chopped parsley or Fines Herbes.
Mayonnaise or Salad Dressing (see pp. 248 and 250).

1. Cut the cooked meats, game, or poultry into small dice, and mix with the vegetables, similarly cut.

2. Season well, and add sufficient of the dressing chosen to hold all together.

3. Arrange the prepared lettuce in a border in the serving bowl, and place the mixture dome-shaped in the middle.

4. Garnish with slices of gherkin and beetroot, and sprinkle the chopped parsley or Fines Herbes over.

SALADE JAPONAISE

5 small cabbage lettuces or hearts.	Lemon juice.
1 orange.	Castor sugar.
6 cubes tinned pineapple.	$\frac{3}{4}$ gill cream salad dressing (see p. 189).
1 large skinned tomato.	Salt.

1. Cut the fruits and tomato into small dice, and season separately as follows—

(a) Slightly acidulate the pineapple with the lemon juice.

(b) Sprinkle the tomato with the castor sugar, a little salt, and a few drops of lemon juice.

(c) Sprinkle the oranges with a little castor sugar.

2. Put the ingredients aside in a cool place while preparing the dressing and cleansing and draining the lettuces.

3. Place a teaspoonful of the prepared fruits inside the heart of each lettuce.

4. Pour over each a spoonful of fresh cream dressing, well seasoned with salt.

5. Hand a sauce-boat of the same sauce separately.

SALADE DE LAITUES

(Lettuce Salad)

2 small cabbage lettuces.	Vinaigrette dressing.

1. Remove any discoloured or withered leaves, and tear the lettuce leaves into small irregular pieces, keeping the hearts intact.

2. Wash the lettuces very thoroughly in cold water, and allow to remain in clear cold water until crisp.

3. Remove, and drain in a basket or cloth, preferably hung in a current of air.

4. Place the prepared lettuce in an eathenware cooking bowl, season with the vinaigrette dressing, sprinkling it from a bottle with a grooved cork in it. Mix lightly but thoroughly, frequently sprinkling with the dressing.

5. Remove to the serving bowl, and serve at once. This salad

should not be seasoned with the dressing until the last possible moment before serving.

Note. This salad is particularly useful for serving with roast game or poultry. A little watercress or curled endive can be added if it is liked. The salad may also be garnished with quarters of hard-boiled eggs.

The yolk of a hard-boiled egg, pressed through a coarse strainer, may be scattered over the above to make Mimosa Salad.

SALADE D'ORANGES

(Savoury Orange Salad)

1 small cabbage lettuce.	1 clove of garlic.
2 large seedless oranges.	Vinaigrette dressing.

1. Trim the lettuce, cut in four, and cleanse thoroughly. Drain well.

2. Place the pieces of lettuce, stalk to centre, in a glass bowl which has rubbed with the clove of garlic cut in half. Pile fillets of orange between.

3. Just before serving, pour over the vinaigrette dressing, made with orange juice in place of vinegar, or hand it separately.

Note. This salad is specially suitable to serve with roast duck, wild duck, widgeon, or teal.

SALADE PANACHÉE EN SURPRISE

Decoration—
 Aspic jelly.
 Truffle.
 Cucumber skin.
Cream Lining—
 4 tablespoonfuls cream.
 2 tablespoonfuls liquid aspic.
Filling—
 2 oz. cooked runner beans.
 2 oz. cooked flageolets.
 2 oz. diced cooked carrot.

2 oz. cooked cauliflower sprigs.
1 gherkin.
1 gill mayonnaise.
½ gill aspic jelly.
½ oz. gelatine.
Garnish—
 Chopped aspic.
 Crescents cut from steamed egg white and beetroot.

1. Line a plain oval charlotte mould, and decorate in strips of cucumber skin, and truffle cut in small batons.

2. Reline the mould, and cover the decoration with aspic jelly.

3. Coat the inside with the cream lining.

4. Cut the cooked vegetables in small pieces, except the flageolets, which are left whole, and mix with the mayonnaise. Season well.

5. Dissolve the gelatine in the aspic, and add to the mixture. When it is thickening, pour all into the prepared mould.

6. When it is set, unmould; garnish with chopped aspic jelly, and crescents of beetroot and steamed egg white.

SALADE DE POMMES DE TERRE

4–5 cooked potatoes.
2 tablespoonfuls French Salad Dressing (see p. 252).
¾ gill mayonnaise (see p. 248).

Chopped parsley or coralline pepper.
Small cress or sprigs of watercress.

1. Cook the potatoes, cut in dice while hot, and sprinkle with the French Salad Dressing.

2. When potatoes are cold, arrange in a mound in the centre of a dish, and coat with thick Mayonnaise.

3. Just before serving, sprinkle with finely chopped parsley, or coralline pepper.

4. Encircle with small cress or sprigs of watercress.

Note. A small portion of the above may be served in an hors d'œuvres dish in that course.

SALADE DE TOMATES

(Tomato Salad)

1 lb. firm even-sized English tomatoes.
½ tablespoonful finely chopped onion.

Vinaigrette dressing.
Chopped parsley or fines herbes.

1. Blanch the tomatoes, and cut in thin slices transversely, preferably with a special slicer. Keep the tomatoes each together in shape.

2. Pile the tomatoes neatly, dome shape, in the salad bowl. Sprinkle with the chopped onion.

3. Season with the vinaigrette, sprinkle with the chopped parsley, or fines herbes, and serve.

SALADE À LA RUSSE (MOULDED)

Liquid aspic.
About half a pint in all of—
    Cooked carrots.
    Cooked turnips.
    Cooked beetroot.
    Cooked peas.
    Cooked French beans.
1 gherkin.

1 teaspoonful capers.
1 oz. cooked tongue.
1 oz. lobster meat.
¾ gill mayonnaise (see p. 248).
Garnish—
    Chopped parsley.
    Chopped aspic.
    Small cress.

1. Line a border mould with aspic, and decorate with neatly cut pieces of vegetable.

2. Set alternate layers of aspic jelly and mixed vegetables, cut in neat pieces, until the mould is full, finishing with a layer of jelly. Allow to set.

3. Mix together the remaining vegetables with the chopped gherkin, capers, chopped tongue, and lobster meat, with sufficient mayonnaise to hold it together.

4. Unmould the jelly on to a silver dish, and place the vegetable salad in the centre, piling it in a mound.

5. Sprinkle the mound with the chopped parsley, and dish with chopped aspic and small cress round.

SALADE À LA RUSSE (UNMOULDED)

2 tablespoonfuls dice of carrot.	2 oz. cooked tongue.
2 tablespoonfuls dice of turnip.	6 anchovy fillets.
2 tablespoonfuls peas.	1 teaspoonful capers.
2 tablespoonfuls French beans, cut in diamonds.	$\frac{3}{4}$–1 gill mayonnaise (see p. 248).
2 tablespoonfuls vinaigrette dressing (see p. 252).	Garnish—
	1 hard-boiled egg.
2 oz. cooked ham.	Fines herbes.

1. Prepare the carrot, turnip, peas, and French beans, and cook each separately.

2. Mix them while still hot, and marinade with the vinaigrette salad dressing in a bowl.

3. Cut up the ham, tongue, and anchovy fillets, and add them with the capers to the bowl. Season, and add sufficient of the mayonnaise to bind, mixing all lightly.

4. Pile the mixture, dome shape, in a salad bowl. Garnish with quarters of hard-boiled egg, sprinkle with fines herbes, and serve.

SALADE DE SANTÉ

2 small cabbage lettuces.	A few Brazil nuts.
2 slices pineapple, fresh or tinned.	Cream Salad Dressing (see p. 189).
1 orange.	

1. Clean and trim the lettuces, after cutting them into four, keeping the sections whole and shell shaped, and the heart uppermost.

2. Place them in a glass dish, garnish with diced pineapple, and lay fillets of orange on top.

3. Prepare the Brazil nuts, dividing them into pieces not too small, and sprinkle these over.

4. Hand the cream salad dressing separately.

SALADE À LA WALDORF

4 rosy dessert apples.
1½ oz. walnuts, after shelling.
2 sticks heart of celery (or cucumber).

½–¾ gill mayonnaise (see p. 248).
Chopped parsley or pistachio nuts.
Celery tops or small cress.

1. Core the apples, not pushing the corer right through to the bottom.

2. Scoop out the bulk of the pulp of the apples, leaving a neat shape. Chop the pulp.

3. Blanch and skin the walnuts, if fresh ones are used, or slightly crisp in the oven if kiln dried. Add them to the chopped apple, with the celery cut small.

4. Mix all with sufficient mayonnaise to bind, and fill the apple cups with this mixture.

5. Sprinkle with chopped parsley or chopped pistachios, and serve each apple on a small individual plate on a paper doily.

6. Garnish with the celery tops or small cress.

CREAM SALAD DRESSINGS

A. COOKED

2–3 egg yolks.
½ pint cream (or cream and milk).
Small teaspoonful mustard.

1 dessertspoonful castor sugar.
Pinch of salt and cayenne.
¾–1 gill vinegar.

1. Beat the yolks, and add the cream.

2. Cook carefully in a double saucepan until the mixture thickens like a custard.

3. Cream the mustard, sugar, salt, cayenne, and vinegar together, and add by degrees to the cream mixture.

4. Stir frequently while cooling, and use as required.

B. UNCOOKED

1 gill cream.
¼ teaspoonful salt.

Lemon juice to taste.

1. Whisk the cream, to which the salt is added, until it begins to thicken.

2. Remove the whisk, and stir in sufficient lemon juice to acidulate the cream pleasantly.

3. Serve very cold as required.

EGG DISHES AND FARINACEOUS FOODS

VERY attractive egg dishes are served nowadays, mainly a luncheon, instead of fish, or as an alternative to fish, and this applies also to dishes composed of some farinaceous product (see p. 197).

EGG DISHES

Egg dishes particularly are of great variety, but can be grouped conveniently according to their method of preparation.

1. FRIED, e.g. Américaine.
2. POACHED, e.g. Œufs Froids à la Niçoise.
3. SUR LE PLAT, or EN COCOTTES, e.g. Œufs Berçi.
4. HARD BOILED, e.g. Œufs aux Sardines.
5. SOFT BOILED (MOLLETS), e.g. Œufs Mollets Mistral.
6. STEAMED, or MOULDED, e.g. Œufs Moulé aux Tomates.

ŒUFS À L'AURORE

(Hard-boiled Eggs, Aurora Sauce)

4 eggs.
½ pint Sauce Aurore (see p. 243). | ½ teaspoonful finely chopped parsley.

1. Hard boil the eggs, and while still warm cut three of them in even slices, preferably with an egg slicer.
2. Pour a thin layer of the sauce into a round gratin dish, and arrange the sliced eggs in lines, the slices slightly tilted and leaning one against the other.
3. Coat with the sauce, which should be nearly boiling.
4. Decorate the two outer lines of slices with lines of sieved egg yolk, and the inner with a line of chopped whites, and place two lines of chopped parsley in the hollows.
5. Sprinkle sieved yolk at one end of the dish, and chopped whites at the other.

ŒUFS BROUILLÉS À LA DIVETTE

(Scrambled Eggs, with Prawns)

1½ oz. butter.
5 eggs.
Seasoning.
1 tablespoonful cream or milk.
1 dozen large prawns.
Sauce—
　½ oz. butter.

½ oz. flour.
1½ gills fish stock.
Seasoning.
½ oz. shrimp butter (see p. 13).
A little cream.

1. For the scrambled egg—

(a) Melt the butter, add the beaten egg mixed with the seasoning, and the cream or milk.

(b) Stir quickly with a metal spoon until the mixture thickens creamily.

2. Add the prepared prawns cut in pieces, and spread the mixture in a flat round, about ¾ in. thick, in the middle of a round dish.

3. Pour the sauce round. Make a small depression in the middle of the egg mixture, and place a tiny puddle of sauce in it.

Note. 1 tablespoonful of white sauce may be used in place of one of the eggs.

ŒUFS BROUILLÉS AUX TOMATES

(Scrambled Eggs, with Tomatoes)

Tomatoes concassé—	Scrambled eggs—
2 firm tomatoes.	1½ oz. butter.
1 oz. butter.	5 eggs.
¼ teaspoonful very finely chopped onion.	Seasoning.
	1 tablespoonful cream or milk.
	Chopped parsley.

1. Prepare the concassé tomatoes (see p. 281).

2. Prepare the scrambled eggs, as in the foregoing recipe, and place in a medium-sized round gratin dish.

3. Hollow out the centre, and place the prepared tomatoes in this neatly.

4. Sprinkle finely chopped parsley on the tomatoes.

ŒUFS EN COCOTTES À LA CRÈME

(Eggs in Cocottes, with Cream)

4 new-laid eggs.	½ gill cream.
1 oz. butter.	

1. Butter and season four cocottes, and place a whole unbroken egg in each.

2. Place the cocottes in a Yorkshire pudding tin with water to come half way up the sides.

3. Place the tin in a moderate oven until the whites of the eggs are jellied, and the yolks set but soft.

4. Pour a little warm seasoned cream on each egg.

Note. Brown sauce might take the place of the cream, or a little purée of game, veal, or chicken might be placed under each egg.

ŒUFS DIABLÉS (CHAUD)

(Hot Devilled Eggs)

4–5 new-laid eggs.	Chilli vinegar.
Cayenne.	Beurre noisette (see p. 12).

1. Fry the eggs in bacon fat or butter, and dish them in a fireproof dish.

2. Sprinkle each with a few grains of cayenne, a few drops of chilli vinegar, and pour the noisette butter over.

ŒUFS DIABLÉS (FROID)

(Cold Devilled Eggs)

5 hard-boiled eggs.	1 oz. butter.
Devil Mixture—	Pepper and salt.
1 small teaspoonful chutney.	A few grains of cayenne.
1 teaspoonful dry mustard.	1 small cabbage lettuce.
2 teaspoonfuls Worcester Sauce.	1 small beetroot.

1. Boil the eggs hard, and plunge them in cold water.

2. Remove the shells of four of them, and cut the eggs in half lengthways with an oiled knife to prevent change of colour.

3. Remove the yolks, mash these with the butter and the Devil Mixture. Pass all through a hair sieve.

4. Fill in the cases, formed by the whites, and join together again, leaving a neat edging of the filling showing round.

5. Prepare the lettuce; peel the beetroot, slice it very thinly, and marinade it in a little vinegar.

6. Arrange the beetroot in the centre of a salad dish, and the lettuce in a border, with the stuffed eggs arranged on the lettuce.

7. Pile the sieved egg yolk in the centre on the beetroot, and garnish with strips of white—using the remaining egg for this purpose.

Note. If preferred, a little of the filling may be reserved for piping the joins of the eggs.

ŒUFS FROIDS À LA NIÇOISE

(Cold Poached Eggs, Niçoise Salad)

4 poached eggs.	Salade Niçoise—
Mayonnaise: 1 yolk, etc. (see p. 248).	3 large tomatoes.
¼ gill aspic.	6–8 cooked new potatoes, small.
½ teaspoonful gelatine.	½ pint cooked runner beans.
large tomato.	French salad dressing.
	2 teaspoonfuls chopped chervil or parsley.

1. Poach the eggs in water, to which a little white malt vinegar has been added.

2. When the eggs are cooked, drop them into a basin of cold water.

3. When quite cold, trim, drain well on a cloth, and coat with mayonnaise chaudfroid.

4. Cut the skinned tomato into four slices, and place aside for dishing.

For the Salad—

1. Skin the tomatoes, and concass them (see p. 281).

2. Cut the potatoes in dice, and roughly chop the beans.

3. Mix all thoroughly with the French salad dressing, seasoning well.

Dishing—

1. Arrange the slices of tomatoes on a round dish.

2. Trim the eggs, and place one on each slice of tomato.

3. Pile the salad in the centre, and sprinkle each egg with a little chopped chervil or parsley.

ŒUFS FROU-FROU

(Eggs in Pastry Cases)

4 pastry croustades.	Scant ¼ gill aspic.
4 poached eggs.	½ teaspoonful gelatine.
1½ gills cooked French beans (or vegetable in season).	Sieved hard-boiled egg yolk. Chopped truffle.
1 gill mayonnaise (see p. 248).	

1. Prepare the croustades. Line four deep patty tins (oval preferably) with lining pastry, rolled out thinly, and from which sugar is omitted. Bake blind in the usual way.

2. Poach four eggs, adding a little white malt vinegar to the water. Rinse them in cold water until perfectly cold. Drain them on a cloth, and trim neatly.

3. Fill the croustades with the cooked French beans, mixed with the mayonnaise, and well seasoned. Lay an egg on top of each.

4. Add the gelatine to the aspic jelly, and both to the remaining mayonnaise. When this is cool, and at the point of setting, coat each egg with the mayonnaise.

5. Cover half of the top with the sieved egg yolk, and half with finely chopped truffle.

6. Arrange on a paper on a silver dish.

ŒUFS AU GRATIN

4 new-laid eggs.	½ teaspoonful made mustard.
2 oz. chopped ham.	½ oz. butter.
½ gill fresh breadcrumbs.	A little hot milk.
Seasoning.	A few shavings of butter.

1. Mix the ham, breadcrumbs, and seasoning, and place 2 tablespoonfuls on one side.

2. Mix the remainder of the ham, etc., with the oiled butter, and just sufficient hot milk to bind. Place this mixture in the bottom of a gratin dish.

3. Make four depressions in the mixture, and slip a whole raw egg into each.

4. Scatter over the remaining ham mixture, and a few shavings of butter.

5. Cover with a greased paper, and bake in a moderate oven until the eggs are set.

ŒUFS MOLLETS AUX ÉCREVISSES

(Soft-boiled Eggs, with Shrimps)

4 new-laid eggs.	1 large truffle.
1¼ gills Sauce Écrevisses (see p. 245).	

1. Place the eggs in a small frying-basket before putting them into a saucepan containing boiling water. (This ensures that the last egg to be removed will not be overcooked.) Boil 4 minutes, or 4½ minutes if large.

2. Place the eggs at once into cold water to check the cooking. Crack and peel the eggs under running water.

3. Place the shelled eggs in cold water for some minutes, and it is then possible to warm them in hot, but not boiling, water without hardening them. Leave them in this water until the moment of serving, then drain well.

4. Place a prepared egg into each of 4 buttered and seasoned cocottes. Cover with shrimp sauce of coating consistency, and lay a slice of untrimmed truffle on top of each.

5. Arrange the cocottes on a flat dish on a dish paper with parsley at one side.

Note. Soft-boiled eggs may be replaced by poached eggs, if preferred, but the former have the advantages of better shape, and of being devoid of any flavour of vinegar.

ŒUFS MOLLETS MISTRAL
(Garnished Soft-boiled Eggs)

4 new-laid eggs.	½ oz. butter.
1 tablespoonful flour.	1 teaspoonful chopped tarragon
½ an egg white.	or parsley.
Fawn coating crumbs.	12 stoned olives.
4 medium-sized tomatoes.	4 anchovy fillets.

1. Prepare the soft-boiled eggs, as in the foregoing recipe.

2. Dip the eggs in flour at the broad end.

3. Whisk the egg white until broken, dip the floured broad end of each egg into this, and then into the fawn crumbs, and repeat for a second time.

4. Concass the tomatoes (see p. 281), and fry them with the butter, adding the tarragon, or parsley, and olives. Keep warm until required.

5. Stand four small round cutters in a small fat bath; place the eggs on these, and fry until the crumbs are crisp.

6. Place a cross of anchovy fillets on the top of each egg.

7. Turn the mixture from the frying-pan on to a hot round gratin dish, and arrange the eggs upon it upstanding. Serve *hot*.

ŒUFS MOULÉS AUX TOMATES
(Moulded Eggs, with Tomato Sauce)

2 oz. chopped cooked lean ham.	Braised rice (see p. 201), 1 gill
4 new-laid eggs.	rice, etc.
	1½ gills tomato sauce.

1. Butter four dariole moulds thickly, and line them with the chopped ham.

2. Break an egg carefully into each mould. Boil some water in a stewpan, and place the moulds so that the water comes two-thirds of the way up the sides.

3. Boil for 5 minutes, then set the top of the eggs by placing them in a hot oven under the browning shelf, covered with paper.

4. Arrange the braised rice in a flat round of about ½ in.–¾ in. thick, on a gratin dish.

5. Unmould the eggs on to this, and pour the tomato sauce round.

Note. Macaroni, spinach, vegetable purée, etc., may be used in place of the rice.

ŒUFS À L'OPÉRA

(Baked Eggs with Garniture)

2 tablespoonfuls Tomato Sauce.	Liver Sauté—
1 doz. tips small asparagus or sprue.	2 oz. calf's liver.
½ oz. butter.	2 teaspoonfuls seasoned flour.
4 new-laid eggs.	½ oz. butter.
	½ teaspoonful chopped parsley

1. Prepare the Tomato Sauce (see p. 252), and cook the asparagus (see p. 107).

2. Butter a fireproof dish thickly. Break each egg separately, and slip it into position on the dish.

3. Bake in a moderate oven, covered with a buttered paper, until set.

4. Wash and dry the liver; cut it into strips; dip it into flour, and sauté the liver briskly for about 3 minutes in the well-heated butter.

5. Sauce over the eggs lightly, when they are set, with the Tomato Sauce. Arrange the liver and asparagus in small separate piles. Sprinkle a little chopped parsley on the liver, and serve at once very hot.

ŒUFS SUR LE PLAT

(Eggs Cooked on a Fireproof Dish)

4 new-laid eggs.	Garnish—
Scant 1 oz. butter.	4 Parisienne sausages.
	3–4 tablespoonfuls tomato sauce.

1. Butter and season a fireproof dish. Place in the whole eggs, and cook over gentle heat, guiding the yolk into place with the finger tips. When slightly set, place in the oven to finish cooking.

2. Prick and grill the French sausages.

3. Have the tomato sauce ready, and pour a ribbon of it round the edge of the dish. Radiate the sausages from the centre between the eggs.

Note. This dish may be left quite plain, if preferred, or may be garnished variously—halved grilled kidneys or tomatoes, grilled rolls of bacon, strips of grilled ham, sautéd chicken livers, etc., are popular.

ŒUFS POCHÉS FLORENTINE

(Poached Eggs, with Spinach)

4 new-laid eggs.	3 tablespoonfuls cooked spinach (see p. 115).
½ pint Béchamel Sauce (see p. 244).	2 oz. grated cheese.

1. Poach the eggs in water, with a little white malt vinegar. Place them in cold water to arrest cooking, then reheat in hot salted water.

2. Place a spoonful or two of Béchamel Sauce in a gratin dish, and arrange the prepared heated spinach on it.

3. Place the eggs on the spinach, and coat with the sauce. Sprinkle with fresh grated cheese and oiled butter.

4. Make sure that all the foregoing components are *hot*, then brown the dish lightly and quickly under a griller.

Note. This dish may be prepared in individual portions, if preferred, in either small gratin dishes or scallop shells.

ŒUFS AUX SARDINES

4 new-laid eggs.
5–6 sardines.
1½ oz. butter.
Pepper and salt.

Small round croûtons of brown bread.
Small cress to garnish.

1. Boil the eggs hard; when they are quite cold remove the shells, and cut the eggs in halves with an oiled knife.

2. Slice a tiny piece from the end of each to make the half stand steadily, and remove the yolks.

3. Skin and bone the sardines, add them to the yolks, butter, pepper, and salt.

4. Rub all through a hair sieve, and pipe a large rose in the centre of each white.

5. Spread the croûtons of brown bread with a little of the sardine butter, and stand a prepared half egg on each.

6. Garnish with the small cress.

FARINACEOUS DISHES
BARQUETTES AU SEMOULE
(Semolina Boats)

½ pint milk.
2½ oz. semolina.
Salt, pepper, and nutmeg.
1 yolk of egg.

Anchovy paste, foie gras, or patum peperium.
Beaten egg, and fawn crumbs.
Fried parsley.
Tomato or Piquante Sauce.

1. Boil the milk, shake in the semolina, and cook for about 10 minutes, stirring meanwhile, until the mixture is thick and leaves the sides of the pan. Season well, and when cool beat in the yolk.

2. Grease some boat-shaped moulds, fill level with the semolina mixture, using a palette knife.

3. Press down the centre with the floured finger, and place in the depression ½ teaspoonful of the filling chosen.

4. Place more mixture on top, and round off neatly with a knife.

5. Unmould the barquettes as soon as set.

6. Roll in flour, then dip in beaten egg, and coat with the crumbs.

7. Fry in butter and oil, or deep fat, until golden brown.

8. Dish on a flat dish on a paper, in a star, with fried parsley in the centre.

9. Hand the Tomato or Piquante Sauce separately.

Note. French mustard is an appetizing addition to almost any farinaceous dish. It is obtainable at any large stores, but an excellent substitute is to mix ordinary mustard with vinegar instead of water, adding a suspicion of very finely chopped onion.

CROQUETTES AU MACARONI

2 oz. macaroni.	½–1 yolk of egg.
Panada—	Pepper, salt, and cayenne.
½ oz. butter.	Beaten egg and coating crumbs.
½ oz. flour	Paprika pepper.
½ gill milk.	Sauce Tomates (see p. 252).
1 oz. grated Parmesan cheese.	

1. Cook the macaroni in boiling salted water for 25 minutes. Refresh and drain thoroughly.

2. Gather the pieces together, and slice into thin rings.

3. Make the Panada, and add the macaroni, cheese, egg yolk, and seasoning. Bind all well over gentle heat.

4. Turn out on a plate to cool.

5. Divide evenly into 8 portions, then form into small flat round cakes.

6. Coat each cake with egg and breadcrumbs, and fry golden colour in deep fat.

7. Drain, and pile on a hot gratin dish on a dish paper. Hand the tomato sauce separately.

Note. 1 oz. chopped lean ham may take the place of the cheese, if preferred.

GNOCCHI AU GRATIN À L'ITALIENNE

(Semolina Cheese)

1 pint milk.	4 oz. fresh grated cheese.
4 oz. semolina.	Salt and pepper.
1 large teaspoonful cornflour.	Browned crumbs.
A little extra milk.	Shavings of butter.

1. Boil the milk, and shake the semolina lightly into it.

2. Stir until it thickens, then remove from heat, and add 1 teaspoonful of cornflour, mixed with a little milk or water.

3. Stir until boiling, and cook for 10 minutes. Add 3 oz. of the cheese, and season with salt and pepper.

4. Grease and flour a small Yorkshire pudding tin, and spread the mixture into it about ¾ in. thick. Leave until cold and set.

5. Cut the mixture in small squares, and arrange them overlapping in a greased fireproof dish.

6. Sprinkle with the remaining cheese, a few of the crumbs, and some shavings of butter.

7. Brown for a few minutes in a hot oven. Serve in the dish *very hot*.

GNOCCHI À LA PARISIENNE

(Poached Choux Pastry, Mornay Sauce)

Choux Pastry—	½ pint Mornay Sauce (see p. 248).
1 gill milk.	1 oz. grated Cheddar cheese.
2½ oz. flour.	Oiled butter.
2 oz. butter.	Paprika pepper.
2 small eggs.	

1. Make a stiff choux pastry (see p. 221), using milk instead of water, adding the extra ½ oz. flour, and the whole of the eggs well beaten.

2. When the pastry is made, place it into a bag, fitted with a ½ in. plain pipe. Squeeze the bag with one hand, and cut off the paste in pieces of 1 in. length, dropping them into a pan of boiling salted water.

3. Poach the gnocchi 15–20 minutes, covered. The pan may be well filled, and should be shaken occasionally. If small gnocchi is needed, cut into ½ in. lengths, and poach 6–7 minutes.

4. Drain on a wire sieve; refresh under cold water, and sauté in a little butter. Season with salt and pepper.

5. Place the gnocchi on a greased gratin dish, and coat with the Mornay Sauce.

6. Sprinkle with cheese and oiled butter, and brown under a griller.

Note. The Gnocchis should be light and well puffed, and should be served at once.

MACARONI AU GRATIN

4 oz. macaroni.	1½ gills flowing white sauce.
4 oz. grated cheese (Parmesan and Cheddar mixed).	Croûtons of fried bread.
	Paprika pepper.
2 oz. butter.	

1. Break up the macaroni, and cook it in boiling salted water about 25 minutes (or blanch, and cook it in milk).

2. Refresh the macaroni, and drain it well. Toss it in about 1 oz. of the butter, and add 3 oz. of the grated cheese to the white sauce.

3. Mix well, season, and place in a greased gratin dish. Sprinkle with the remaining grated cheese and oiled butter. Brown lightly under a griller.

4. Sprinkle with the Paprika pepper, and garnish with crescent-shaped croûtons of bread, fried in a little butter.

NOUILLES AU BEURRE

(Buttered home-made Macaroni)

Nouille pastry (see p. 220). | **Finely chopped parsley or**
1-2 oz. butter. | **grated cheese.**

1. Prepare the nouille pastry, and leave it to dry for an hour before cutting.

2. Flour it lightly, fold over in four, and cut in shreds. Take these up in the fingers, and shake them lightly apart.

3. Poach the nouilles in boiling salted water 5-8 minutes. Keep them separated with a fork while cooking, and avoid flattening them.

4. Drain and refresh in cold water. Again drain very thoroughly. Sauté the nouilles in butter, and season well.

5. Sprinkle with a little finely chopped parsley or the grated cheese.

RISOTTO AU FOIE DE VOLAILLE

(Savoury Rice with Chicken Livers)

Few threads of saffron. | $\frac{1}{2}$ **pint strong stock.**
Scant $\frac{1}{2}$ gill hot water. | **3 chicken livers.**
$\frac{1}{2}$ **onion.** | **Little butter and oil for frying.**
2 oz. butter. | **Juice of half a lemon, or $\frac{1}{4}$ gill**
$\frac{1}{4}$ **lb. Patna rice.** | **white wine.**
Salt and cayenne. | **1 gill brown sauce.**

1. Infuse the saffron. Shred the onion, and sauté it in 1 oz. of the butter. Add the rice, mix well, and cook for 2 minutes. Add the salt and cayenne, stock, and strained saffron.

2. Cover with a greased paper with a hole in the centre, and cook in a moderate oven 20-25 minutes.

3. Remove and add 1 oz. of butter (the rice should have absorbed the stock completely). Place in a greased border mould, and press down well with a teaspoon.

4. Cut the chicken livers into thin escalops, and fry them in the butter and oil. Season well, and cook about 3 minutes, being very careful not to overcook them.

5. Make the sauce by adding the lemon juice or wine to the congealed blood of the liver on the bottom of the pan; add the brown sauce, and boil up.

6. Add ½ oz. butter to the sauce in small pieces. Add the livers, and reheat without boiling.

7. Turn out the rice, and warm it in the oven. Pile up the liver sauté in the middle.

RIZ PILAFF

(Braised Rice)

2 oz. chopped onion.	1 pint veal stock.
3 oz. butter.	A little Paprika pepper or
½ pint Patna rice.	chopped parsley.

1. Sauté the chopped onion in 2 oz. of the butter, without colouring.

2. Add the rice, and heat through, stirring with a wooden spoon. Add the pint of veal stock, boil up, and place in the bottom of the oven to braise for 20 minutes. All the stock should be absorbed.

3. Remove and add the remainder of the butter, mixing with a fork, so that all grains are loosened.

Serve in a hot dish, sprinkled with a little Paprika or finely chopped parsley, or use as part of a dish, as desired.

SPAGHETTI À LA MILANAISE

6 oz. spaghetti.	About 1 gill tomato sauce.
1½ oz. butter.	1 oz. grated cheese.
1½ oz. lean cooked ham.	Seasoning.
1½ oz. cooked tongue.	Chopped parsley.
1 oz. champignons.	

1. Cook the spaghetti in salted water for about 15 minutes. Refresh, and drain.

2. Melt the butter in a saucepan, add the spaghetti, and toss well. Add the ham, tongue, and champignons (each cut into julienne), the tomato sauce, and the cheese.

3. Correct the seasoning, and serve piping hot in a fireproof dish. Sprinkle with grated cheese and the chopped parsley.

Note. Julienne of truffle may also be added.

OMELETTES AND SOUFFLÉS

OMELETTES are most palatable if carefully cooked, and a French omelette is easily and quickly prepared. Writing or reading about making an omelette takes longer than actually doing it, for a perfect French omelette is made and ready to serve within a minute—and the eater should be in waiting for the omelette, never vice versa.

Because it is so quickly made an omelette forms an excellent emergency dish. Eggs are usually available, and there are often scraps of cooked food in the larder, which can be used as stuffing for the omelette or added to the mixture, giving bulk and additional nutriment, substance, and variety.

Omelettes are divided into three classes—

1. Plain or French omelettes. These are the most general, and in making them whole eggs are beaten together.

2. Puffed or English omelettes; which have a soufflé strain in their composition—yolks and whites of eggs being separated.

3. Filled or stuffed omelettes—either plain or puffed. The filling can be either savoury or sweet.

POINTS IN THE PREPARATION AND COOKING OF OMELETTES

1. The pan used for cooking omelettes must be thick and strong, with a smooth level surface to prevent sticking, and well "proved" (see Note on p. 15).

(a) It must be suitable in size to the number of eggs to be used, or the omelette will be over-thick and under-cooked, or too thin and leathery. It is always better to have two or more small omelettes as necessary, rather than to make a large one. A pan of 5 in. diameter will take two eggs; one of 6 in. diameter is required for three eggs.

(b) The pan must be made of steel, iron, or tin-lined copper, as eggs are most liable to stick in an aluminium or enamelled pan.

(c) It is not essential to keep a pan specially for omelettes only, so long as the inner surface of the pan can be kept perfectly smooth.

2. The eggs must be perfectly fresh and well beaten—although not to a froth for a French omelette. When the whites are separated, they must be whisked stiffly.

3. Correct proportions must be allowed for a French omelette— $\frac{1}{4}$ oz. of fresh butter to each egg.

1 tablespoonful of water, cream, or milk to each 3 eggs.

Water makes a very light omelette, and is preferable, but cream or milk improve its food value.

4. Everything must be in readiness for mixing, frying, and dishing before work is begun. Any material added to an omelette or used as filling must be cooked first if it requires cooking.

5. For success in frying a French omelette—

(*a*) It must be rapidly cooked in smoking butter. Avoid burning the butter, but when used really hot it isolates the egg mixture and prevents sticking.

(*b*) The manipulation of the egg mixture while it is setting must be quick and deft (see below).

6. In cooking a puffed omelette, do not leave it on the top heat for longer than half a minute, and place the pan at once into a hot oven for 8–10 minutes. When ready, the omelette should be golden brown, just firm to the touch, yet spongy. If it rises too rapidly, or if insufficiently cooked, it becomes very wrinkled on the outside, collapsing quickly.

Note. A well-made French omelette is quite set, but moist, no part being actually raw. The middle of the omelette is, however, a little less cooked than the outer coat.

I. PLAIN, OR FRENCH, OMELETTES
PLAIN OR FRENCH OMELETTE
(Foundation)

4 eggs.	Seasoning.
1 oz. butter.	½ teaspoonful chopped parsley.
1 large tablespoonful water, milk, or cream.	

1. Prove the frying-pan (see p. 15).

2. Beat the eggs in a small basin until no streaks of white are showing; add the liquid chosen to thin the egg, seasoning, and the chopped parsley.

3. Melt the butter, skim thoroughly, and when it is just smoking pour in the egg mixture.

4. Stir the top briskly, not touching the bottom of the pan; when the edges begin to set, push the side of the omelette nearest the worker to the centre of the pan. Any egg which is not quite set will run out at the sides and set quickly, and can be added into the middle of the omelette.

5. Work the omelette to the far side of the pan. Remove the pan from the heat; holding it in the left hand, knock the handle briskly two or three times near the pan end. This raises the further edge, so that the omelette is thus easily folded in three. Add any filling that may be required before the final folding.

6. Allow the under part of the omelette to colour for half a

minute, then tip it right over on to a piping hot dish. The dish may be garnished with a thin trail of some suitable sauce to match the filling, if desired.

Note. If a sweet foundation omelette is needed, omit the seasoning and parsley, and add 1 teaspoonful of castor sugar and a small pinch of salt.

SOME SUGGESTED FILLINGS FOR FRENCH OMELETTES

Name of Omelette	Ingredients	Method
Champignons.	2 oz. white button Mushrooms. 1 oz. butter. Seasoning. 1 tablespoonful of Madeira Sauce (optional).	Prepare the mushrooms, and cut in dice. Fry in butter, adding seasoning. Fold the centre with a little of the butter, or strain and heat the mushrooms in the sauce.
Confiture.	1 tablespoonful stiff jam.	Place hot jam inside the omelette. Dredge with castor sugar when placed on a hot dish. Brand with a red hot metal skewer in 3 lines across the omelette.
Foie de Volaille.	2 chicken livers. $\frac{1}{2}$ oz. butter. Seasoning. $\frac{1}{4}$ teaspoonful of chopped parsley, and of chopped onion.	Cut the livers in slices. Fry quickly over sharp heat for a minute or two. Add the seasoning, parsley, and onion.
Jambon.	3 oz. cooked ham. $\frac{1}{2}$ oz. butter. Seasoning. $\frac{1}{2}$ teaspoonful chopped parsley.	Shred the ham. Toss it in the butter until heated. Season, and add the parsley.
Petits Pois.	2 tablespoonfuls green peas. A nut of butter. Seasoning.	Cook the peas in the usual way and toss them in the butter. Add the seasoning.
Pointes d'Asperges.	1 cupful cooked asparagus points. $\frac{1}{2}$ oz. butter. Seasoning.	As for Petits Pois.

SOME SUGGESTED FILLINGS FOR FRENCH
OMELETTES—*(Contd.)*

Name of Omelette	Ingredients	Method
Rognons.	2 sheep's kidneys. ½ oz. butter. Seasoning. ¼ teaspoonful of chopped parsley, and of onion.	As for Foie de Volaille.
Tomates.	2 firm tomatoes. A nut of butter. ½ teaspoonful chopped parsley. Seasoning.	Have the tomatoes concassé (see p. 281). Toss them in the butter to heat through over gentle heat. Add the parsley and seasoning. A little tomato sauce may be poured round the dish with advantage.

ADDITIONS TO FRENCH OMELETTE MIXTURE

Fines Herbes.	½ teaspoonful chopped tarragon, and of chervil. 1 teaspoonful chopped parsley. A pinch of sweet herbs. A clove of garlic.	Add the finely chopped herbs to the egg mixture. Cut the garlic in half, and wipe inside of omelette pan with the cut side.
Fromage.	Scant 1 oz. cheese.	Add to the egg mixture, reserving a little to sprinkle over before serving.
Oseille.	4 oz. sorrel. 1 oz. butter.	Pick and wash the sorrel thoroughly. Cut leaves in fine juliennes, and cook in the butter. Add to the egg mixture.
Rhum.	2 tablespoonfuls rum.	Dish the omelette, and sprinkle with sugar. Pour over it the rum, which has been briskly warmed. Set it alight, and serve blazing.

OMELETTE À LA CRÈME

4 eggs.	Finely grated cheese.
6 oz. white button mushrooms.	1 gill cream, or cream and milk.
1 oz. butter.	2 yolks of eggs.

1. Clean and peel the mushrooms. Cut them in pieces, and fry in the butter for 5 minutes.

2. Season with salt and pepper, and add half the cream. Heat barely to boiling-point, add the yolks, and mix all well.

3. Prepare a French omelette with the four eggs, and place the above mixture inside before folding it.

4. Separately, take another yolk of egg, and mix it with the remaining cream, or cream and milk, and seasoning.

5. Sauce over the omelette with this when it has thickened, sprinkle with the grated cheese, and glaze under a griller.

6. Sprinkle with chopped parsley, and serve at once.

OMELETTE À LA MORNAY

French omelette.	1 gill flowing Mornay Sauce
2 tablespoonfuls cooked flaked	(see p. 252).
smoked haddock.	1 oz. grated cheese.

1. Prepare the French omelette in the usual way with four eggs, adding the fish, free from skin and bone, to the egg mixture before cooking.

2. Dish on a fireproof dish, pour thin Mornay Sauce over, sprinkle with the grated cheese, and brown lightly under a griller.

II. SOUFFLÉ, OR ENGLISH, OMELETTES
SOUFFLÉ OMELETTE (AU CONFITURE)

4 eggs.	1 tablespoonful castor sugar.
A few drops of vanilla essence	1 tablespoonful hot jam.
or some flavouring substance.	

1. Prove a frying- or omelette-pan (see p. 15), grease it with clarified butter, and keep it hot.

2. Cream the yolks of the eggs thoroughly with sugar until thick.

3. Add the flavouring, then fold in the stiffly whisked whites very lightly, but making sure that they are completely incorporated to make one pale yellow mixture.

4. Pour in the mixture lightly, and spread it level. Shake for a minute or two over moderate heat, then place the pan in the hot oven to set the mixture, 8–10 minutes. Dredge with icing sugar 2 minutes before the mixture is cooked, returning it to the oven to glaze.

5. Turn out the omelette on to a sugared paper, place the hot jam in the centre, fold in half, and serve at once on a lace paper doily.

Note. If a savoury foundation omelette is needed, omit the sugar and flavouring, and substitute salt and pepper. This omelette can be glazed by rubbing a small nut of butter over the hot surface, instead of using the icing sugar.

OMELETTE AUX BANANES

As for **Soufflé Omelette** (see p. 206).
Omit the jam, and substitute—

2 sliced bananas. 1 tablespoonful apricot marmalade (see p. 11).	1 tablespoonful orange or lemon juice.

Warm these together to form the filling.

OMELETTE AUX FRUITS

As for Omelette aux Bananes.
Omit the bananas and fruit juice, and substitute—

1 tablespoonful Metz fruits, cut in small pieces.	1 tablespoonful apricot marmalade (see p. 11). $\frac{1}{2}$ tablespoonful liqueur.

OMELETTE AUX ORANGES

As for Soufflé Omelette.
Omit the vanilla essence and jam, and substitute—

The grated rind of one orange. 1 tablespoonful marmalade.	The juice of half a sweet orange.

Add the grated rind when creaming the yolks and sugar. Heat the marmalade and orange juice to form the filling.

OMELETTE AU POISSON

As for Soufflé omelette, savoury foundation. Add—

2–3 tablespoonfuls flaked cooked fish.

Prepare the omelette in the usual way, adding the fish to the creamed yolks and seasoning.

III. SOUFFLÉS

POINTS ABOUT SOUFFLÉS

1. The word "Soufflé" correctly translated means "blown up," this being the characteristic of a carefully prepared soufflé. It is a very light mixture.

2. Eggs are an essential component of soufflés and are frequently used in the proportion of one more white than yolk.

3. Some soufflés are enriched with cream.

4. Many soufflés consist of a characteristic foundation called a panada.

VARIETIES OF SOUFFLÉS

I. Savoury. II. Sweet.
(*a*) Steamed, e.g. Soufflé au Vanille.
(*b*) Baked, e.g. Soufflé au Fromage.
(*c*) Fried, e.g. Beignets Soufflés.
(*d*) Cold, e.g. Soufflé a la Milanaise.
(*e*) Iced, e.g. Soufflé au Café Frappé.

COOKING HOT SOUFFLÉS

All soufflés should be exposed to moderate heat.

1. If baked or fried, intense heat causes a crust to form on the top, which prevents the soufflé from rising.

2. If steamed, too much heat causes the soufflé to rise very rapidly, all the air is expelled, and the soufflé falls as rapidly as it has risen.

3. Too low a temperature prevents the egg from rising, and causes the soufflé to be heavy.

RULES FOR STEAMING SOUFFLÉS

1. Measure all ingredients very accurately.

2. Avoid over-cooking the panada.

3. Have perfectly fresh eggs, whisking the whites until stiff and dry.

4. Steam the mixture at once when prepared.

5. Fill the tin about three-quarters full, preparing it as on p. 213.

6. Remove the soufflé from the saucepan as soon as it is cooked, but allow it to shrink slightly before turning out.

Note. To test when cooked, a soufflé should be firm in the centre. When pierced with a skewer, the latter should be quite clean on removal.

COLD SOUFFLÉS

These may be savoury or sweet.

CHARACTERISTICS OF COLD SOUFFLÉS

1. The eggs are separated, and for a sweet soufflé are often whisked with the sugar over hot water until thick. The whites are stiffly whisked.

2. Cream is added.

3. A small proportion of gelatine is melted in water and added, to make the soufflé set.

ICED SOUFFLÉS

These are similar to cold soufflés, but the gelatine is omitted, and the mixture frozen in an ice cave.

SOUFFLÉ AUX ANANAS

Panada (see p. 15).
 1 oz. butter.
 1 oz. flour.
 1 gill milk.
3 yolks and 4 whites of new-laid eggs.

2 oz. castor sugar.
4 oz. sieved pineapple.
Rounds of pineapple, and angelica to decorate.
Mousseline Sauce (see p. 255).

1. Prepare a soufflé tin as for Soufflé au Vanille (see p. 213). Decorate the bottom with rounds of pineapple and pieces of angelica.

2. Prepare the Panada, and beat in the yolks, one at a time. Add the sugar and sieved pineapple.

3. Finish as for Soufflé au Vanille.

SOUFFLÉ D'ÉPINARDS

(Spinach Soufflé)

2 lb. spinach, prepared as for Épinard a la Crème (see p. 115).

2 eggs.

1. Prepare the spinach. When all the processes are completed (prior to dishing), beat in the yolks of eggs one by one, and add the stiffly whisked whites.

2. Pour lightly into a greased soufflé case, of 5 in. diameter, round which a protecting band of greased paper has been tied.

3. Bake in a moderately hot oven for 15 minutes.

4. Remove the paper from the case, and serve at once very hot.

SOUFFLÉS DE FROMAGE

(Chaud)

Panada—
 ½ oz. butter.
 ¼ oz. flour.
 ½ gill milk.
1½ yolks of eggs.

Few grains cayenne and salt.
2 whites of eggs.
1½ oz. grated Parmesan.
Coralline pepper.

1. Grease 5 small china or paper soufflé cases.

2. Make the panada with the butter, flour, and milk.

3. When it is slightly cooled, beat in the yolks very thoroughly, adding the salt, and a few grains of cayenne.

4. Mix in the finely grated cheese lightly, reserving two teaspoonfuls for dishing.

5. Mix in 1 tablespoonful of the stiffly beaten egg whites, then fold in the remainder very lightly.

6. Divide the mixture into the prepared soufflé cases.

7. Bake in a moderately hot oven (400° Fahr.) for about 15 minutes.

8. Serve *at once*, sprinkled with grated cheese and coralline pepper.

SOUFFLÉ DE MERLANS

(Whiting Soufflé)

4 oz. filleted whiting.
Panada (see p. 15)—
 ½ oz. butter.
 ½ oz. flour.
 ½ gill fish stock, or milk.
2 small eggs.
Cayenne, salt, and lemon juice.

½ gill cream.
1½ gills coating, Béchamel
 Sauce (see p. 244).
Garnish—
 Coralline pepper.
 Fans of lemon.
 Sprigs of parsley.

1. Grease a half-pint plain charlotte tin, and fit a disk of greased paper in the bottom.

2. Shred the fish finely, make the panada, and allow to cool.

3. Place fish and panada in a mortar, and pound well. Add beaten eggs by degrees, continuing the pounding.

4. Rub through a wire sieve.

5. Season the soufflé mixture, add the lemon juice, and lightly fold in the cream.

6. Place the mixture in the prepared tin, twist a greased paper over, and steam gently about 45 minutes, until firm.

7. Unmould on to a small oval gratin dish, coat with the prepared sauce, and decorate with coralline pepper, lemon, and parsley.

SOUFFLÉS DE MERLUCHE FUMÉE

½ oz. butter.
½ oz. flour.
½ gill milk.
1½ yolks of eggs.
Salt, pepper, and cayenne

2 tablespoonfuls chopped, cooked, smoked haddock.
2 whites of eggs.
Coralline pepper.

1. Make the panada with the butter, flour, and milk. Beat in the yolks when it is slightly cooled.

2. Add the salt, pepper, and cayenne, and the prepared haddock, from which all skin and bones have been removed.

3. Whisk the egg whites stiffly, and fold in lightly.

4. Divide into five small greased china or paper soufflé cases, and bake in a moderate oven until well puffed and golden brown.

5. Sprinkle a little coralline pepper on top, and serve at once as a hot savoury.

Note. If preferred, this mixture may be baked in one large soufflé case with a suitable sauce, handed separately, and served in the fish course.

SOUFFLÉ À LA MILANAISE
(Milan Soufflé)

3 eggs.	$\frac{1}{2}$ gill water.
$\frac{1}{2}$ lb. castor sugar.	Decoration—
$2\frac{1}{2}$ lemons.	2 tablespoonfuls of ratafia crumbs.
$\frac{1}{2}$ pint cream.	Chopped pistachios.
$\frac{1}{2}$ oz. gelatine.	

1. Place the yolks of the eggs, sugar, grated lemon rind, and juice into a basin.

2. Have a saucepan half full of boiling water, and remove to table. The water must not touch the bottom of the basin. Keep the basin tipped and constantly turned to avoid over-heating.

3. Whisk the mixture until thick and creamy. Remove from heat, and whisk for 5 minutes until cool.

4. Mix in the half-whipped cream. Dissolve the gelatine in the water, and strain into the mixture.

5. Fold in the whites of the eggs, stiffly whisked.

6. When it is thickening creamily pour into a soufflé case of $5\frac{1}{2}$ in. diameter, with a band of paper tied round the outside (the mixture should come above the top of the case).

7. Put aside to set; when firm remove the paper, and decorate the sides, which are upstanding, with crushed ratafias and the top with the finely chopped pistachio nuts.

SOUFFLÉ AUX ORANGES
(Orange Soufflé)

As for Soufflé à la Milanaise, using the rind and juice of three oranges, and the grated rind of half a lemon instead of the $2\frac{1}{2}$ lemons. Use 5 oz. castor sugar only, and add a little orange colouring.

SOUFFLÉ AU MOKA PRALINÉ

(For 6 persons)

4 new-laid eggs.
2 oz. castor sugar.
1½ gills cream.
½ oz. gelatine.
½ gill water.
Strong coffee essence.

2 oz. praline, pounded to powder.
Decoration—
  Scant ½ gill cream.
  Sugar and vanilla essence.
  Chopped pistachios.
  Ratafia crumbs.

1. Put the yolks of the eggs with the sugar in an earthenware basin, and whisk over a pan of steaming hot water, until thick and rope-like.

2. Remove from the heat and whisk for 4 or 5 minutes.

3. Half whisk the cream, and add it to the egg mixture, flavour with the coffee, and dissolve the gelatine gently in the water.

4. Strain the gelatine into the mixture and fold in the stiffly whisked whites of eggs.

5. Fold in the pounded praline and stir gently until the mixture thickens creamily.

6. Pour into a china soufflé case (4¾ in. bottom diameter), around which a band of stiff paper has been tied, the paper coming about 3 in. above the edge.

7. When it is set remove the paper and press ratafia crumbs against the upstanding sides. Decorate with roses of whipped sweetened flavoured cream and chopped pistachios.

SOUFFLÉ À LA PRINCESSE

(Princess Soufflé)

½ pint apricot purée.
4 eggs.
2 oz. castor sugar.
1 gill cream.
½ oz. gelatine.
½ gill water.

Carmine.
Decoration—
  2 tablespoonfuls of sieved ratafias.
  ½ gill cream.
  Chopped pistachios.

1–4. Prepare as for Soufflé à la Milanaise, steps 1–4, using fruit purée in place of the grated lemon rind and juice.

5–6. Colour with 1 or 2 drops of carmine, then complete steps 5 and 6 as for Soufflé à la Milanaise.

7. When it is firm, remove the paper, and decorate the upstanding sides with sieved ratafias.

8. Sweeten and whip the cream until it hangs on the whisk. Place it in a paper cornet, fitted with a coarse rose pipe, and decorate the top with this.

9. Sprinkle with finely chopped pistachio nuts and serve upon a paper doily.

SOUFFLÉ AU VANILLE (BAKED)

(Baked Vanilla Soufflé)

1½ gills pastry cream (see p. 16). | Vanilla essence.
Yolks of 2 eggs. | Sauce au Chocolat (see p. 254).
Whites of 3 eggs. |

1. Prepare the pastry cream, and set aside to cool.
2. Beat in each yolk separately; add the vanilla essence.
3. Whisk the whites stiffly, and fold into the mixture.
4. Pour the mixture lightly into a buttered, sugared soufflé case of 6 in. diameter. Knock the case lightly on the table to settle the mixture, and level it with a palette knife.
5. Place on a baking-sheet, on a piece of cardboard to protect the bottom of the soufflé, or place a little water in the tin.
6. Cook in a fairly hot oven for 5 minutes, then loosen the edges quickly with a sharp-pointed knife.
7. Return to the oven, and cook for a further 5–8 minutes. Dredge well with castor sugar, and cook for about 5 minutes further.
8. Serve on a lace paper doily, handing Sauce au Chocolat separately.

SOUFFLÉ AU VANILLE (STEAMED)

Panada (see p. 15)— | ½ teaspoonful vanilla essence.
  1 oz. butter. | 3 yolks and 4 whites of new-
  1 oz. flour. | laid eggs.
  1 gill milk. | Chocolate Sauce or one of the
1 dessertspoonful castor sugar. | Sweet Wine Sauces.

1. Preparation of Tin—

(a) Grease a 1½ pint soufflé tin, which is fitted with a disk of greaseproof paper at the bottom.

(b) Tie a three-fold band of paper round the upper half of the tin, so that it extends 3 in.–4 in. above the top.

(c) Grease the inside of the paper band, and also a small square of paper to rest on the top of it.

2. Prepare the panada in a quart saucepan. When it is cooked, beat in the yolks, one at a time and very thoroughly. Beat in the sugar and vanilla essence.

3. Whisk the whites of eggs until very stiff and dry. Fold a tablespoonful into the panada to soften it, then fold in the remainder very lightly until a uniform pale yellow mixture is obtained.

4. Pour the mixture lightly into the prepared tin, and lay the greased paper on top.

5. To Steam the Soufflé—

(*a*) Prepare a large saucepan, filled ¼ full with gently simmering water. Invert an old saucer at the bottom, or stand a pastry cutter in it. Stand the saucepan half over the gas ring only, so that the soufflé will not steam too fast.

(*b*) Steam gently until the centre feels firm, 40–45 minutes, and do not lift the lid until it is expected that the soufflé will be cooked.

6. Remove the paper and string, and leave the soufflé to shrink for half a minute. If it is necessary, ease it away very gently with a rounded knife.

7. Invert on to a hot dish, draw off the tin gently, and pour the prepared sauce round.

SOUFFLÉ AU CAFÉ

Use **strong coffee** and **milk** to make the **panada.** Proceed as for Vanilla Soufflé.

SOUFFLÉ AU CHOCOLAT

As for Vanilla Soufflé, dissolving **2 oz. shredded chocolate** in the milk before making the panada.

PASTRY MAKING, PIES, FLANS, AND VOL-AU-VENTS

PASTRY has importance in the preparation of meals, apart from its value in confectionery. Meat and Game pies, both raised and in pie dishes, are popular at luncheon, while rich raised game pies are frequently prepared for a Ball or Dance Supper. Savoury Vol-au-Vents make attractive light entrées for luncheon or dinner, and patties or small bouchées of fish can be served in the fish course, or for party refreshments.

Savoury Flans make good luncheon dishes, and Sweet Flans form attractive sweets for any occasion. Puff, Genoese, and Choux pastries are all used in a variety of fancy sweets.

A batch of rich pastry (such as rich short crust, flaky, rough puff, or puff) can be made, wrapped in greaseproof paper, kept in a cool place, and used on several successive days as required. This saves time, and does not harm the pastry in any way. Any pastry which does not contain baking-powder is best left for at least an hour before use, placed between two floured plates, in order that it may lose the elasticity gained in even the most careful manipulation.

VARIETIES OF PASTRY

1. Pastry with rubbed-in shortening—
   (a) Short crust—plain or rich.
   (b) Lining pastry.
   (c) Cheese pastry.
2. Flaky.
3. Rough puff.
4. Puff.
5. Suet.
6. Hot-water crust.
7. Nouille.

FANCY PASTRIES

1. Genoese.
2. Choux.

Short and Puff are the two most in use in French cookery, together with Nouille and Genoese and Choux. Rough Puff and Flaky are essentially English pastries.

GENERAL POINTS ABOUT PASTRY MAKING

FLOUR. That used should be of the best quality; choose a fine starchy variety for puff, Genoese, and choux pastries.

SHORTENING. Best English lard, firm roll margarine, or butter may be used, according to the kind of pastry made.

WATER. This should be freshly drawn, perfectly cold, and in sufficient quantity to form a dough—firm for short and suet pastries, and more pliable for flaky, rough puff, and puff. Average amount—$\frac{3}{4}$–1 gill to each $\frac{1}{2}$ lb. of flour.

BAKING POWDER. This should be added to the plain flour for short or suet pastry when the amount of shortening used is only half, or less than half, the amount of flour used. Add then a small teaspoonful to each $\frac{1}{2}$ lb.

MANIPULATION—

(a) Keep the pastry cool.

(b) Avoid elasticity, and manipulate the dough quickly and lightly.

(c) Roll the pastry lightly and evenly. A heavy rolling-pin used lightly is better than *vice versa*.

BAKING. Pastry should always be baked in a hot oven, the general rule being—the richer the pastry, the hotter the oven required.

RICH SHORT PASTRY

(Pâte Brisé)

$\frac{1}{2}$ lb. flour.
Large pinch of salt.
1 level tablespoonful castor sugar (optional).

5–6 oz. butter (or lard and butter).
1–2 yolks of eggs.
Water to mix.

1. Sieve the flour, salt, and sugar if used.

2. Cut in the shortening (which should not be too hard) with a knife, then rub it in with the finger tips lightly until well mixed.

3. Beat the yolks with 1 tablespoonful of water and mix to a firm paste, adding a little more water as required.

4. Place the dough on a floured slab or board. Draw the rough edges to the centre lightly, turn the ball of pastry over, press it with a floured rolling-pin, and leave to relax.

Note. For plain short pastry, use the smaller proportion of shortening, omit the yolks, and slightly increase the water. If the shortening is still further reduced to 4 oz. shortening to $\frac{1}{2}$ lb. flour, add a small teaspoonful of baking powder.

USES. For fruit pies, Tartlets, and Flans.

LINING PASTRY

$\frac{1}{2}$ lb. flour.
Large pinch of salt.
$\frac{1}{4}$ lb. butter.

1 oz. castor sugar.
1 egg.
Scant $\frac{1}{4}$ gill water.

1. Sieve the flour, add the sugar and butter, rubbing in the latter with the finger tips.

2. Make a well in the centre of the flour. Add the unwhisked egg with the water.

3. Mix firmly, making up the pastry as quickly as possible to avoid elasticity.

4. Put the pastry aside to mellow and relax for at least $\frac{1}{2}$ hour.

USES. The whole egg added to pastry makes it rather more tenacious, so it is specially suitable for lining flan rings, or for making rissoles.

CHEESE PASTRY

3 oz. flour.	Seasoning.
2 oz. butter.	Few grains of cayenne.
2 oz. finely grated cheese (preferably half Cheddar and half Parmesan).	About 1 tablespoonful egg yolk and water.

1. Chop the butter into the flour very finely on a board. Add the grated cheese and seasoning, and chop all well together. At this stage remove the ingredients to a basin, if preferred.

2. Make a well in the centre, and mix to a stiff dough with the egg yolk and water, using the finger tips.

3. Cut the pastry to shape as required. Place it on a greased paper on the baking-tin, and bake for a short time in a hot oven.

4. Remove at once from the tin when cooked.

Note. If the butter is soft, leave the pastry to chill before rolling out.

USES. For cheese straws and biscuits, and for canapés and croûtons for hors d'œuvres and savouries. When shaped and baked, cheese pastry keeps well if stored in a small airtight tin. If its crispness should have abated, the pastry may be warmed through in a very moderate oven and left to cool before use.

FLAKY PASTRY

$\frac{1}{2}$ lb. flour.	3 oz. best English lard.
Large pinch of salt.	Water to mix.
3 oz. butter.	

1. Sieve the flour and the salt together. Cut the butter in half and the lard in half, and rub in one portion of the butter as for short pastry.

2. Mix to a pliable, but not sticky, dough.

3. Place the pastry on a floured board or slab. Draw the rough edges to the centre lightly, turn the ball of pastry over. Press lightly with a floured rolling-pin, and roll to an oblong strip

about three times as long as it is broad, and slightly less than $\frac{1}{4}$ in. thick.

4. (a) Place one portion of the lard in small pieces over the top two-thirds of the pastry. Dredge lightly with flour.

(b) Fold the plain piece upward, and bring the top third down (this should form practically a square). Seal the edges with a rolling-pin.

(c) Give the pastry a half turn, so that the top fold is placed to the left. Press with the rolling-pin to amalgamate the fat and pastry, then roll to an oblong strip as before.

5. Repeat step 4, using the remainder of the butter, then the remainder of the lard, and once again dredging the oblong strip with flour only.

6. Leave the pastry folded into a square with the edges well sealed. Set aside to relax for at least 1 hour.

USES. For the plainer meat pies, sausage rolls, savouries, tartlets, and fancy tarts.

PUFF PASTRY

(Feuilletage)

$\frac{1}{2}$ lb. flour.	1 teaspoonful lemon juice.
Large pinch of salt.	Cold water to mix.
$\frac{1}{2}$ lb. butter or firm roll margarine.	

1. Sieve the flour and salt together; rub in a piece of butter of the size of a walnut. Make a well in the centre.

2. Add the lemon juice and water, and mix to a dough which is very pliable but not sticky.

3. Place the dough on a floured slab, and draw the rough edges to the centre with the floured fingers until the dough is smooth. Avoid elasticity.

4. Roll out to a square and leave to relax.

5. Cream the butter on a plate with a rounded knife, mashing it smooth, then press it together in a smooth flat cake of the same consistency as the dough.

6. Flour the top of the butter lightly and invert it on to one half of the dough. Flour again lightly, and fold over the dough to enclose the butter. Seal the edges.

7. Place the fold to the left hand, and press the dough lightly with a floured rolling-pin to an oblong strip. Any rolling at this stage should be in very short strokes, or the butter will break through.

8. Fold up the lower third, fold down the top third, seal the edges with the floured rolling-pin, and press lightly with it over

the surface to join the layers. This constitutes one rolling and folding.

9. Roll and fold the pastry 7 times in all (after the butter is placed on the dough), placing the fold to the left-hand side each time, and leaving the pastry to relax 10–15 minutes between each two rollings.

10. Leave for 1 hour before rolling the pastry out to shape.

Notes. (*a*) Have the butter and dough of the same consistency, or they will slide one on the other in working, and the pastry will be difficult to manipulate.

(*b*) Place the pastry aside in the cool between the rollings, but not directly on ice, or the butter is stiffened too much.

(*c*) Roll the pastry very evenly, keeping it square-cornered, and fold it so that the layers rest evenly above each other to ensure uniform rising.

USES. For meat and game pies in dishes, Vol-au-vents, Bouchées, and Patties, both savoury and sweet. For lining tartlet tins, for savoury and sweet fillings, etc.

ROUGH PUFF PASTRY

(Demi-Feuilletage)

½ lb. flour.	A teaspoonful lemon juice.
Large pinch of salt.	Cold water to mix.
6 oz. butter or firm roll margarine.	

Make as for puff pastry; but as there is less fat to be incorporated, give only 3 complete rollings and foldings after the butter has been laid on the dough.

USES. As for flaky pastry.

SUET PASTRY

½ lb. flour.	4 oz. finely chopped suet.
Large pinch of salt.	Cold water to mix.
Small teaspoonful baking-powder.	

1. Sieve the flour, salt and baking-powder together.

2. Remove all the skin from the suet, shred and chop, using some of the weighed flour to prevent sticking.

3. Mix to a firm dough with the cold water.

4. Knead lightly for a few moments on a floured board to remove any cracks.

USES. For lining pudding basins; for meat, poultry, game, or fruit puddings to be served as luncheon dishes.

HOT-WATER CRUST

10 oz. flour.
Large pinch of salt and pepper.
3 oz. best English lard.

¾ gill milk or water (good measure).
1 yolk of egg (optional).

1. Warm the flour and sieve it with the seasoning.

2. Heat the lard with the liquid chosen until boiling, and pour it rapidly into a well made in the warm flour.

3. Work all the ingredients together with a wooden spoon.

4. If the egg yolk is used, beat it with a tablespoonful of the measured liquid, before heating the remainder with the lard. Add, when the great heat of the boiling fat and liquid has passed off.

Note. This pastry is the exception to the rule of keeping everything cold. Avoid working it in a draught or cold place, and keep the portions of pastry not actually worked upon at the moment in a warm basin covered with a cloth. Make sure that the filling for the pie is completely ready before making the pastry.

Uses. For making Raised Pies.

NOUILLES

(Pâte Nouilles)

½ lb. flour.
Large pinch of salt.
About 2 tablespoonfuls milk or water as necessary.

2 oz. butter.
1 egg.

1. Sieve the flour and salt on to a slab and mix in the butter. Make a well in the centre and put in the whole egg and a little milk or water.

2. Mix slowly round and round, forming a rather stiff dough; work it well.

3. Place dough aside on floured slab, making two cross cuts on top. Leave to mellow for ¼ hour.

4. Roll the dough as thin and flat as possible, then hang it over pieces of string (like a clothes line) to dry for an hour before cutting.

Uses. For entrées, Farinaceous Dishes, and Savouries.

GENOESE PASTRY

(Pâte Génoise)

3 oz. butter.
3 oz. flour.
4 eggs.
4 oz. castor sugar.

Alternative ingredients for GÉNOISE COMMUNE (a more economical variety)—
2¼ oz. butter.
4½ oz. flour.
4 eggs.
4½ oz. castor sugar.

1. Soften the butter gently in a pie dish until just pourable, and dry the flour.

2. Whisk the eggs, add the sugar, and place the bowl to rest on a pan of water which has been brought to boiling-point, and thence to the table. See that the water does not touch the bottom of the basin.

3. Whisk until the mixture becomes thick and white. By that time it will have increased in quantity, and may be tested by dropping a little from the whisk, when a rope-like coil should show.

4. Remove from the heat and whisk for 5 minutes until cool. Add half the butter, folding it in very lightly with a metal spoon, then shake in half the flour through a coarse strainer. Add the remainder of each, still very lightly.

5. Pour into the prepared tin, and bake in a moderate oven. If Genoese pastry is over-cooked it shrinks and becomes tough.

Note. When poured into the tin, the mixture should be very light and elastic. If it shrinks and is heavy, the pastry has been over stirred or stirred too heavily.

USES. This is the lightest and best form of sponge cake, and is used for making sponge foundations for luncheon sweets, and for confectionery in various forms. Genoese Commune is of rather firmer texture, which is sometimes useful.

CHOUX PASTRY

1 gill water.
1 oz. butter.
2 oz. flour.
$\frac{1}{2}$-1 yolk of egg.

1 whole egg.
Few drops of vanilla essence (if used for a sweet dish).

1. Dry the flour, and pass through a hair sieve on to a stiff piece of paper.

2. Boil up the water and butter in a small saucepan, draw it aside from the heat, and slide in all the flour at once.

3. Stir round briskly with a small wooden spoon; when the paste leaves the sides of the saucepan, set it aside to cool for a few minutes.

4. Beat in the yolk, then the well-whisked egg in very small amounts, beating well. If the egg is added too fast, the mixture will become thin.

5. Beat very thoroughly.

USES. As a foundation for various savouries and sweets.

VOL-AU-VENTS

A Vol-au-Vent is a case of baked puff pastry which has a filling of some rich mixture, either savoury or sweet. The case may be either round or oval. If preferred, small cases, each sufficient for one person, may be made instead of one large one.

A savoury Vol-au-Vent is cut with a plain cutter, and is served with the lid of pastry placed on slightly slantwise, to show tidily a little of the filling within. It is dished on a plain dish paper and garnished with parsley sprigs, or small cress if served cold.

A sweet Vol-au-Vent is cut with a fluted cutter, no lid being served; the top is frequently decorated with whipped cream or meringue, and it is dished on a lace paper.

A Vol-au-Vent should not be filled until just before serving, or it is liable to become soddened by its contents.

To Shape a Vol-au-Vent

1. Roll out the pastry to scant $\frac{1}{2}$ in. thickness and leave to relax and cool.

2. Stamp out two ovals of the pastry, removing the centre from one of them. Be careful not to cut nearer to the edge of the pastry than $\frac{1}{2}$ in.

3. Damp round the edge of the oval with white of egg, taking care that it does not run down the side.

4. Place the oval ring vertically on this, fixing it firmly, and place aside in the cool for at least half an hour.

5. Brush the top of the ring with beaten egg yolk, and bake in a hot oven for 40–45 minutes.

6. When baked, scrape out the soft centre and place the case back again in a more moderate oven to dry.

7. The small lid of pastry is baked, after being brushed with egg yolk, at the side of the vol-au-vent case, where it can be quickly removed when cooked. If a sweet vol-au-vent is being made this piece may be used up with the trimmings for some other dish.

FLAN CASES

A Flan is an open tart, the pastry case being baked inside a flan ring, which can be round or oval, fluted or plain, and of about 1 in. depth. Firm short-crust pastry containing some beaten egg is necessary for the flan to keep its shape; and, further to ensure this, it is filled with rice or haricot beans on a greased paper for baking. When it is baked and dried, a filling is placed inside, which may be savoury or sweet, hot or cold.

Note. For a savoury flan omit sugar from the pastry.

To Shape a Flan.

1. Grease a 6 in. flan ring to ensure that the pastry will adhere.

2. Roll out the pastry 1 in. bigger than the flan ring all round.

Fold it over in half to lift without stretching it, and fit it into the flan ring, pressing firmly with the fingers.

3. Press the pastry down from the rim to make a small bulging roll. Roll off any superfluous pastry with a rolling-pin, then press up the edge again, and decorate it with pincers or a fork if the flan ring is a plain one.

4. Place on it a round of greaseproof paper, large enough to come up the sides, and snipped at the edges to make the paper set well and keep the flan a good shape.

5. Fill with raw rice or haricot beans, bake in a fairly hot oven, 380° Fahr.

6. When it is set, remove the paper, rice or beans, and ring, and return the crust to dry off in the oven. This method is known as preparing an "empty" or "baking blind."

PASTRY RECIPES

FLAN AUX BANANES

(A Luncheon Sweet)

Lining pastry ($\frac{1}{4}$ lb. flour, etc., see p. 216).
Pastry cream ($\frac{1}{2}$ pint milk, etc., see p. 16).

2 bananas.
Apricot marmalade (see p. 11).

1. Prepare a flan case as on p. 222.
2. Fill the flan case with boiling pastry cream and leave to set until quite cold.
3. Arrange thin slices of the bananas, overlapping, over the surface; and glaze with well reduced apricot marmalade.

FLAN AUX FRUITS

(Open Fruit Tart)

I. FOR FRESH FRUITS

1 baked flan case (see p. 222).
$\frac{1}{2}$–$\frac{3}{4}$ lb. fresh fruits (Strawberries, raspberries, sliced bananas, etc.).
Castor sugar.

Maraschino, Kirsch, or sherry.
$\frac{1}{2}$–$\frac{3}{4}$ gill Crème Chantilly.
$\frac{1}{2}$ teaspoonful chopped pistachios.

1. Prepare the fruit in small pieces, or leave in whole berries, according to its kind.
2. When almost ready to serve, arrange a layer in the bottom of the flan case, dredge with castor sugar, and sprinkle with the liqueur or wine.
3. Prepare the cream, and place it in a forcing bag fitted

with a coarse rose pipe, and decorate the surface, completely covering it.

4. Sprinkle with chopped pistachios and serve.

Note. Well-drained tinned fruits might be treated in this way.

FLAN AUX FRUITS

II. FOR TINNED OR STEWED FRUITS

Baked flan case (see p. 222).

Filling—
Small tin of fruit.
1 gill syrup and water.
1½ oz. loaf sugar.
1 teaspoonful arrowroot.
1 teaspoonful lemon juice.

1 teaspoonful red, yellow, or green jam, or jelly (according to the colour of the fruit).
Colouring, if necessary.
Scant ½ gill Crème Chantilly.

1. Drain the fruit thoroughly and place it in the case.

2. Dissolve the sugar in the water, mix the arrowroot smoothly with a little water, add, and boil well.

3. Add the lemon juice, jam or jelly, and colouring, and correct the consistency of the sauce.

4. Strain over the fruit completely to cover it.

5. Decorate the edge with small rosettes of the Crème Chantilly. As an alternative finish to this method, leaves of baked puff pastry may be placed on the surface, leaving spaces to show the fruit between them.

FLAN AUX FRUITS MERINGUÉS

Baked flan case (see p. 222).
Fruit, etc., according to either of the foregoing recipes.

Meringue—
1 white of egg.
2 oz. castor sugar.

1. Arrange the fruit in the baked flan case according to the method chosen.

2. Prepare the meringue, and place it in a bag fitted with a coarse rose pipe.

3. Pipe the meringue over the fruit completely to cover it. Dredge with the castor sugar.

4. Place in a cool oven for about ½ hour, until the meringue is crisp and biscuit coloured.

FOR THE MERINGUE. Whisk the egg white until it is dry and stiff. Sprinkle 1 teaspoonful of the castor sugar over, and whisk until smooth for ½ minute. Shower over it the remaining sugar, folding it in very lightly.

FLAN AU MACARONI

1 baked flan case (see p. 222).
Filling—
    2 oz. macaroni.
    1½ gills Béchamel Sauce
        (flowing).
    2 oz. grated cheese.
	Seasoning.
	½ teaspoonful mixed mustard.
	Few shavings of butter.
	Few browned crumbs.
	Coralline pepper.

1. Prepare the flan case and have it warm.
2. Add the cooked macaroni to the Béchamel Sauce, season well, and add the cheese, reserving a little for sprinkling on the surface later.
3. Scatter brown crumbs, cheese, and shavings of butter over the surface.
4. Brown lightly in a hot oven or under a griller.
5. Scatter the coralline pepper over and serve *hot*.

FLAN À LA NORMANDE

Lining pastry (4 oz. flour, etc., see p. 216). Apple Marmalade (see p. 11).	Thin slices of apple. Boiling apricot marmalade.

1. Prepare a flan case as on p. 222 to the end of point 3. Do not bake it.
2. Put some cold apple marmalade in the bottom.
3. Arrange thin slices of apple over it, overlapping, and all converging on the centre. Peel the apples from top to bottom to make good-shaped slices.
4. Dust with castor sugar, and bake in a fairly hot oven (380° Fahr.) for ½ hour.
5. When cold, glaze with boiling apricot marmalade.

FLAN DE RIS D'AGNEAU TOULOUSE

(Sweetbread Flan)

1 baked flan case (see p. 222). ¼ lb. lamb's sweetbreads. Mirepoix to braise (see p. 14). ¼ pint coating Velouté Sauce (see p, 251). 1 yolk of egg.	¼ gill cream. Few drops of lemon juice. 4 champignons. ½ a small bottle of cockscombs. 1 truffle. Jus lié.

1. Blanch, trim, and press the sweetbreads. Braise on a mirepoix for 1 hour.
2. Prepare the sauce, add liaison of yolks and cream, and see that the sauce is of coating consistency.
3. Mix together the cockscombs cut in pieces and the kernels

(found in the bottle with the cockscombs—these are the kidneys of the fowl), chopped champignons, and the prepared well-seasoned sauce.

4. Place these into the warmed flan case.

5. Place the braised sweetbreads on top. Dip slices of truffle in the jus lié, and arrange them on the sweetbreads.

6. Serve hot, garnished with parsley sprigs.

Note. Cockscombs may be omitted to make a plain sweetbread flan, or the filling may be placed in a vol-au-vent case.

FLAN DE VOLAILLE AUX ASPERGES

(Chicken and Asparagus Flan)

A flan case, baked blind (see p. 222).	1½ gills thick white sauce. Seasoning.
Remains of cold cooked chicken (3-4 oz.).	1 tablespoonful thick cream (optional).
1 teacupful cooked asparagus tips.	Duchesse potato mixture (see p. 119).

1. Prepare the flan case and keep it warm.

2. Cut the chicken into dice and add it, with the asparagus tips, to the sauce. Heat through thoroughly, season with salt and pepper, and add the cream if it is used. Pour the mixture into the prepared flan case.

3. Prepare the duchesse potato mixture, and put it into a forcing bag fitted with a coarse rosette vegetable forcer.

4. Cover the top of the mixture in the flan with the prepared potato, piping it in rosettes or circles.

5. Brush with beaten egg; brown lightly under a hot griller. Serve hot.

PÂTÉ DE GIBIER À LA FRANÇAISE

(Raised Game Pie)

Hot-water crust (see p. 220). Filling—	1 teaspoonful finely shredded pistachios.
1 game bird.	1 teaspoonful finely chopped ham.
¼ lb. veal.	Finishing the Pie—
¼ lb. pork.	¼ gill good stock.
Salt, pepper, cayenne, and nutmeg.	1 teaspoonful gelatine, if necessary.
2 teaspoonfuls chopped champignons.	Chopped aspic.
2 truffles, cut in strips.	Sprigs of fresh parsley.

1. Prepare everything for the filling first. Mince the veal and pork together, and season.

2. Prepare the hot-water crust and cut off two quarters of it.

3. Line a warm, greased, raised pie mould with the pastry, using one of the quarters for the bottom, the large piece for lining the sides, and reserving the remaining quarter for the lid.

4. Brush the inside of the drum thus formed with slightly beaten egg white.

5. Place a layer of the minced meat all round the mould, inside the pastry, and fill in the centre with fillets of the game bird (grouse, partridge, pheasant, pigeons, quails, etc.). For a large pie, use a variety of game.

6. Sprinkle the champignons, truffles, pistachios, and seasoning in layers between the fillets, and cover the top with the remainder of the mince.

7. Damp the edge with egg white. Lay over the cover of pastry, trim, decorate, and glaze with egg yolk.

8. Tie a band of greased paper round the mould to come about 3 in. above the top of the mould.

9. Bake in a moderate oven steadily 1¾–2 hours. Slacken off the heat towards the end of cooking.

10. When the pie is nearly cold, pour in some good stock, to which a little gelatine has been added unless it is jellied before melting—this liquid must be cold but not set.

11. When perfectly cold, garnish the pie with chopped aspic and parsley and serve.

An Alternative Method of finishing the pie is to cover it for baking with a perfectly plain lid of pastry. When cold, cut off the lid carefully, run stock into the pie—prepared as above—and when quite set cover the surface with chopped aspic, raising it slightly in the centre. Stick a hâtelet skewer through the pie. This method is, however, more suitable for a large pie.

PÂTÉ DE PIGEON À L'ANGLAISE

1 pigeon.
1 small onion.
1 piece carrot.
1 stick celery.
2 rashers streaky bacon.
6 oz. rump steak.
Puff pastry made with 6 oz. flour, etc. (see p. 218).

2 oz. fresh mushrooms.
1 hard-boiled egg.
2 tablespoonfuls white wine.
Seasoning.
1 level tablespoonful chopped parsley.
Sprigs of parsley.

1. Pluck and draw the pigeon. Cut it in half, and again across.

2. Put it in a small saucepan with tepid water barely to cover and boil up. Skim, and add the vegetables. Simmer gently for 1 hour.

3. Strain, remove vegetables, and allow stock and pigeon to become cold.

4. Blanch the bacon and cut in narrow strips; slice the steak thinly.

5. Arrange in layers in a pie-dish of $\frac{3}{4}$ pint capacity, with chopped parsley and seasoning between. Arrange the sliced hard-boiled egg on top.

6. Fill the dish half full with the pigeon stock, to which the white wine is added.

7. Cover with pastry in the usual way, decorate with leaves of pastry, and brush with yolk of egg.

8. Bake in a hot oven at first (400° Fahr.), then slacken; cook 45–50 minutes in all.

9. Add $\frac{1}{2}$ gill extra stock, with gelatine dissolved in it if the pie is to be served cold.

10. Serve hot or cold, garnished with parsley.

PETITS PÂTÉS D'ÉCREVISSES

Puff pastry, 4 oz. flour, etc. (see p. 218).
Filling—
$\frac{1}{2}$ gill Béchamel or Velouté Sauce (thick) (see pp. 244, and 251).

Few drops of lemon juice.
Salt, pepper, cayenne.
1 tablespoonful thick cream.
9–10 large prawns.
Sprigs of parsley or small cress to garnish.

1. Prepare the pastry and roll out $\frac{1}{2}$ in. thick.

2. Cut out four rounds of pastry with a plain cutter of 2 in. diameter, being careful to cut well within the edge of the pastry.

3. With a cutter of scant 1 in. diameter, cut half through the centre of each round. Leave to relax in a cool place for $\frac{1}{2}$ hour.

4. Work up some of the trimmings, roll out $\frac{1}{4}$ in. thick, and cut out 4 rounds for lids of 1 in. diameter.

5. Brush the tops of the rounds with beaten egg yolk, also the tops of the lids.

6. Bake the pâté cases 25–30 minutes, removing the lids as soon as ready.

7. Scoop out the centres and place the cases back in the oven to dry.

8. Prepare the filling, and, when hot, fill into the cases.

9. Place on the lids sideways, with one or two prawn heads sticking out on the other side.

Note. Petits Pâtés are usually served hot in the fish course. If preferred, substitute for the prawns: 2–3 oz. cooked lobster cut in dice, 8–9 oysters cut in halves, or 2 oz. diced cooked chicken; and name accordingly

BOUCHÉES. As above, but smaller, making at least 6 from the same quantities. More usually served cold for Buffet refreshments.

PITHIVIERS DE PIGEON

Short crust, 3 oz. flour, etc. (see p. 216).	Beaten egg.
Puff pastry, 4 oz. flour, etc. (see p. 218).	Stuffing—
1 boned pigeon.	6 oz. sausage meat.
2 oz. sausage meat.	1 oz. cooked tongue.
	1 doz. pistachios.

1. Stuff the pigeon with 4 oz. of the sausage meat, add the tongue cut in small strips, and the pistachios. Roll in a pudding cloth and tie.

2. Boil in stock for 1¼ hours. Put on a fresh pudding cloth, and press with a weight on top until cold.

3. Cut an oval of short crust pastry, brush a rim 1 in. wide at the edge with beaten egg. Put the pigeon in the middle, and soften the edges with extra sausage meat to make a shapely oval mound.

4. Season, and cover with a larger oval of puff pastry, pressing down a rim of 1 in. all round. Again brush with the beaten egg.

5. Finish with a ¾ in. rim of puff pastry, laid all round on the top edge, pressing firmly on to the egged pastry, and making a very neat join.

6. Notch the edges and brush the whole over with egg. Bake in a hot oven at first, 45 minutes in all.

7. Serve hot as a luncheon dish, or cold for picnics.

PUITS D'AMOUR

(Jam Puffs)

Puff pastry, 4 oz. flour, etc. (see p. 218).	Jam in varied colours.

Prepare as for Petits Pâtés (see p. 228). Use a 1½ in. fluted cutter, and do not make the lids. Fill in with jam when cold after drying. Serve cold on a lace paper doily.

VOL-AU-VENT AUX FRUITS

1 baked Vol-au-Vent case.	Fresh or well-drained tinned fruits.
Pastry Cream, or Rice Cream, omitting gelatine (see pp. 16 and 144).	Castor sugar to dredge.
	Scant ½ gill Crème Chantilly.

1. Prepare the Vol-au-Vent case and allow it to become cold.

2. Prepare the pastry cream, or rice cream, and place a layer in the bottom of the case.

3. Fill the case with the fruit, dredging the layers lightly with castor sugar.

4. Decorate with the Crème Chantilly, piped in rosettes, and serve.

VOL-AU-VENT PRINCESSE

1 baked Vol-au-Vent case (see p. 222).	Seasoning.
	4 or 5 champignons.
3 oz. cooked chicken, shredded.	2 truffles.
1–1½ gills Béchamel or Velouté Sauce.	Parsley or small cress to garnish

1. Prepare the pastry case and keep it warm.

2. Prepare the sauce, season it highly, and add a good proportion of cream.

3. Add the prepared chicken, with the champignons and truffles cut in pieces.

4. Pour the prepared sauce into the centre of the case, ensure that all is well heated, and serve, garnished with the sprigs of parsley or small cress.

Note. Do not place the filling in the case until sending to table. A savoury Vol-au-Vent is more usually served hot, and if required cold is more usually served in the form of small Bouchées for Buffet refreshments, etc.

NOTE

PLAIN FLOUR

Plain flour should be used for all the foregoing recipes, and, in fact, should always be used in good cooking. In a self-raising flour the amount of raising agent is fixed, and cannot be lessened or removed altogether when necessary—as in the case of making rich cakes or pastries. It is also more expensive to use self-raising flour for making sauces, or for dredging, where the raising agent in its composition is unnecessary.

SANDWICHES AND SNACKS

THIS section might be termed the lighter side of Cookery, but it is one which no one who claims competence in Cookery can afford to decry, because modern conditions demand a large variety of "Finger Foods," and savoury oddments which can be easily served.

Reasons for this are the modern taste for such foods, also the comparatively recent trend towards more informal entertaining, the motor habit, which lends itself to picnics, and the week-end cottage with its short and unconventional meals.

SANDWICHES

The usefulness of sandwiches is beyond all question for the most varied occasions, and in unending variety. The objection is sometimes raised that they involve the eating of a great deal of bread, but nothing can quite be substituted for them.

CLASSIFICATION—

Sandwiches can be divided into five main classes—

1. Those which are substantial, and suitable for an impromptu meal which is easily portable if necessary. Slices of white or brown bread, small rolls, and water, cream cracker, or digestive biscuits, can be used for these.

2. Hot Sandwiches and Toasts—an emergency meal which can be appetizing and satisfying. Slices of bread, evenly toasted and freshly buttered, are an essential factor in making these successful.

3. Light Sandwiches, made from bread and butter more thinly cut, and with less substantial fillings—suitable for afternoon tea or for a buffet at a party.

4. Tiny sandwiches, having piquant flavoured fillings spread between wafery slices of bread and butter, suitable as hors d'œuvres.

5. Sweet Sandwiches. Fillings prepared from chopped dried fruits, mashed fresh fruit, grated nuts, grated chocolate, honey, preserved ginger, etc., can be spread between bread and butter, and cut into fancy shapes, or between ice wafers or thin biscuits of shortbread texture.

A FEW ESSENTIALS

1. Consider the occasion for which the sandwiches are required.

2. Have bread one day old for ease in cutting, but avoid that which is stale.

3. Use good butter, and cream it with a little salt and pepper so that it can be spread evenly and with economy. Mixed mustard, if it is to be used, should be added to the butter.

4. Trim off the crusts before filling. Make an even layer of the filling ingredients, press well, cut smartly, and label clearly with flags, if more than one variety is served.

5. Well-washed small cress, from which all seeds are scrupulously removed, looks attractive sprinkled over sandwiches, and helps to keep them moist, though the more ordinary fresh sprigs of parsley may be used if preferred.

SANDWICH FILLINGS

The following sandwich fillings may be spread between thin slices of white or brown bread, trimmed of crust, and spread with well creamed, seasoned butter, to which a little mustard is added where suitable. Press the sandwich well, cut in small squares, fingers, or triangles, and garnish with sprigs of parsley or small cress.

MEAT AND FISH FILLINGS

Anchovy and Egg.
Anchovy paste.
Scrambled egg (see p. 191).

Spread a thin layer of anchovy paste on slices of bread and butter. Cover with a layer of scrambled egg, cooked to creamy consistency, and allowed to become cold.

Beef (minced).
Slices of lean beef.
Mustard.
Chopped mixed pickles.
Beef dripping.

Mince the beef, and add a little mustard, and finely chopped mixed pickles at discretion. Spread thin slices of bread with some of the beef dripping, using any of the jelly present under it. A nourishing picnic sandwich, which is very appetizing.

Beef and Tomato.
Small thin slices of underdone beef.
Salt. Store Tomato Sauce.

Carve the meat in small thin slices. Lay on slices of bread and butter. Sprinkle first with a little fine dry salt, then with tomato sauce.

Crab (fresh).
1 small freshly cooked crab. Oil, vinegar, mustard, salt and pepper.
1 bunch watercress.

Prepare the flesh of the crab as for dressed crab (see p. 49). Add the seasonings, to flavour the mixture of light and dark crab meats, beaten to a paste. Chop some watercress leaves finely and sprinkle over each layer of crab paste, spread on bread and butter. Garnish with watercress.

MEAT AND FISH FILLINGS—(Contd.)

Ham and Egg.	¼ lb. cooked ham; ⅓ should be fat. 1 hard-boiled egg. Mustard.	Chop the ham very finely, and the egg coarsely. Chop both together with some mixed mustard to form a paste.
Lax.	Lax. Vinaigrette (see p. 252). Pepper.	Prepare thinly shaved, small slices of Lax (either freshly smoked, or preserved in tins in oil). Steep in the vinaigrette for ½ hour. Drain well, and arrange on bread and butter.
Liver Sausage.	Thin slices of Liver Sausage. French mustard or thin mayonnaise.	Spread the thin slices of liver sausage VERY THINLY with the French mustard or mayonnaise, and arrange on bread and butter.
Mayonnaise of Tongue.	3–4 oz. cooked Tongue. Pepper. Thick mayonnaise.	Chop the tongue finely, and season with pepper. Mix with just sufficient mayonnaise to hold it together. Spread as required.
Princess.	4–6 oz. cooked chicken. 1 tablespoonful thick cream. Salt. Lemon juice. Paprika. 4 oz. walnut kernels. Sprigs of water-cress.	Pound the chopped chicken until smooth. Add the cream and seasonings. Blanch, drain, and skin the walnut kernels, or use kiln-dried halves which have been crisped in the oven. Slice them across roughly, and sprinkle them on the chicken mixture; spread on slices of bread and butter. Garnish with sprigs of watercress.
Salmon.	1 steak Canadian Salmon. Salt, cayenne, paprika. Anchovy essence. Oiled butter to make a smooth spreadable paste.	Steam the salmon, and remove the skin and bones. Add the seasonings and anchovy essence, and work in a little oiled butter by degrees. Pass through a wire sieve, adding a little more butter as necessary. Placed in small pots, this paste will keep some few days.

MEAT AND FISH FILLINGS—*(Contd.)*

Spiced Beef and Watercress.	Small thin slices of spiced beef. Chopped watercress. Salt and mustard.	Shave the beef to wafer thinness. Place on slices of bread, spread with butter, appreciably flavoured with mustard. Sprinkle finely chopped watercress over, and add a little salt.
Veal and Olive.	Cooked minced Veal. Oiled butter and seasoning. Chopped olives.	Mince the veal, season it well ; add a little oiled butter to hold it together, and work it smooth. Cover with a thin layer of chopped olives.

SAVOURY FILLINGS OTHER THAN MEAT AND FISH

Apple, Lettuce, and Nut.	1 large firm apple. 2 oz. Brazil nuts. Thick mayonnaise. Shredded lettuce.	Chop apple and Brazil nuts separately, but not too finely. Chop them together, and mix with sufficient well-seasoned thick mayonnaise to bind. Place a layer on bread and butter, covered with fine lettuce shreds.
Beetroot.	Thinly sliced beetroot. Vinaigrette (see p. 252).	Steep the beetroot in the vinaigrette for at least 1 hour. Drain well on crumpled paper, and sandwich between bread and butter.
Bengal.	1 hard-boiled egg. Pinch of curry powder. Few drops of anchovy essence. Few drops of lemon juice. ½ oz. creamed butter. ½ tablespoonful thick cream.	Chop the hard-boiled egg finely and add the remaining ingredients to form a paste.
Carrot.	Firm carrots. Salt.	Grate finely the red parts of some carrots. Add the salt, and spread between brown bread and butter.

SAVOURY FILLINGS OTHER THAN MEAT AND
FISH—(*Contd.*)

Cheese (potted)	Dry Cheshire or Cheddar cheese. Seasoning. Mixed mustard. Creamed butter.	Grate full-flavoured cheese, add the seasoning, mustard, and a few drops of vinegar if it is liked. Add just enough creamed butter to make a spreadable paste. This mixture stores well in small jars.
Cheese Biscuit.	Digestive biscuits. Butter. Cheddar or Cheshire cheese.	Butter the biscuits lightly, and sandwich each two together with thin slices of new Cheddar or Cheshire cheese. A useful sandwich to pack in a knapsack.
Chutney and Walnut.	Chutney. Walnut kernels.	Chop the chutney if necessary, and spread a suspicion on slices of brown buttered bread. Prepare the walnuts as for Princess sandwiches, and scatter over sparsely.
Cream cheese and Watercress.	1 packet cream cheese or soft cheese. Watercress leaves. Pepper and salt.	Season the cheese with pepper, and spread on slices of bread. Sprinkle with the chopped watercress, seasoned with salt. Lay a buttered slice on top.
Cucumber.	Thin slices of cucumber. Vinaigrette dressing (see p. 252). 1–2 chopped spring onions.	Marinade the cucumber in the vinaigrette for half an hour. Sprinkle it with very finely chopped onion. Drain very well on crumpled paper, and include the onion in the sandwich or not as desired.
Devilled Egg.	1 hard-boiled egg. ½ teaspoonful mixed mustard. A few grains of cayenne. Large pinch of salt. A few drops of Worcester Sauce. ½ teaspoonful chopped parsley. 1 tablespoonful mayonnaise.	Sieve the yolk, and chop the white of the hard-boiled egg. Add the seasonings, chopped parsley, and sufficient mayonnaise to enable the mixture to be spread easily on slices of bread. Cover with the chopped egg white, and lay a buttered slice on top.

SAVOURY FILLINGS OTHER THAN MEAT AND
FISH—(Contd.)

Pineapple and lettuce.	Tinned or fresh pineapple. Thick mayonnaise. Fine shreds of lettuce.	Drain the pineapple if necessary, and chop it very finely. Lay on the lettuce shreds placed on thin slices of bread; spread with thick mayonnaise. Lay buttered slices on top.
Walnut and Cheese.	2 oz. kiln-dried walnut halves. 2 oz. cream cheese. Seasoning.	Pass walnuts through a rotary grater or nut mill, and press a thin layer on to thin brown bread and butter slices. Beat the cheese smooth, with seasoning, and spread it on to an equal number of slices. Press firmly.

SNACKS

Snacks can be of unlimited variety, and a great many dinner savouries made slightly larger salads and egg dishes can be utilized.

FAVOURITE INGREDIENTS

Sausages, liver sausage, cooked ham and tongue, cooked smoked haddock, hard-boiled eggs, cheese, sardines, lax, lobsters, prawns and salmon; thin slices of home-made galantines, cheese straws and biscuits, curled shreds of celery, green saladings, and potato chips.

These may be reinforced by such piquant etceteras as French mustard, pickled walnuts, pickled beetroot, or Spanish onion shreds, salted almonds, olives, gherkins, capers, mayonnaise, scraped horseradish, thick horseradish cream, chutney, etc.

SOME WAYS OF SERVING

1. Savoury mixture in small boat-shaped Cassolettes of baked rich short crust or cheese pastry—rolled out very thinly. Cheese custard may be baked in these, or they may be filled with prawns, lobster, or salmon flaked and each mixed with mayonnaise.

2. Savoury mixture on canapés of brown bread and butter.

3. Small bridge rolls, filled with mayonnaise of eggs, prawns, or chicken.

4. A savoury ingredient, such as flaked cooked smoked haddock or chopped lean ham, mixed with a white sauce, heated and piled on heated water biscuits. Cap each with a slice of pickled walnut.

5. Small individual salads. For these, savoury ingredients may be piled in a leaf of a lettuce heart.

6. Stuffed hard-boiled eggs and savoury stuffed olives.

7. Tiny bouchée cases of puff pastry, filled with a savoury salpicon of chicken, tongue, oyster, etc.

8. Grilled chipolata sausages, brushed with glaze and served cold, dished on a small strip of toast.

9. Many savoury preparations can be served in small paper soufflé cases, which economizes washing up.

AMERICAN CLUB SANDWICH

Lettuce.	Slices roast chicken.
Mayonnaise.	Frizzled bacon.
Buttered toast.	Tomato.

Arrange crisp shredded lettuce sprinkled with mayonnaise on the first piece of buttered toast, and cover with another slice. Arrange slices of roast chicken and small pieces of frizzled bacon on top, cover again with a slice of toast, covered in its turn with thin slices of heated seasoned tomato. Serve very hot.

ANCHOVY AND HAM RELISH

3 oz. lean cooked ham.	Thin cheese biscuits.
4 anchovy fillets.	A few drops of anchovy essence.
1 yolk of egg.	Grated cheese.
2 tablespoonfuls white sauce.	Strips of anchovy fillets to
Cayenne and salt.	garnish.
Mustard.	Parsley.

1. Chop the ham finely, and cut the anchovy fillets into small pieces.

2. Pound these together into a paste, add the yolk of egg and sauce, season with the cayenne and dry mustard, and mix well. Put these in a small saucepan and heat.

3. Butter the biscuits, dust lightly with a little salt and pepper, and sprinkle with a few drops of the anchovy essence. Make them hot in the oven.

4. Spread the biscuits with the mixture, dredge with a little finely grated cheese, and place under the grill for a minute or two to brown the surface.

5. Place two crossed anchovy strips on top, and dish on a paper on a hot dish, garnished with the parsley. Serve *very hot*.

ANGELS ON HORSEBACK

8 oysters.	4 fingers of buttered toast.
8 small thin pieces of streaky bacon.	Parsley.

1. Beard the oysters and roll a piece of streaky bacon round each. Thread on a skewer and grill for about 3 minutes.

2. Dish each two on a finger of buttered toast, and place them on a piping hot dish, garnished at one side with sprigs of parsley.

Note. Chicken livers may be used in place of the oysters.

BENGAL CROÛTES

Cheese pastry (see p. 217).
Savoury Butter—
 ½ oz. butter.
 A few grains cayenne.
 A dash of stiffly mixed mustard.

Yolk of half a hard-boiled egg, sieved.
Chopped gherkins.
Small cress.

1. Roll out the cheese pastry, cut into fingers 2¼ in. × ¾ in., and bake until golden brown.

2. When cold, spread with the savoury butter.

3. Spread the sieved egg yolk evenly over one half, and the chopped gherkin over the other.

4. Dish in a star, the colours to the centre alternating, and the small cress in the middle.

CHEESE D'ARTOIS

Flaky pastry, ¼ lb. flour, etc. (see p. 217), or 6–7 oz. puff pastry trimmings.
1 egg.

2 oz. grated cheese.
1 oz. butter, oiled.
Salt, pepper, cayenne.
Beaten egg.

1. Roll out the pastry very thinly into an oblong and divide it equally.

2. Beat the egg, add the cheese, the oiled butter, salt, pepper, and cayenne.

3. Spread this mixture on one half of the pastry, wet the edges, and place the other piece on it.

4. Press the edges, brush with egg, and score across in long narrow fingers. Bake in a quick oven, and cut in fingers as marked.

CHEESE CUSTARD TART

¼ lb. lining pastry (see p. 216).
½ lb. small firm cooked potatoes.
2 oz. grated cheese.
1 gill milk.

1 egg, and 1 yolk.
Salt, pepper, and nutmeg.
A few shavings of butter.

1. Make the pastry (omitting sugar) and line a plain 6 in. flan ring with this (see p. 222).

2. Prick the bottom, and arrange the cooked potatoes, cut in slices, then into small rounds, in circles overlapping.

3. Season the potatoes. Beat the egg and yolk, add the milk, salt, cayenne, and nutmeg. Add this mixture and the grated cheese.

4. Place a few thin shavings of butter on top, bake until set and brown. Cut in small slices when cold.

CROÛTES À L'INDIENNE

2 oz. lean cooked ham.	Salt and a few grains of cayenne.
A nut of butter.	Rounds of hot buttered toast.
1 large tablespoonful curry sauce (see p. 247).	A few breadcrumbs.
	3–4 herring roes (soft).

1. Chop the ham and sauté it in the butter. Add the curry sauce, salt, and cayenne.

2. Heat all thoroughly together and place on rounds of hot buttered toast; sprinkle with the breadcrumbs.

3. Place the savouries on a baking-tin in a moderate oven for 5 minutes.

4. Lay half a soft herring roe, poached, on top of each, and serve at once.

To Poach Herring Roes. Soak in salt and water to remove the blood. Poach in a small saucepan with salt, pepper, lemon juice, and 1 or 2 tablespoonfuls of hot fish stock or water.

HADDOCK CROÛTES

2 tablespoonfuls cooked smoked haddock.	Seasoning.
	2 small firm tomatoes.
2 small tablespoonfuls white sauce.	2 or 3 pickled walnuts.
	Croûtons of fried bread.

1. Remove the skin and bones from the haddock.

2. Mix the fish with the white sauce, add the seasoning, and spread the mixture on the croûtons of fried bread.

3. Place a slice of baked tomato on each with a small round of pickled walnut in the middle.

4. Serve hot on a plain dish paper, garnished with parsley.

HAM SNACKS

3–4 oz. cooked ham.	Pepper, and made mustard.
1 slice onion.	1 teaspoonful chopped parsley.
1 oz. butter.	Fingers of baked cheese pastry
2 eggs.	(see p. 217).

1. Use lean ham, and chop it finely.

2. Chop the onion very finely and fry it in the butter without browning. Add the ham and beaten eggs.

3. Stir over gentle heat, until the eggs begin to thicken; add the seasoning and half of the parsley.

4. Cover the fingers of baked cheese pastry thickly with the mixture, sprinkle with the remainder of the parsley, and serve *very hot* or *quite cold*.

JELLIED HAM AND EGG

¼ lb. cooked ham.
1 tablespoonful boiled macaroni, cut in rings.
1 tomato-concassé (see p. 281).
Seasoning.
1 teaspoonful chopped parsley.
Scant ½ oz. gelatine.

½ gill strong white stock.
½ gill aspic jelly.
Decoration and Garnish—
  ½ gill aspic jelly.
  1–2 hard-boiled eggs.
  1 teaspoonful chopped parsley.
  Green salad plants.

1. Chop or mince the ham, add the prepared macaroni, tomato, seasoning, and 1 teaspoonful of finely chopped parsley.

2. Line a small flat tin 5 in. × 8 in. with the aspic jelly. Decorate with slices of hard-boiled egg and chopped parsley.

3. Dissolve the gelatine in the stock and aspic jelly, and when cool add to the mixed ingredients.

4. Pour into the prepared tin, when quite cold, and leave to set.

5. Unmould and cut in strips; garnish with green salad.

Note. If preferred, the eggs may be coarsely chopped and added to the mixture.

LOBSTER CROÛTES

1½ oz. butter.
3 yolks of egg.
2 oz. lobster purée.

1 tablespoonful port wine.
Seasoning.
Fingers of buttered toast.

1. Melt the butter in a small saucepan gently, add the yolks of eggs, and stir over gentle heat for a few *seconds*, long enough to heat without curdling.

2. Remove from heat, add the lobster purée, port wine, and seasoning. Stir well.

3. Cut some fingers of freshly toasted bread and put a thick layer of the mixture on each.

4. Place the fingers on a baking-sheet and bake for 2 minutes in a very hot oven.

5. Dish up, and serve *very hot* or *quite cold*.

PIQUANTE ROLLS

Small unsweetened Bridge Rolls.
1–2 oz. cooked chicken, rabbit, or veal.
½ oz. cooked ham.

1 teaspoonful chopped gherkin or capers.
Mayonnaise.
1 teaspoonful lemon juice.
A few grains of cayenne.
Salt.

1. Split and butter the rolls.
2. Mix together the minced chicken, rabbit, or veal, and the ham, gherkins or capers, with sufficient mayonnaise to bind.
3. Add the lemon juice, season well, and place some of this mixture in each of the prepared rolls.
4. Fit together again, sprinkle with some small cress, and serve.

PRAWN ROLLS

Small unsweetened Bridge Rolls.
Small jar of prawns.

Salt and pepper.
Mayonnaise.
Small cress.

1. Take a thin piece from the top of each roll, stretching for the chief part of its length.
2. Hollow out some of the soft inside, and spread the remaining boat shape inside with a little seasoned butter.
3. Cut the prawns if they are large, and add just sufficient mayonnaise to hold all together.
4. Pile some of this mixture in the prepared rolls; sprinkle with the small cress, and serve.

SARDINE ROLLS

Flaky pastry or puff pastry trimmings (see pp. 217 and 218).
Small sardines or brisling.

Salt, pepper, lemon juice.
2–3 teaspoonfuls grated Parmesan cheese.
Beaten egg.

1. Roll out the pastry chosen to wafer thickness, and cut in squares large enough to enclose one fish, as for sausage rolls.
2. Lay a fish on each piece, sprinkle with a little seasoning, lemon juice, and grated cheese.
3. Finish and mark the rolls as for a very small sausage roll.
4. Brush with beaten egg, and bake in a *hot* oven until the pastry is golden brown and cooked through.
5. Serve *cold*, garnished with the small cress.
Note. Fillets of anchovy or small strips of par-boiled sausages can take the place of the sardines—omitting cheese and lemon juice for the latter.

SMOERRBRODE

Take 4 slices of toasted bread, buttered and allowed to become cold (slices of brown bread and butter, $\frac{1}{4}$ in. thick, or rye crisp bread may be substituted). On each slice put respectively—

1. Thin slices of smoked salmon or lax, creamy, scrambled egg, sprinkled with finely chopped parsley.

2. Anchovy fillets, or fillets of sardines, sprinkled with chopped hard-boiled egg and coralline pepper.

3. Cooked ham, sliced to wafer thinness, concassé tomato, sprinkled with finely chopped parsley.

4. Cream cheese, with a suspicion of chutney.

Multiply the above to the required number, cut in fingers or fancy shapes, and sprinkle with small cress lightly.

SAUCES

(Savoury and Sweet)

VARIETIES OF SAUCES

I. SAVOURY. Examples are—

White	*Brown*	*Plain or English*	*Cold*
Béchamel.	Espagnole.	Bread.	Mayonnaise.
Velouté.	Réforme.	Brown.	Rémoulade.
Hollandaise.	Italienne.	White.	Tartare.
Soubise.	Financière.	Mustard.	Chaudfroid.
Cardinal.	Madère.	Mint.	Raifort.
Mornay.	Chasseur.		Cumberland.
Béarnaise.	Robert.		
	Orange.		
	Demi-glace.		

II. SWEET. Examples are—

Hot	*Cold*
Abricot.	Dur.
Anglaise.	Whipped Cream Brandy.
Cerises.	Custard.
Chocolat.	Chocolate Cream.
Gingembre.	
Marmelade.	
Mousseline.	
Pralinée.	
Sabayon.	
Vin Rouge.	
,, Blanc.	

USES OF SAUCES

1. To supply additional flavour and richness to food.
2. To improve the appearance of food when dished.
3. To hold certain ingredients together.

SAVOURY SAUCES
SAUCE AURORE

½ pint Béchamel or Velouté Sauce (see pp. 244 and 251). | ½ pint Tomato Purée or Tomato Sauce (see p. 252).
1 oz. butter.

243

1. Heat the Béchamel or Velouté until boiling, and add the Tomato Purée or Sauce.

2. Boil up together and tammy. Draw aside, whisk in the butter in small pieces, and correct the seasoning and consistency.

SAUCE BÉARNAISE

1 gill thick Béchamel Sauce (see below).	¼ gill of tarragon vinegar.
1 shallot.	2 yolks of eggs.
¼ gill white wine vinegar.	1 oz. butter.
	Seasoning.

1. Prepare the Béchamel sauce and place it in a small basin.

2. Chop the shallot finely and put it into a small saucepan with the vinegars. Reduce to about half in quantity.

3. Add the strained vinegars to the white sauce carefully, then mix in the yolks, one at a time.

4. Place the basin over a small saucepan of steaming water and whisk well. Add the butter in small pieces, whisking each piece in thoroughly before the next is added.

5. Be *very careful* not to overheat the sauce, or it will curdle.

6. Tammy the sauce, which should be of about the consistency of mayonnaise. Season and use as required.

SAUCE BÉCHAMEL

1 shallot.	1 pint milk.
Piece of carrot.	2 oz. butter or margarine.
Stick of celery.	2 oz. flour.
12 white peppercorns.	Salt.
Blade of mace.	½ gill cream.
½ a bayleaf.	

1. Put the sliced vegetables and herbs in the milk. Bring slowly to boiling-point. Cover the saucepan and set it aside for 10–15 minutes to infuse.

2. Strain off the milk, and make a white sauce with a roux of butter and flour and the flavoured milk. Note that the roux is allowed to become cold if the milk is used while it is still hot.

3. Simmer for 10 minutes, and pass through a tammy strainer or wring through a tammy cloth.

4. Reheat, correct the seasoning, add the cream, again reheat carefully, and use as required.

SAUCE CUMBERLAND

Rinds of 1 orange and 1 lemon.	2 tablespoonfuls red currant jelly.
1 shallot.	
¾ gill port wine.	

1. Cut the rinds of the orange and the lemon into fine julienne strips, and chop the shallot finely.

2. Put these on in cold water and cook for about 15 minutes. Strain.

3. Boil up the wine and jelly, and when the jelly has quite dissolved pour the mixture on to the rinds and cook for a further 10 minutes.

Note. This sauce is always served cold, and should be just chilled. It is much improved if kept for a few days. It is served with cold grouse and boar's head.

SAUCE DEMI-GLACE

½ pint Espagnole Sauce (see p. 246).
½ pint brown meat stock.

1 tablespoonful full-flavoured sherry.

1. Reduce the Espagnole Sauce and stock to slightly less than half.

2. Strain, correct the seasoning and consistency, add the sherry, and keep warm until required.

SAUCE DIABLÉ

½ pint brown stock.
1 tablespoonful Worcester Sauce.
½ tablespoonful peppercorns.
1 tablespoonful vinegar.
½ tablespoonful mixed mustard.

½ tablespoonful mushroom ketchup.
½ tablespoonful chutney.
Scant 1 oz. butter.
Scant 1 oz. flour.
½ tablespoonful red currant jelly.
1 tablespoonful sherry.

1. Heat together the stock, peppercorns, sauce, vinegar, mustard, ketchup, and chutney. Simmer for 10 minutes.

2. Blend the butter and flour, add the strained liquid, and stir until boiling.

3. Add the jelly and sherry—reheat, tammy, and hand with any kind of grill.

SAUCE ÉCREVISSES

2 heaped tablespoonfuls picked prawns or shrimps.
1 teaspoonful Paprika pepper.
½ oz. butter.
1 gill Hollandaise Sauce (see p. 246).

1 gill Béchamel Sauce (see p. 244).
1 tablespoonful white wine.
Seasoning.

1. Pound all trimmings from the prawns in a mortar with butter.

2. Fry the Paprika in butter, and add the pounded trimmings.

3. Prepare and mix the sauces add a little white wine, and reduce.

4. Add sufficient shrimp butter to colour and flavour the sauce, and pass all through muslin.

SAUCE ESPAGNOLE

2 oz. raw ham or bacon.	1 pint brown stock.
2 oz. butter or dripping.	6 champignons (or stalks).
1 small onion.	1 gill tomato pulp.
1 small carrot.	1 large tablespoonful sherry.
1 shallot.	Salt and pepper.
2 oz. flour.	

1. Cut up the ham or bacon and sauté it in the butter or dripping.

2. Slice the vegetables and fry them until they shrink slightly, but are not coloured.

3. Add the flour and brown the whole gradually to a rich russet colour. This takes about $\frac{1}{2}$ hour, and scorching must be avoided or the flavour of the sauce is ruined.

4. Add the stock and champignons; stir until boiling. Skim and simmer for 30 minutes.

5. Add the tomato pulp and sherry, season the sauce, and simmer for a further 10 minutes.

6. Pass the sauce through a tammy strainer, or wring through a tammy cloth. Correct the seasoning, and use as required.

Note. Espagnole Sauce is the foundation of many rich brown sauces.

SAUCE HOLLANDAISE I

1 gill white sauce.	Salt and pepper.
2 yolks of eggs.	Juice of half a lemon.
1 oz. butter.	

1. Make the white sauce, and put it into a small basin over a saucepan of hot water.

2. Whisk in the yolks, one by one. Then whisk in the butter, a small piece at a time, until the sauce thickens.

3. Season with salt and pepper, and lastly add the lemon juice.

SAUCE HOLLANDAISE II

Juice of half a lemon.	4$\frac{1}{2}$ oz. butter.
1 teaspoonful water.	Salt, cayenne, lemon juice.
2 yolks of eggs.	

1. Place the lemon juice and water in a small basin over a saucepan containing hot water.

2. Add the beaten yolks and ½ oz. of the butter. Whisk well.

3. Continue whisking until the marks of the whisk show.

4. Leave at the side of the stove, and whisk in the remainder of the butter by degrees with salt, cayenne, and lemon juice at discretion.

5. Wring through muslin and use.

JUS LIÉ
(Thickened Gravy)

½ pint strong brown stock.	Carmine.
2 teaspoonfuls arrowroot.	Salt and pepper.
A few drops of browning or a little meat extract.	1–2 tablespoonfuls sherry.

1. Use some of the stock to mix the arrowroot smoothly, heat the remainder, and pour it on to the slaked arrowroot.

2. Return to pan, stir until boiling. Colour with browning, and add 1 drop of the carmine to make the sauce of a clear red-brown colour. Stir briskly all the time.

3. Correct the seasoning, add the wine, and boil until the arrowroot is quite clear.

4. Strain, and use as required.

Note. Poultry stock or veal stock may be used, according to the nature of the dish with which the sauce is to be served.

SAUCE AU KARI
(Curry Sauce)

2 oz. dripping.	1 oz. tamarinds or 1 tablespoonful plum jam.
1 pint stock.	
½ lb. peeled and sliced onions.	2 oz. chopped apple.
Lemon juice.	1 oz. desiccated coconut.
1 tablespoonful curry powder.	2–3 allspice.
1 oz. ground rice.	6 peppercorns.
2 oz. chutney.	1 tablespoonful tomato purée or a sliced ripe tomato.

1. Melt the dripping in a saucepan, and when hot add the onions. Fry them until quite cooked and of pale golden colour.

2. Add the curry powder and ground rice, and fry all together for 3–4 minutes.

3. Add the chutney, tamarinds or jam, apple, coconut (which has been soaking in a little warm water), spices, tomatoes, and stock.

4. Boil all together while stirring, then simmer gently for 1 hour, stirring frequently.

5. Press the sauce through a fine sieve.

6. Return the sauce to the saucepan, and correct the consistency and seasoning. Add a little lemon juice as required.

SAUCE MADÈRE

½ pint Espagnole Sauce (see p. 246).
½ pint stock.

Seasoning.
Meat glaze.
Scant ½ gill Madeira.

1. Reduce the Espagnole Sauce and stock to half quantity.

2. Correct the seasoning and add a little meat glaze.

3. Add the Madeira. Tammy the sauce and keep warm until required for use.

SAUCE MAYONNAISE

1 egg yolk.
Salt, pepper, and mustard.
1–2 gills olive oil.

2 teaspoonfuls tarragon vinegar.
2 teaspoonfuls white malt or French wine vinegar.

1. Place the yolk of the egg, free from all trace of white, in a small basin, round which a kitchen cloth is pinned, weighted at one end.

2. Add the seasoning and cream well with a small wooden spoon.

3. Add the oil from the point of a teaspoon, dropping it slowly at first.

4. As the sauce thickens, add the vinegar by degrees to keep the sauce from becoming too thick.

5. After some of the vinegar has been added, the oil may be added more rapidly without fear of curdling, so it is advisable to add some of the vinegar as soon as possible.

Notes. (*a*) If the mayonnaise is too thick when the required amount of vinegar has been added, whisk in a little boiling water as required.

(*b*) The mayonnaise may also be acidulated by the use of lemon juice in place of the vinegar. A little whipped cream may be folded in before serving.

SAUCE MORNAY

½ pint Béchamel Sauce (see p. 244).
½ gill fish essence or strong fish stock.

1 oz. grated Cheddar or Gruyère cheese.
1 oz. grated Parmesan.
1 oz. butter.

1. Boil the Béchamel Sauce and fish essence until well reduced, and add the cheeses.

2. Return to heat for a minute or two, stirring with a whisk to melt the cheese.

3. Whisk in the butter in small pieces away from the heat.

SAUCE D'ORANGES

1 orange.
½ pint Espagnole Sauce (see p. 246).
½ pint brown stock.

1 teaspoonful lemon juice.
1 teaspoonful red currant jelly.
Pepper and salt.

1. Cut the thinly peeled rind of the orange into julienne shreds, cover with water, boil up, and boil for 5 minutes.

2. Place the Espagnole Sauce and stock in a saucepan, with the juice of half the orange, and reduce to half its quantity.

3. Tammy the sauce, and add the shreds, the lemon juice, red currant jelly, and seasoning. Boil up and serve.

SAUCE PIQUANTE

1 oz. dripping.
Small piece of carrot and of onion.
1 oz. flour.
1 large tablespoonful vinegar.
¾ pint stock.

4 or 5 champignons.
1 tablespoonful Worcester Sauce or ketchup.
Blade of mace.
Small bay leaf.
Pepper and salt.

1. Melt the dripping and fry the vegetables until shrivelled.

2. Add the flour, and brown carefully.

3. Add the vinegar, and reduce for 4–5 minutes.

4. Add the stock by degrees and a pinch of salt.

5. Boil up, skim thoroughly, and add the Worcester Sauce or ketchup and herbs.

6. Simmer for ½ hour, skimming when necessary.

7. Strain, reheat, and correct the seasoning and consistency.

Note. If fresh mushrooms are used, remove the stems and skins in the usual way, also excess of black part. Chop them up and fry with the vegetables. If preserved champignons are used, cut them in pieces and add with the stock.

SAUCE RAIFORT FROIDE

(Horseradish Sauce, cold)

1½ oz. grated horseradish.
1 teaspoonful castor sugar.

Scant tablespoonful white malt vinegar.
Mustard, salt, cayenne.
½ gill cream.

1. Mix the grated horseradish, sugar, seasonings, and vinegar.

2. Half whip the cream and stir the mixed ingredients lightly into it.

Note. If evaporated horseradish is used, take 1 level tablespoonful, and soak it in 2 tablespoonfuls of milk for 1 hour before adding the remaining ingredients.

SAUCE RÉFORME

½ pint Espagnole Sauce (see p. 246).
½ tablespoonful red currant jelly.

1 tablespoonful port wine.
Few grains cayenne.

1. Prepare the Espagnole Sauce, adding half only of the usual amount of sherry.

2. Boil up the sauce, stir in the jelly, wine, and cayenne.

3. Simmer for 10 minutes, strain and use.

SAUCE RÉMOULADE

Few leaves of tarragon, parsley, and burnet.
Few chives.
1 gill mayonnaise.
1 level teaspoonful mustard.

1 tablespoonful tarragon vinegar.
Pinch of castor sugar.
Few drops of anchovy essence.

1. Blanch the herbs, drain well, and chop finely; chop the chives.

2. Prepare the mayonnaise with extra mustard, adding tarragon vinegar only whilst making it. Add the chopped herbs, chives, etc., and finally the anchovy essence.

Note. The flavour of mustard is characteristic of this sauce.

SALAD DRESSING

(Mock Mayonnaise)

½ teaspoonful mustard.
½ teaspoonful castor sugar.
¼ teaspoonful salt.
¼ teaspoonful pepper.

½ gill evaporated milk.
½ gill salad oil.
1 large tablespoonful vinegar.

1. Place mustard, sugar, salt, and pepper in a small basin, and mix smoothly with the milk.

2. Add the oil gradually, whisking briskly meanwhile.

3. Whisk in the vinegar, which forms an emulsion with the oil and thickens the dressing.

Note. If Mustard Dressing is required, double the quantity of mustard used in making the dressing.

SAUCE SOUBISE

3 medium-sized onions.
1 gill white stock.
½ pint stiff Béchamel Sauce (see p. 244).

Salt and white pepper.
A pinch of sugar.
1 tablespoonful thick cream.

1. Peel the onions and boil until soft in the white stock.
2. Drain the onions very thoroughly, and chop them finely or press on a wire sieve.
3. Return to the saucepan, and stir over moderate heat until *all* moisture is absorbed. Rub through a fine wire sieve.
4. Add the sauce and reduce to the desired consistency.
5. Season and add the cream.

SUPRÊME, OR VELOUTÉ, SAUCE

1 oz. butter.
4 white peppercorns.
A few parsley stalks.
Trimmings of white mushrooms or a few stalks of champignons.

Salt.
¾ oz. flour.
½ pint white stock.
Juice of ¼ lemon.
¼ gill cream.

1. Melt the butter in a small saucepan. When it is melted, stir in the peppercorns and parsley stalks, then the flour, and cook for a few minutes without browning.
2. Add the stock gradually; stir again until the whole has well boiled. Add the lemon juice, mushroom trimmings, and salt.
3. Simmer gently for 20 minutes, stirring frequently.
4. Tammy the sauce, reheat, carefully adding the cream, and use as required.

SAUCE TARTARE

1 gill mayonnaise sauce.
½ tablespoonful cold Béchamel Sauce.
½ tablespoonful chopped gherkins.

¼ tablespoonful chopped capers.
¼ tablespoonful chopped parsley.
½ teaspoonful chopped tarragon and chervil.

1. Prepare the mayonnaise and work in the Béchamel Sauce.
2. When it is required for use, add the prepared chopped ingredients.

SAUCE TOMATES
(or Américaine)

½ oz. butter.	1 teaspoonful tomato conserve.
½ rasher of bacon.	1 gill white stock.
1 small onion.	Salt and pepper.
½ small carrot.	1 teaspoonful cornflour.
½ lb. tomatoes.	

1. Melt the butter in a small saucepan and add the bacon cut into strips.

2. Fry slightly and add the sliced onion and carrot. Cook without colouring until the fat is absorbed.

3. Add the sliced tomatoes, boil all well, crushing with a wooden spoon.

4. Add the tomato conserve to colour, stock, salt, and pepper. Boil up and skim.

5. Simmer for 30 minutes, stirring occasionally.

6. Pass through a hair sieve, and thicken with the cornflour slaked with a little stock or water. Boil 5 minutes.

7. Correct the seasoning and consistency, and use as required.

Note. If this sauce is to be served with fish, substitute two anchovy fillets for the bacon, and fish stock for the white stock.

VINAIGRETTE DRESSING

Salt, pepper, dry mustard—¼ teaspoonful of each.	3 tablespoonfuls olive oil.
	1 tablespoonful vinegar.

1. Place the salt, pepper, and dry mustard in a small basin, and mix them smoothly with the oil.

2. Whisk in the vinegar to form an emulsion.

3. Put the mixture into a bottle, fitted with a cork grooved on opposite sides to form a sprinkler.

SAUCE AU VIN BLANC

½ oz. butter.	1 yolk of egg.
½ oz. flour.	1 tablespoonful cream.
1 gill white or fish stock.	½ tablespoonful Sauterne or
Cayenne and salt.	sherry.

1. Blend the butter and flour, add the stock, and boil well.

2. Add the cayenne and salt. When mixture is cool add the egg yolk and cream, beaten together.

3. Cook until thickened, add the wine, reheat carefully, and serve.

SAUCES

SWEET SAUCES
SAUCE D'ABRICOTS
(Apricot Sauce)

2 tablespoonfuls of apricot jam, made up to ½ pint with water. | 2 teaspoonfuls arrowroot. Carmine.

1. Boil up the jam and water, reserving a little of the latter for slaking the arrowroot.
2. Thicken with the prepared arrowroot and boil until clear. A little sugar or lemon juice may be added at discretion. Strain and use.

SAUCE ANGLAISE

2 yolks of eggs. | ¾–1 oz. cornflour (according to
1 oz. castor sugar. | degree of thickness required).
½ pt. milk. | Vanilla essence.

1. Separate the yolks and place them in a basin with the sugar. Mix well.
2. Mix the cornflour smoothly with the milk; boil up, and cook for a few minutes, then pour on to the yolks and sugar.
3. Add the essence, return to pan, and cook until the sauce coats the spoon smoothly. Use as desired.

SAUCE AUX CERISES
(Cherry Sauce)

Juice of half a lemon. | 1 teaspoonful red currant jelly
1–2 tablespoonfuls sherry. | or raspberry jam.
Water. | 1 oz. granulated sugar.
1 teaspoonful powdered arrow- | 1½ oz. glacé cherries, cut in
root. | quarters.
Carmine. |

1. Squeeze the juice from half a lemon, add the sherry, and make up to 1½ gills with the water.
2. Mix the arrowroot smoothly with some of the liquid, heat the remainder, and stir in the prepared arrowroot.
3. Boil until clear (5–7 minutes) while stirring, adding 1 drop of carmine, the jam or jelly, and the sugar.
4. Strain, add the cherries, reheat, and use as required.

SAUCE À L'ANANAS (Pineapple Sauce). Substitute 1 large tablespoonful of pineapple, cut in tiny cubes. Omit the jam or jelly.

SAUCE AUX BANANES (Banana Sauce). Substitute 1 banana sliced and cut in quarters. Omit the jam or jelly, using a little carmine only as colouring. Preferably substitute Maraschino syrup for the sherry.

SAUCE AU CHOCOLAT

2 oz. plain chocolate.	1 teaspoonful castor sugar.
2 tablespoonfuls water.	½ gill cream or evaporated milk.
1 small teaspoonful cornflour.	½ teaspoonful vanilla essence.
¾ gill milk.	

1. Scrape the chocolate with a knife, dissolve it in the water, and boil well until it becomes a smooth batter.

2. Mix the cornflour smoothly with the milk, add it to the chocolate, with the sugar, and stir until boiling. Boil for 5 minutes.

3. If the sauce is to be served hot, add the cream and vanilla essence, when it has cooled somewhat, and reheat carefully without boiling.

4. If the sauce is to be served cold, set the sauce aside to cool, stir in the cream, and serve as cold as possible.

Note. If the sauce is required thick to be served as a coating in making Chocolate Sundaes, halve the amount of milk used, and take a piled teaspoonful of cornflour.

SAUCE DUR

2 oz. butter.	1 oz. ground almonds and a
3 oz. castor sugar.	few drops ratafia essence.
Flavouring—	Grated nutmeg or chopped
2–3 teaspoonfuls rum or brandy; or	pistachios.

1. Cream the butter thoroughly, add the castor sugar, and cream until white.

2. Add the flavouring chosen, and pile or pipe the sauce on a small fancy dish.

3. Sprinkle with grated nutmeg or chopped pistachios.

4. Place aside in the cool to become quite firm and hard. Serve with any rich steamed or boiled sweet pudding.

SAUCE GINGEMBRE

(Ginger Sauce)

Caramel (see p. 146).	½ in. cinnamon stick.
Water, to make up ½ pint.	1 teaspoonful arrowroot.
Rind and juice of half a lemon.	4 oz. preserved ginger.

1. Prepare the caramel, and thin it down to ½ pint with the water. Add the rind and juice of the lemon and the cinnamon stick. Heat, and leave to infuse for ½ hour.

2. Mix the arrowroot smoothly (if the ginger is taken from a jar, some of the syrup may be used for mixing; otherwise use water), and thicken the sauce with it.

3. Add the preserved ginger and use as desired.

SAUCE MARMELADE

(Marmalade Sauce)

1 gill water.	1 **large tablespoonful orange**
6 lumps sugar.	**marmalade.**
	The juice of ½–1 sweet orange.

1. Make a syrup with the water and sugar, and reduce.

2. Add the marmalade, boil up, and add fresh orange juice at discretion, to improve the flavour and correct the consistency.

3. Pour round the pudding or serve in a sauce-boat. Do *not* strain.

SAUCE MOUSSELINE

(Froth Sauce)

Yolks of 2 eggs.	¾ oz. castor sugar.
White of 1 egg.	1 tablespoonful maraschino.
¼ gill cream.	

1. Put the above ingredients into a small basin, and stand it over a saucepan half filled with hot water.

2. Whisk until the sauce becomes creamy and frothy, being careful not to over-cook it. Do not make the sauce until it is required for use.

SAUCE PRALINÉE

Sauce Anglaise (see p. 253).	Praline—
2 oz. Praline (after sieving).	1½ oz. almonds.
	1½ oz. castor sugar.

1. Prepare Sauce Anglaise.

2. Add the Praline, and serve.

PRALINE

1. Rub the almonds in a damp cloth, but do not blanch them.

2. Place them in a small strong saucepan with the castor sugar, and work them together gently until the sugar has melted around the almonds.

3. Turn out on to an oiled tin; when cold, pound and sieve.

SAUCE SABAYON

Yolks of 2 eggs.	¾ gill sherry or fruit juice.
1 dessertspoonful castor sugar.	Small strip of lemon rind.

1. Put all the ingredients together in a small basin, and stand it on a small saucepan half filled with steaming hot water.

2. Whisk briskly until the sauce becomes creamily frothy. If overheated the sauce will curdle, but if it is under-cooked the egg will separate from the liquid very quickly on standing.

3. Remove the lemon rind and serve *at once*.

Note. Do not make the sauce until it is required for use.

SAUCE AU VIN ROUGE (SUCRÉE)

(Sweet Red Wine Sauce)

1 oz. granulated sugar.	1 teaspoonful arrowroot.
1 gill water.	1–2 tablespoonfuls claret.
Rind and juice of ¼ lemon.	Carmine.
2 tablespoonfuls raspberry jam.	

1. Dissolve the sugar in the water, add the jam, lemon rind, and juice, and boil up.

2. Cook gently for 8–10 minutes; thicken with the arrowroot, slaked with a little water, and boil until clear. Add the claret, and carmine if necessary. Strain, reheat, and serve.

SAUCE AU VIN BLANC (Sucrée). (Sweet White Wine Sauce.) Substitute apricot jam or orange marmalade for the raspberry jam, omit the carmine, and use sherry in place of the claret.

WHIPPED CREAM BRANDY SAUCE

1 gill cream.	Grated nutmeg or finely chopped
2 teaspoonfuls castor sugar.	pistachios.
2 teaspoonfuls brandy.	

1. Whisk the cream until beginning to thicken. Add sugar and brandy, and continue whisking carefully until the cream is stiff enough to hang on the whisk.

2. Pipe the cream into a small fancy dish, using a coarse rose pipe.

3. Scatter grated nutmeg or chopped pistachios over, and serve as cold as possible.

GARNISHING AND DISHING

GENERAL PRINCIPLES

THE OBJECT OF GARNISHING is to make the dish as effective as possible, and to accompany it with some suitable adjunct.

A FEW SPECIAL POINTS

1. The garnish should be ornamental and appropriate.
2. The colour and design should harmonize.
3. The garnish should not be over-abundant.
4. It should be cooked if it is usual to cook the materials which are used.
5. With a hot dish the garnish should be heated.
6. If a garnish is to be arranged on a hot dish, it should not be too elaborate; otherwise the dish is apt to be cold by the time it is garnished.
7. The dish chosen for dishing should be suitable in size.

VARIETIES OF GARNISHES

1. SIMPLE GARNISHES

(a) *For Savoury Dishes*. E.g. Fresh parsley, chopped or in sprigs. Fried parsley. Scraped horseradish. Small cress. Salad plants of all kinds. Cucumber. Beetroot. Eggs, hard boiled, poached or fried. Croûtes or croûtons. Macaroni. Rice. Capers. Chilli skin. Gherkins. Lemon. Vegetables, cut into various shapes. Fleurons of pastry. Pimento. Aspic jelly. Panurette. Coralline or Paprika pepper. Olives.

(b) *For Sweet Dishes*. E.g. Glacé Cherries. Angelica. Crystallized fruits. Silver sweets (Dragées). Coconut, white, browned, or coloured. Stiffly whisked white of egg or meringue. Whipped cream. Chopped jelly. Almonds. Coloured sugar.

2. ELABORATE GARNISHES, suitable for Hot Entrées.

(a) *Vegetables*, cut into various shapes.
(b) *Potatoes*. E.g. Ribbons. Balls. Straws. Piped potato purée.
(c) *Forcemeat* made into balls.
(d) *Quenelles, truffles, olives, sweetbreads, mushrooms*.
(e) *Garnishes suitable for Fish Dishes*. E.g. Prawns. Oysters. Fried smelts. Scallops.
(f) *Sauce used as garnish*. E.g. Lobster. Oyster. Mayonnaise.

3. HÂTELETS, or Silver Skewers, used mostly for decorating cold dishes.

STANDARD NAMES OF DISHES AND THEIR TYPICAL GARNISHES

The use of a certain name for a dish means that a definite ingredient or ingredients have been used in making it, or form the garnish, and these are standardized.

AMÉRICAINE	Tomatoes in some form.
AURORE	Yellow or flame-coloured dishes, in which sieved egg yolk is frequently used, with red pepper or lobster coral (often in lines to indicate the rays of the sun).
BELLE VUE	For cold dishes. Masked with white Chaud-froid Sauce, decorated with slices of truffle and ox tongue.
BOUQUETIÈRE	Groups of carrots and turnips (cut Paysanne shape), French beans, cauliflower buds, button onions, and asparagus tips. Jus Lié or Demi-glace as sauce.
BRETONNE	Haricot beans, whole or in purée.
CHASSEUR	Dice of game and mushrooms in Chasseur Sauce.
CRESSY	Carrots, in purée, dice, or balls.
DUBARRY	Cauliflower sprigs (or as purée in soup).
ÉCARLATE	Cooked smoked ox tongue, cut in slices or dice, or chopped.
FINANCIÈRE	Slices of blanched sweetbread, tiny quenelles, chicken forcemeat, heads of champignons, stoned olives, slices of truffle and cockscombs.
FLORENTINE	Spinach in the form of a purée, or steamed (with egg yolk, or white sauce), to form small fancy shapes.
INDIENNE	Applied to curried dishes—usually served with chutney and plain boiled rice.
LYONNAISE	Denotes the use of onions. As a garnish the onions are frequently shredded and fried.
JARDINIÈRE	Groups of young spring vegetables or a Mace-doine, served with brown gravy or demi-glace.
JOINVILLE	A fish garnish, consisting of slices of truffle and mushrooms, and crayfish tails. Lobster or shrimp sauce.
MILANAISE	Cooked macaroni or spaghetti, with julienne strips of ham or tongue, and mushrooms, in tomato sauce.
MINUITE, à la	Something cooked very rapidly, e.g. food cut in thin slices and cooked by frying or grilling —Omelettes, etc.

STANDARD NAMES OF DISHES AND THEIR TYPICAL GARNISHES—(contd.)

NAPOLITAINE   Spaghetti, mixed with tomato sauce and Parmesan cheese. Or it may mean tri-coloured in stripes, e.g. Crème Napolitaine.

NESSELRODE   Denotes the use of chestnuts in some form (usually).

NORMANDE   Usually implies that apples are used, though the standard fish dish "Filets de Sole à la Normande" is an exception.

PARMENTIER   Implies the use of potatoes (Parmentier introduced the potato into France in 1786).

PRINCESSE   Denotes the use of chicken.

PRINTANIÈRE   (From *Printemps*, Spring.) Early spring vegetables, used as garnish—left whole or cut, served in separate groups or as Macedoine.

SOUBISE   Onion purée—frequently mixed with thick white sauce.

ST. HUBERT   Implies dishes made with game (St. Hubert is the patron saint of hunters).

VIN BLANC (au)   Cooked with white wine.

CORRECT ACCOMPANIMENTS FOR STANDARD DISHES

SOUP

Clear   A small dish of finely grated Parmesan cheese is frequently handed.

Purées, or any thickened soup without garnish   Small croûtons of fried or toasted bread handed separately. Cheese straws are now often served with a vegetable purée instead of croûtes.

Game Purées   Small forcemeat balls handed separately.

Curried   Plain boiled rice, handed separately.

FISH

Boiled   Garnish with fresh parsley and cut lemon, or prawns, and "fish" potatoes. (Alternatively to the latter, hand plainly boiled potatoes separately.) Serve with a suitable sauce.

Fried   Garnish with fried parsley and cut lemon. Hand a suitable sauce separately.

Grilled   Spread Anchovy, Maître d'Hôtel, or Tomato Butter on top before serving.
(For suitable fish sauces, see "Savoury Sauces.")

Oysters   Hand thinly cut brown bread and butter, cayenne, quarters of lemon, and white vinegar separately.

CORRECT ACCOMPANIMENTS FOR STANDARD DISHES—(contd.)

FISH

Salmon	
(Boiled, Hot)	Hand Hollandaise, Lobster, or Shrimp Sauce separately. Garnish with sliced cucumber.
(Cold)	Mayonnaise or Tartare Sauce. Cucumber salad.
Mackerel	
(Boiled)	Fennel or Parsley Sauce.
Herrings	
(Grilled)	Mustard Sauce.
Skate	
(Boiled)	Nut brown butter or Parsley Sauce.
Red Mullet	
(Grilled)	Parsley butter. Tomato or Piquante Sauce.

MEAT, JOINTS

BEEF (Roast)	Yorkshire Pudding. Hot or cold Horseradish Sauce, or scraped horseradish. Browned potatoes. Gravy.
Boiled (Fresh)	Boiled cabbage. Carrots, turnips, etc., which have been cooked with the meat, as a garnish. Parsley Sauce. Some of the meat liquor.
Boiled (Salt)	Suet dumplings. Carrots, turnips, and onions. Parsley Sauce. Some of the meat liquor.
CALF'S HEAD	
(Boiled)	Parsley or Brown Sauce. Brain purée. Boiled bacon.
LAMB	Mint Sauce. Gravy. Mint-flavoured new potatoes and peas, if in season.
MUTTON	
(Boiled Leg or Neck)	Caper Sauce. Carrots, turnips, and onions.
(Roast Saddle, Leg or Loin)	Red currant jelly. Gravy.
(Roast shoulder)	Onion Sauce. Baked potatoes.
VEAL (Roast)	Grilled bacon rolls, or a piece of boiled ham. Thyme and parsley stuffing. Gravy.
VENISON (Roast)	Red currant jelly. Sour Cream Sauce. Gravy.
PORK (Roast)	Sage and onion stuffing. Apple sauce. Gravy.
(Boiled Pickled)	Pease pudding. Parsnips or carrots. White or Mustard Sauce.
RABBIT (Boiled)	Pickled pork. Onion sauce.
(Roast)	Parsley or sage stuffing. Fried savoury balls. Thickened brown gravy. Tomato or Piquante Sauce.

CORRECT ACCOMPANIMENTS FOR STANDARD DISHES—*(contd.)*

VEGETABLES

Asparagus (Hot)	Oiled butter or Hollandaise Sauce.
(Cold)	Mayonnaise or French Salad Dressing.
Artichokes	
(Globe)	Oiled butter. Hollandaise or Piquante Sauce.
(Jerusalem)	Parsley, Béchamel, Velouté, or Tomato Sauce.
Vegetable Marrow	Béchamel, Parsley, Brown or Piquante Sauce.
Sea-kale	
(Hot and Cold)	As for Asparagus.
Cauliflower	White, Béchamel, or Hollandaise Sauce. For Cauliflower au Gratin, add grated cheese to the white sauce, and sprinkle with grated cheese after pouring sauce over. Brown and serve in the gratin dish.
French Beans	Oiled fresh butter, in which the beans are tossed.
Broad Beans	Skin these when boiled unless they are very young. Toss them in a flowing White or Parsley Sauce.
Green Peas	Mint used to flavour in cooking. Oiled fresh butter in which the peas are tossed.
Celeriac	Béchamel, Egg, or Hollandaise Sauce.
Celery (Boiled)	White, Béchamel, or Velouté Sauce.
(Braised)	Brown or Piquante Sauce, or Jus Lié.
Aubergines	Brown or Piquante Sauce.
Spanish Onions	
(Boiled)	White or Parsley Sauce.
(Roast)	Browned thickened gravy.

Suitable Vegetables

With Roast Poultry	When poultry is served to take the place of a roast joint, it is frequently stuffed, and one of the following vegetables, according to season, might be served with it: Asparagus. French Beans. Green Peas. Cauliflower. Vegetable Marrow. Brussels Sprouts or Savoy Cabbage. Château Potatoes.
With Boiled Turkey or Fowl	As for Roast Poultry, and also the following are specially suitable—Cauliflower. Stewed Celery. Parsnips. Jerusalem artichokes. Plainly boiled potatoes.

CORRECT ACCOMPANIMENTS FOR STANDARD DISHES—(contd.)

POULTRY AND GAME

Chicken or Fowl (Roast)	Grilled or baked bacon rolls. Watercress to garnish. Bread Sauce. Thin brown gravy. Chips or fried potatoes. Green salad.
Duck or Duckling	Sage and onion stuffing. Thickened gravy. Apple, Cranberry, or Orange Sauce; or Orange Salad.
Turkey (Roast)	Grilled sausages, and Veal or Chestnut Stuffing, or Sausage Meat Stuffing. Bacon rolls. Bread Sauce. Gravy.
Goose (Roast)	Sage and Onion Stuffing. Apple Sauce. Thickened gravy.
Guinea fowl, Grouse, Ptarmigan, Partridges, Pheasants, Quails (Roast)	As for Roast Fowl, but with the addition of fried crumbs, and the bacon rolls omitted.
Wild Duck, or Widgeon (Roast)	As above, but serve Orange Sauce or Orange Salad.
Hare (Roast)	Red currant jelly. Fried Savoury Balls. Port Wine Sauce.

MAKING MENUS : DINNER MENUS

THE word "Menu" is a French one, and its literal translation is "Small or minute detail." Its English equivalent is "Bill of Fare."

The actual menu card acts as the programme of the meal, and gives the details of the food to be served. It consists of a list of the dishes, written or printed on small cards, and placed on the table for each guest, or for each two guests.

The use of menu cards appears to date from the Middle Ages, and the cards have diminished in size. Originally one was placed at each end of a long table, and was of large dimensions.

COMPILATION OF MENUS

It is of no use to be able to produce a few perfect dishes, however elaborate. These must be combined to form a suitable meal.

The making up of menus is a great art, requiring correct technical knowledge and good judgment. Skill is needed to provide a meal which will combine well-balanced diet with a pleasing colour scheme, and can also be cooked adequately and served in the time allotted and with the equipment available.

Nothing takes the place of experience in these matters, but the following rules form good guidance—

1. Consider the number of people to partake of the meal and the occasion for which it is required.

2. Also consider the season of the year, so that the materials used are at their best and of full flavour.

3. Make allowance for the seasonableness of the various foods— the warmth-giving dishes of winter are out of place in summer.

4. Choose dishes which are distinctive and offer variety in method of cooking. Avoid, for example, a series of foods cooked in sauces, or two fried dishes following one another.

5. Arrange that the dishes are all on a similar plane. It is not well-balanced judgment to mingle elaboration in one course with extreme homeliness in another. A dish may be simply cooked to form a contrast, but must still be distinctive and smart.

6. Have a pleasing variety in the colour of the dishes, so that they contrast yet harmonize. The exception to this rule would be in the arrangement of a "freak" meal, such as a "Pink Dinner" or a "Green and White Luncheon." In this case all the food used should consist of the colour chosen, or should be coated with that colour.

263

7. Do not repeat any distinctive ingredient in a later course. It would be incorrect to follow Potage St. Germain by Côtelettes d'Agneau aux Petits Pois.

8. Avoid over-elaboration. In a successful dinner menu the dishes are often limited, but must be choice.

PREPARING A SPECIAL OCCASION MEAL

1. On the day beforehand, find time for foundational work: Stock, basic Sauces, Jellies, etc. Estimate quantities and also make careful lists of ingredients required, arranging for perishable articles to be delivered early on the next day.

2. Plan out a good method of work, writing it down if inexperienced.

3. Allow sufficient time for the thorough cooking of each dish and for smart garnishing and dishing.

4. Pay careful attention to seasoning and flavouring.

5. Serve all the hot dishes perfectly hot, and all the cold ones perfectly cold.

6. Allow each course to be served promptly. Rapid purposeful work is always necessary at dishing time, but rush is to be deprecated in the best interests of the meal.

THE COMPLETE DINNER MENU

The elaborate full-course dinner is now rarely served except at public functions. At its hey-day, in the latter half of Queen Victoria's reign, it often took two hours to pursue, and provided the evening's amusement except for a little music or card-playing. Time is now too precious to be spent in that way, and a dinner is not an end in itself, but must form the prelude to the evening's enjoyment.

The dinner party is not, however, less important on these grounds. The menu is still chosen with the greatest care, and the meal is choice, distinctive, and smartly served.

The menu for a full course dinner still provides the framework on which to build—it remains as the standard and is curtailed of certain courses as desired.

The complete dinner consists of eight courses, if the Entremet course, which has three sections, is considered as one course.

The courses are as follows—

1. Hors d'Œuvres.   Appetizers.
2. Potage.   Soup.
3. Poisson.   Fish.
4. Entrée.   Made dish—always more or less elaborate.
5. Relevé.   Joint.

After this a Sorbet is sometimes served.

6. Rôti.   Roast game, poultry, or birds.
7. Entremet—
    (a) Entremet de légumes.   Dressed vegetables.
    (b) Entremet Sucré.   Sweet.
    (c) Entremet Savoureux.   Savoury.
8. Dessert.

Café

SHORTENING THE MENU

1. Nowadays it is usual to omit Hors d'Œuvre or Savoury—more frequently the former in a dinner menu.

2. In many cases only one meat course is served. Usually either the Entrée (with suitable accompanying vegetables) or Rôti. Or a light Entrée may be followed by a roast bird.

3. If a Bisque is served, the fish course is sometimes omitted.

4. Thus, a smart modern dinner may consist of—

Soup.   Roast.
Fish.   Sweet.
Light Entrée   Savoury.

A LITTLE DINNER FOR EACH MONTH OF THE YEAR

MENU	BILL OF FARE
January	
Potage Dubarry	Cauliflower Cream Soup
Sole Américaine	Steamed Sole, Tomato Sauce
Faisan Rôti au Cresson	Roast Pheasant, Accompaniments
Bavarois au Rhum	Moulded Rum Custard
Bonnes Bouches aux Pruneaux	Savoury Stuffed Prunes
February	
Bisque aux Huîtres	Oyster Soup
Côtelettes Réforme	Fried Mutton Cutlets, Reform Sauce
Pommes Duchesse	Fried Potatoes
Maïs en Coquilles	Scalloped Sweet Corn
Flan de Cerises	Cherry Flan
Jambon Diablé	Devilled Ham
March	
Consommé Madrilène	Clear Tomato Soup
Poulet Maryland	American Fried Chicken
Chou de mer à la Hollandaise	Sea-kale in Hollandaise Sauce
Fruits Rafraîchis au Kirsch	Fruit in Kirsch Syrup
Soufflés de Merluche Fumée	Smoked Haddock Soufflés

A LITTLE DINNER FOR EACH MONTH OF THE YEAR—(contd.)

MENU	BILL OF FARE
April	
Potage d'Amandes	Almond Soup
Petites Bouchées de Crevettes	Prawn Patties
Selle d'Agneau Bretonne	Roast Saddle of Lamb
Pommes Châteaux	Haricot Purée
Crème Napolitaine	Browned Potatoes
Beignets de Gruyère	Neapolitan Cream
	Cheese Fritters
May	
Crème aux Concombres	Cucumber Cream Soup
Homard à la Newburg	Hot Lobster—Newburg Style
Noisettes d'Agneau	Boned Lamb Cutlets
Asperges Froides, Sauce	Cold Asparagus, Mayonnaise
Mayonnaise	Sauce
Bavarois aux Fruits	Moulded Custard with Fruit
June	
Consommé Frappé	Iced Clear Soup
Blanchailles au Citron	Fried Whiting and Lemon
Caneton Rôti aux Petits Pois	Roast Duck
Pommes Nouvelles	Green Peas—New Potatoes
Coupes Glacées Tutti-Frutti	Ices garnished with Metz fruits
July	
Cantaloup Frappé	Iced Melon
Bisque de Homard	Lobster Soup
Mousse de Jambon, Sauce	Moulded Ham, Cumberland
Cumberland	Sauce
Salade de Saison	Seasonable Salad
Soufflé D'Épinards	Spinach Soufflé
Omelette au Confiture	Sweet Omelet
August	
Consommé Double en Gelée	Jellied Clear Soup
Mayonnaise de Homard	Lobster Mayonnaise
Longe de Veau Braisé	Braised Loin of Veal, Vege-
Bouquetière	table Garnish
Pommes Parisienne	Fried Potato Balls
Salade à la Japonaise	Japanese Salad
Pouding Glacé aux Framboises	Iced Raspberry Pudding

A LITTLE DINNER FOR EACH MONTH OF THE YEAR—(contd.)

MENU	BILL OF FARE

September

Velouté de Volaille Froide	Cold Chicken Soup
Kari de Crevettes Parisienne	French Curried Prawns
Salmis de Perdrix	Stewed Partridges
Aubergines Frites	Fried Egg-plant
Pêches Melba	Peach Melba
Champignons Farcis	Stuffed Mushrooms

October

Huîtres de Whitstable	Whitstable Oysters
Purée aux Épinards	Spinach Soup
Côtelettes d'Agneau Braisées	Braised Lamb Cutlets
Carottes Glacées	Glazed Carrots
Poires au Vin Rouge	Pears stewed in Claret
Noix au Fromage	Cheese-Stuffed Walnuts

November

Consommé de Tomates Royale	Tomato Clear Soup
Sole Meunier	Sole Fried in Butter
Filets Mignons aux Bananes	Small Beef Fillets and Bananas
Pommes Mousseline	Baked Shapes of Mashed Potatoes
Charlotte à la St. José	Pineapple Charlotte
Pailles au Parmesan	Cheese Straws

December

Potage Mulligatawny	Mulligatawny Soup
Darne de Cabillaud, Sauce aux Huîtres	Braised Cod, Oyster Sauce
Sarcelle Rôti	Roast Teal
Salade d'Oranges	Orange Salad
Bombe Nesselrode	Ice Pudding
Mignardises	Dessert Dainties
Olives Madras	Stuffed Olives

THE SERVICE OF WINE

THE study of Wine is very technical, and the Wine Trade in all its branches is the business of a lifetime, but at the same time any one who deals with the service of good food should understand something of the wines suitable to accompany it, and the correct method of storing and serving them.

CHOOSING WINES FOR THE MEAL

FORMERLY it was considered necessary that a different wine should accompany each course. They were served in the following order—

OYSTERS (with the). Chablis, Sauterne, or Barsac.

POTAGE (Soup). Dry Sherry.

POISSON (Fish). Still Hock, or those allotted to oysters.

ENTRÉES. Red Burgundy. Either Beaujolais, Beaune, Volnay, Pommard, or Chambertin.

RELEVÉ (Joint). Vintage Claret—Châteaux Margaux, Lafite, Mouton Rothschild, etc.

RÔTI ET ENTREMETS (Roast, Vegetables, Sweets and Savouries). Champagne.

DESSERT. Port wine or Marsala.

COFFEE. Benedictine, Curaçao, Kummel, Green or Yellow Chartreuse.

Now the number of wines served with a meal is considerably reduced.

1. Sometimes Sherry is served with the soup, after which Champagne is served until the Dessert, when Vintage Port or Vintage Claret can take its place.

2. Frequently one or at the most two kinds of wine are served throughout the meal. Popular varieties are red wines, such as Claret or Burgundy, French white wines, such as Graves, Barsac, Sauterne or Chablis, as well as Rhine Wines, Italian Chianti, or, of course, Champagne. As an alternative to Champagne, Sparkling Moselle (White or Red) or Samur may be substituted; but fashion changes in wine, as in other matters, from time to time. Before a meal Sherry and Angostura, Italian or French Vermouth, Gin and Orange Bitters are often served.

TEMPERATURE OF WINES

1. Ice should never be put into wine, and this should apply also to Claret Cup and similar beverages.

2. Champagne and similar sparkling wines should be served

cold, but should be cooled in bottle. In summer, the bottles are served in silver wine coolers, filled with ice.

3. Claret or Burgundy, on the contrary, should not be chilled, and in winter time may be very gradually warmed by a fire to develop their characteristic bouquet. If exposed to too cold a temperature the character of port is quite spoiled.

SERVING WINE

1. Wine should be kept lying down until required, so that the liquid touches the corks, and keeps them wet and swollen.

2. Sherry and Port are the wines which are most frequently decanted, and this should be done some little time (at least 1 hour) before they are required.

3. When decanting a bottle, remove all wax and dust near the cork, insert the corkscrew in the middle, and draw out the cork steadily, disturbing the wine as little as possible. Decanting an old crusted port is really "two-handed" work, as the cork should be drawn while the bottle is still in a horizontal position and the wine caught in a decanter or another bottle by means of a funnel. This care is, of course, to prevent the crust breaking and spoiling the wine.

4. Wipe the mouth of the bottle thoroughly before serving.

5. Some of the wine should be poured first into the host's glass—a custom which survives from times when poison was conveniently administered in the wine offered to a guest, and that the host was served with the same wine first was accepted as a gesture of good faith.

6. All glasses and decanters should be spotlessly clean. Do not fill the glasses more than three parts full, and replenish them before they are empty.

THE WINE CELLAR

Any disturbance is bad for wine if it is desired to serve it in perfection. For this reason it is desirable to keep a cellar entirely for storing wines, beers, and liqueurs when these are served regularly on a large scale—this would be in the care of the butler in a private house, or a competent cellarman in the case of a hotel or restaurant.

A cellar which has a concrete floor is the best, because it is the most stable, and would not be subject to vibration from traffic. It is also draught-proof, and this helps to keep the temperature steady. It will also be fitted with a reliable thermometer, which is regularly checked, and kept night and day to approximately 50° Fahr.

The ventilation should be good, and the cellar kept normally in darkness, though electric lighting is convenient for working.

Efficient labelling is essential—each bin and row of bins being numbered and labelled with the name of the wine and year of vintage.

ARRANGEMENT OF CELLAR

If the cellar is large enough it may be divided by wooden partitions, and it is most important in arranging it to remember that warm air rises. Place those wines needing the lowest temperature at the bottom, e.g. sparkling wines, still white wines, and barrels of beer. Red wines should be stored above these and the temperature may be a little higher.

MENUS FOR LUNCHEON AND OTHER LIGHT MEALS

(Menus de Déjeuners à la Fourchette, etc.)

RULES FOR COMPILING LUNCHEON MENUS

1. The menu is not so long as that for a dinner, as there are fewer courses and fewer dishes. More cold dishes are served, especially in summer.

2. Hors d'œuvres are most popular at a luncheon of the present day, especially a good selection of Hors d'Œuvres Variés.

3. Soup is not always served, though a clear soup is frequently included, and may be served "en tasses." In any case the soup must be of a light variety.

4. Omelettes, egg or farinaceous dishes are frequently served, either instead of fish or as an alternative to fish.

5. As a rule an entrée is served, or such dishes as grilled meats, meat pies, and boiled poultry. Cold joints, galantines, etc., may be served as side dishes.

6. A fruit sweet or one composed of Genoese or choux pastry is popular in a luncheon menu, or one hot and one cold sweet may be served.

7. After the sweets a savoury, or biscuits, butter, and cheese, may follow. Serve at least two kinds of cheese, together with tiny butter balls, dry plain biscuits, and, if liked, pulled bread. Coffee follows.

8. Although fewer in number, the dishes which make up a smart luncheon menu are as carefully chosen as those for a dinner, and they are attractively garnished.

It may be noted that in a large household quantities allowed for luncheon must be somewhat elastic, to provide for chance callers who may be asked to remain for the meal.

A SMALL LUNCHEON FOR EACH MONTH

MENU	BILL OF FARE
January	
Hors d'Œuvres Variés	Various appetizers
Spaghetti Milanaise	Spaghetti and Ham with
Rognons sautés Turbigo	Tomato Sauce
Pommes rissolées	Grilled Kidneys, Sausages,
Gâteau d'Ananas	and Mushrooms
	Brown strips of Potato
	Pineapple Cake

A SMALL LUNCHEON FOR EACH MONTH—*(contd.)*

MENU	BILL OF FARE
February	
Minestroni	Broth with Vegetables and Cheese
Sole Grillé Parisienne	Grilled Sole
Escalopes de Veau Viennoise	Veal Scallops with Garnish
Pommes croquettes	Potato Balls
Charlotte Russe	Sponge-finger Mould
March	
Filets de Hareng portugaise	Herring Fillets and Tomatoes
Barquettes au Semoule	Savoury Semolina
Poulet Bouilli, Sauce Béchamel	Boiled Fowl, Béchamel Sauce
Choux Pralinées au Sucre	Choux Pastry and Caramel Sugar
April	
Canapés Variés	Various Appetizers
Gnocchis à la Romana	Italian Gnocchis
Bouchées Alexandra, Sauce Piquante	Small Savoury Patties, Sharp Sauce
Choux de Mer à la Hollandaise	Sea-kale, Hollandaise Sauce
Crème Caramel	Caramel Cream
May	
Darne de Saumon en Aspic	Salmon Steak in Aspic
Côtelettes d'Agneau en Cuirasse	Lamb Cutlets in Pastry Cases
Asperges, Sauce Mousseline	Asparagus, Froth Sauce
Meringues Glacées	Iced Meringues
June	
Crabe Garni	Dressed Crab
Suprêmes de Caneton aux Cerises	Breast of Duck in Aspic with Cherry Garnish
Salade aux Petits Pois	Green Pea Salad
Pouding Diplomate	Cream Sponge Pudding
Croûtes de Jambon	Ham Savoury
July	
Œufs Brouillés aux Tomates	Scrambled Eggs and Tomatoes
Mayonnaise de Volaille	Mayonnaise of Chicken
Salade Pommes de Terre	Potato Salad
Salade Mimosa	Lettuce and Egg Salad
Abricots Colbert	Apricot Fritters and Creamed Rice

A SMALL LUNCHEON FOR EACH MONTH—*(contd.)*

MENU	BILL OF FARE
August	
Bouillon Glacé en Tasses	Iced Beef Broth in Cups
Saumon en Coquilles	Salmon in Shells
Galantine de Veau en Chaudfroid	Veal Galantine
Salade Américaine	American Salad
Zambaione	Whisked Eggs, Cooked in Wine
September	
Olives Madras	Stuffed Olives
Délices de Sole aux Raisins	Fillets of Sole and Grapes
Veau Sauté Milanaise	Stewed Veal and Spaghetti
Pommes Duchesse	Baked Shapes of Mashed Potato
Aubergines au Gratin	Stuffed Egg-plant
Gelée à la Madeleine	Fruit Jelly and Cream
October	
Salade Waldorf	Apple, Nut, and Celery Salad
Omelette aux Champignons	Mushroom Omelet
Émincé de Volaille Duchesse	Minced Chicken
Tomates Pochées	Poached Tomatoes
"Day Dreams"	"Day Dreams"
November	
Bouillon en Tasses	Beef Broth in Cups
Turbot Caprice	Garnished Fried Turbot
Pithiviers de Pigeons	Stuffed Pigeons in Pastry
Chou-fleur Polonaise	Cauliflower and Brown Butter
Bavarois au Café	Moulded Coffee Custard
December	
Velouté de Tomates	Tomato Cream Soup
Nouilles au Parmesan	Macaroni Paste and Grated Cheese
Fritto Misto	Mixed Fried Meat and Vegetables
Beignets de Chou-fleur	Cauliflower Fritters
Omelette au Rhum	Rum Omelet

10—(G.3150)

TWO ENGLISH LUNCHEON MENUS

Autumn

Grape-fruit
Boiled Turbot, Lobster Sauce
Spatchcock of Chicken
Fried Potatoes
Apple Pie, Cream
Angels on Horseback

Winter

Ox-tail Soup
Boiled Cod, Oyster Sauce
Mixed Grill
Orange Pudding, Marmalade Sauce
Stilton Cheese, Water Biscuits

SUPPER MENUS

(a) HOMELY

Suppers of this character are served only in households where late dinner is not the rule, and individual tastes are studied in this meal more than in any other.

A selection from such dishes as Soups, Fish, Cold Meat, Salads, simple Sweets, Fruit, Cheese and Cheese Dishes are served, together with simple beverages such as Coffee, Cocoa, Barley Water and Lemonade. In any case the dishes chosen should be digestible and they can often be prepared partly earlier in the day. Often left-over portions can be réchauffèd or re-dished.

(b) THEATRE

Theatre suppers are like short dinners. Hors d'œuvres are served—fish, entrée, sweets, ices, and coffee.

(c) BALL OR DANCE SUPPERS

These can be more or less elaborate according to circumstances, but all follow along certain lines.

1. Usually no hot dishes are served—certainly not more than two or three, if the function is long and late. These might take the form of Breakfast Dishes—although this is not to be taken as a serious point of technique.

2. A variety of cold entrées can be served, as well as sandwiches, pâtes, and similar dishes.

3. A good variety of sweets should be chosen, together with ices, petits fours, and beverages.

4 Hot clear soup can be served on the arrival of the guests, and again at departure, and frequently this is the only hot item served, other than coffee.

SPECIMEN SUPPER MENUS

Buffet for an Evening Reception

Consommé en Tasses

Petites Bouchées de Homard

Mousses de Jambon

Mayonnaise de Volaille

Denises Assortis

Crèmes de Cerises

Gâteau d'Ananas

Gelées au Vin

Pâtisserie

Glaces Napolitaine

Vins.   Café Glacé.   Limonade Frappée

Theatre Supper

Bouillon en Tasses

Suprêmes de Sole aux Raisins

Poulet Sauté Marengo

Petits Pois

Fruits Rafraîchis au Kirsch

Mignardises

Café

COMPARISON OF DINNERS, LUNCHEONS, AND SUPPERS

DINNER	LUNCHEON	SUPPER
I. Hors d'œuvres	Usually served	Served at a Theatre Supper
II. Potage	Frequently omitted. Consommé en Tasses, hot or cold, is popular	Hot Clear Soup served at a Ball Supper. Served at a Theatre Supper. Frequently served at a homely Supper
III. Poisson	Usually served, unless Egg or Farinaceous dishes take its place	Served in the form of a Mayonnaise or Chaud-froid at a Ball Supper. Served at a Theatre Supper. Frequently served at a homely Supper
IV. Entrée	May be omitted and grilled meat, cold meat, boiled fowl, or meat pie substituted	A large variety of cold Entrées served at a Ball Supper. A light Entrée is served at a Theatre Supper
V. Relevé	Not served (unless cold)	Not served
VI. Rôti	Not served	Not served
VII. Entremets— (a) Légumes (b) Sucrés (c) Savoureux	May be served / Always served / Biscuits, butter, and cheese substituted, especially if hors d'œuvres are served	Not served / Served in each kind of Supper / Not served
VIII. Dessert	Not served	Frequently served

OTHER LIGHT MEALS

BREAKFASTS

1. Vary the menu as much as possible.

2. Make any possible preparations the day before, as time is short for cooking in the morning. Many dishes can, however, be made or partly made the day before.

3. See that the porridge is well cooked and free from lumps, and have the toast thin and crisp.

4. Have the tea and coffee freshly made, and serve milk, just below boiling-point, with the latter.

5. Whenever possible, serve fresh or stewed fruit at breakfast.

6. Have the table carefully arranged, and serve all hot dishes *really hot*.

COURSES FOR BREAKFASTS

I. *Cereals or Fruit.* In winter, porridge is best, though grape-fruit is sometimes preferred at any time of the year. In the summer, wheat flakes or some light breakfast food can be sub-stituted for the porridge with advantage.

II. *Fish*, fresh, or smoked.

III. *Savouries*, such as eggs in varied forms, omelettes, savoury meat, ham, etc.

IV. *Sundries*, such as toast, rolls, scones, preserved or fresh fruit, marmalade, home-potted meat or fish.

AFTERNOON TEA

I. BEVERAGES. The tea should be allowed to infuse for only 3 minutes (5 minutes for China tea); it should be made imme-diately the water *boils* to ensure the flavour being extracted. Water that has boiled twice will also spoil the flavour of the tea.

The cream should be fresh from the dairy.

Coffee is often served as well for those who may prefer it.

Iced Tea and Coffee may be served in the summer time, and Russian tea may be provided at any time of the year.

II. BREAD AND BUTTER. Thin white and brown bread and butter should be cut, and if liked it may be rolled. White tin bread one day old is most convenient for cutting, or a milk loaf may be used; but brown bread is nicer and cuts better when quite new. Bridge or milk rolls are best new, and may also be used as sandwiches.

III. SANDWICHES. Savoury sandwiches should be cut into small squares or triangles, dished lightly on a doily, and sprinkled with carefully washed small cress.

Sweet sandwiches, spread with preserve, etc., may be provided, and should be cut into round or fancy shapes.

Note. If sandwiches have to be cut some time before they are needed, a damp muslin should be placed over them.

IV. SCONES, POTATO CAKES, TEA CAKES, ETC. These should be well buttered and served hot in cold weather.

V. CAKES AND BISCUITS. A good variety of cakes and biscuits should be served, and help to make the table very attractive. Fingers of rich cake, biscuits, and small fancy or iced cakes may be served separately or mixed on plates, which should not be too crowded.

CATERING FOR GARDEN PARTIES

Catering for Garden Parties, or similar special occasions, brings the complication of providing for a larger number of people, and adequate arrangements must be made for the following—

1. Good catering, and estimation of quantities.

2. A sufficient quantity of china, glass, cutlery, tables, and table linen, together with sufficient space and seating accommodation. It is not fair to herd guests to the stage of discomfort. A long buffet table, and small tables to seat four, six, or eight persons, make the most comfortable form of arrangement; and provide a chair for every guest. Arrangements can be made for hiring all of these.

3. Efficient service, with satisfactory means of boiling water, etc. Service is considerably aided if plates of certain foods are placed on each small table before the guests are seated.

4. A method of keeping food fresh and dainty—which is less easy when it has to be served out of doors.

Preliminary arrangements are all-important on these occasions, and lists must be most carefully prepared of everything required—even to the smallest details.

A FOUNDATION MENU

Various Sandwiches
(Tomato, Cucumber, Shrimp, Nut, Cress, Egg, etc.)
White and Brown Bread and Butter
Small Fancy Cakes
Chocolate Layer Cake
Dundee Cake   Almond Pound Cake
Strawberries or Raspberries and Cream, or
Fruit Salad
Cream and Water Ices
Tea and Coffee
Iced Coffee
Iced Lemonade or Orange Squash
Iced Claret or Cider Cup

QUANTITIES FOR 50 PEOPLE

Amounts to provide are always debatable, but the following quantities are average.

Tea. Half a pound. If possible make this in small quantities in china pots as required.

Coffee. Make 4 quarts of strong coffee early, leave it to become cold, then ice it, and serve with cream. Have one quart of strong hot coffee and one quart of hot milk in readiness.

Sandwiches. 3 half-quartern sandwich loaves will give about 120 slices, i.e. 60 whole sandwiches, which would yield 240 small square sandwiches. Some of these may be replaced by small bridge rolls, if preferred.

Bread and Butter. 2 milk loaves and 2 new brown loaves cut in thin slices should be sufficient.

Cakes. 1½–2 lb. each of Dundee and Almond Pound Cakes. 2 small fancy cakes per person, i.e. 100. 4 layer cakes, each to cut into eight pieces.

Strawberries and Cream. 4–6 oz. per person—hulled and placed on small plates in readiness. 2 quarts of cream, whipped and slightly sweetened.

Fruit Salad. 7 quarts—1 quart serves about 8 people. Cream as above.

Iced Lemonade, etc. 4 quarts of strong lemonade or orange squash, diluted as required, with iced water or soda water, to double this amount.

Iced Cup. Allow 2 pony glasses per person.

FRENCH CULINARY TERMS

Aiguille à Brider.	Larding needle used in braising (see p. 60).
Aiguillettes (*F.*).	Small strips of cooked meat.
Ajouté.	Added or mixed. In feminine pl. means a small garnish, i.e. something added.
Allumette (*F.*).	Lit. a match. Here a small strip.
Aromatiser.	To flavour with herbs.
Arroser.	To moisten or baste.
Assaisonnement.	Seasoning or condiment.
Assiette (*F.*).	Plate.
Atelets (**Hâtelets**).	Silver skewers used in decorating a cold entrée.
Au four.	Cooked in the oven.
Au Gras.	Applied to meat served with a rich sauce.
Au Gratin.	Food (frequently coated with sauce) sprinkled with browned crumbs and butter shavings, and possibly cheese, and served in the dish in which it is cooked.
Au Jus.	Applied to food served with its own juice or with gravy.
Au Maigre.	Meatless.
Bain-Marie (*M.*).	Water Bath. A large flat open vessel, half filled with water, in which sauces, garnishes, etc., may be stored after preparation to keep warm.
Barquette (*F.*).	A small boat. Applied to dishes prepared in boat-shaped moulds.
Batterie de Cuisine (*F.*).	A set of cooking utensils.
Bavaroise (*M.*).	A moulded custard, usually set with gelatine.
Beignets (*M.*).	Fritters.
Beurre Manié.	An equal quantity of butter and flour kneaded together and added to form a thickening.
Beurre Noir (au).	Food cooked in brown butter.
Beurre Noisette.	Melted skimmed butter, fried until lightly browned.
Blanc.	Strong white stock. Au Blanc means cooked in white stock or served with white sauce.
Blanquette (*F.*).	A rich stew of veal or fowl, served in a white sauce, enriched with egg yolk.
Bonne Bouche.	A small savoury mouthful.

Bouquet Garni (*M*.).   A small bag of herbs. On a small square of muslin place: a pinch of mixed herbs, a clove, 3–4 peppercorns, 2–3 parsley stalks, a tiny piece each of bay leaf and mace. Tie up, and add to sauces, soups, stews, etc.

Brider.   To truss (with a needle and thread).

Broche (à la).   Grilled or roasted before the fire.

Brouillé(e).   Scrambled (as applied to eggs).

Canapés (*M*.).   Small foundations (see p. 19).

Cannelons.   Small rolls of puff pastry filled with a mince of game, poultry, etc., and baked.

Cassolette (*F*.).   Small pastry cases, baked "blind," and filled as desired.

Casserole (*F*.).   Literally a saucepan, usually applied to a utensil of earthenware or oven glass. Or it may be a case of baked potato crust, or pastry.

Chair (*F*.).   Flesh. Chair à saucisse—Sausage meat.

Chartreuse (*F*.).   A moulded preparation of meat, vegetables, or fruit. Also the name of a liqueur.

Charlotte.   A sweet preparation which may be of the variety which is served hot (in which slices of bread, dipped in butter and baked, form a case for fruit) or that served cold (in which sponge finger biscuits form a case for a cream or cream and fruit mixture, set with gelatine).

Chiffonade (*M*.).   Finely shredded green salad plants, or herbs—usually added to soup.

Cocottes (*F*.).   Small fireproof pans—usually of the size for individual portions.

Compote (*F*.).   May denote a carefully prepared dish of stewed fruit, or fruit set in sweet jelly; or it may denote a game stew, served as an entrée.

Concasser.   To chop coarsely. To concass tomatoes, peel them and cut in half transversely, squeeze out juice and pips, and cut in $\frac{1}{4}$ in. pieces.

Coquilles (*F*.).   Shells. En Coquilles, small portions of food served in scallop shells.

Crêpes (*M*.).   Pancakes.

Cuillère (*F*.).   Spoon.

Cuit(e).   Cooked.

Darne (*F.*).	A thick cut from the middle of a large fish, such as salmon or cod.
Découper.	To carve or to cut.
Dégraisser.	To skim off fat—from soups, sauces, etc.
Denises.	Sandwiches.
Désosser.	To bone.
Diablé(e).	Devilled, i.e. cooked with mustard, Worcester Sauce, cayenne, etc.
Doré(e).	Literally gilded. In cookery—brushed over with beaten egg.
Émincer.	To cut in thin slices, or shred.
En.	"in." Denotes that food is served in some particular utensil, e.g. Saumon en Coquilles.
Escalopes (*F.*).	Thin slices of meat, and usually applied to veal.
Escargots (*M.*).	Edible snails.
Estouffade.	Slow cooking in little water or stock.
Étuvé.	Stewed.
Fagot (*M.*).	As Bouquet Garni, but shaped into a bunch and tied round, fresh thyme being used instead of powdered herbs.
Farci(e).	Stuffed.
Fécule (*F.*).	Fine flour.
Fleurons (*M.*).	Small shapes (usually crescents) of puff pastry, egged, baked, and used as a garnish.
Foie Gras (*M.*).	Fatted goose liver, used in the preparation of hors d'œuvres and savouries. Alsace is the country celebrated for the preparation of Pâté de Foie Gras.
Fondu(e).	Melted.
Fourchette (*F.*).	Fork.
Fouetté(e).	Whisked.
Four (*M.*).	Oven. Au four—baked in the oven.
Frappé(e).	Iced (temperature).
Friandines.	Small patties containing a salpicon, egged, crumbed, and fried.
Friandises (*F.*).	A selection of dessert dainties, or petits fours.
Frisé(e).	Curled, e.g. Chicorée Frisée, curled endive.
Frit(e).	Fried.
Friture (*F.*).	This may apply either to the fat used in the deep fat bath, or to the article fried in it.

Fumet (*M.*).	The essence, usually of game or fish, reduced with wine, and added to a dish to increase the flavour.
Gâteau (*M.*).	Cake.
Gaufre (*F.*).	Wafer or light biscuit.
Glace de Viande (*F.*).	Meat glaze.
Glacé(e).	May mean something iced, frozen, coated with meat glaze or jelly, or prepared in a sugar syrup.
Goût.	Taste or savour. *Petit Goûter* (*M.*)— the equivalent of afternoon tea.
Gras.	Fat or plump.
Gratiner.	To brown the surface of food in a dish under the griller or in a hot oven.
Hacher.	To chop.
Hachis (*M.*).	A hash or réchauffé of meat.
Julienne (*F.*).	Cut into fine match-shaped shreds. Usually applied to shreds of vegetables placed in a clear soup.
Kari (*M.*).	Curry.
Kirsch or **Kirschwasser.**	A liqueur prepared from cherries, and very useful as a flavouring.
Kromeskies.	Rolls of minced meat (usually white), flavoured with ham, chopped mushrooms, bound by a soft panada, wrapped in a thin piece of bacon, dipped in batter, and fried.
Kummel.	Kümmel, a liqueur distilled from carraways and coriander.
Lax.	Smoked salmon fillets, obtainable in oil in small flat tins.
Liaison.	A mixture of beaten egg yolks and cream, used for thickening rich white sauces and soups.
Luting.	A paste of flour and water used for sealing the edges of a saucepan or casserole, when it is necessary to prevent the escape of steam; or for covering a joint of venison or spiced beef for baking.
Macédoine.	A mixture of vegetables cut of even size, and used as a garnish; or of fruits of various kinds, frequently set in jelly.
Macéré(e).	Steeped, or macerated.
Marbré.	Marbled.

Marinade. To steep, or to leave to soak. This may also apply to the brine in which meat is pickled before cooking.

Marmite. A large earthenware stock-pot in which stocks and soups are made. Petites Marmites are small soup pots in which individual portions may be served.

Mélange. Mixture.

Mignardises. See **Friandises.**

Mignonette (Pepper). White peppercorns coarsely ground in a little pepper mill, which may be placed to hand while cooking, or on the table for the meal.

Mousse. Literally, mossy. A very light mixture, which may be savoury or sweet, hot, cold, or iced.

Naturel (au). Very simply served, or served uncooked.

Navarin. Lamb or Mutton stewed—frequently in one piece, and garnished with turnips.

Népaul (Pepper). An Indian pepper—not so pungent as cayenne, but more so than Paprika.

Nids (*M.*). Nests. Savoury and sweet preparations are sometimes so shaped, with tiny eggs of suitable edible material placed inside them.

Noisettes. Literally, nuts. Applies to the small rounds of lean meat taken from lamb or mutton cutlets.

Nourrir. To enrich—by adding cream, eggs, etc., to a partly prepared dish.

Noyau, Noyeau. A liqueur made from peach kernels.

Olives. The chief uses of olives are as hors d'œuvres, for cleansing the palate between courses, as a garnish for salads, for savouries, and as a garnish for brown entrées (see also p. 19).

Olives. Thin slices of raw beef rolled round a little veal forcemeat, tied, and stewed in brown sauce.

Pailles (*F.*). Straws—applied to potatoes, and to baked strips of cheese pastry.

Paillé(e). Straw coloured, or pale golden.

Panaché(e). Literally, plumed, but as a culinary term means striped.

Panurette.	Reddish coloured, seasoned, fine bread-crumbs, used for egging and crumbing where a red colour is desirable, e.g. Lobster Cutlets.
Papillotes (en).	Paper twisted over certain articles of food for cooking, or food served in paper cases.
Paprika.	Hungarian red pepper, useful in garnishing, as it is not pungent. It is best fried in a little butter if it is necessary to add it to other materials.
Parfait (*M*.).	Literally, perfect. A light rich ice cream —may also be applied to a light mixture of fish, game, etc.
Passer.	To pass through a sieve, strainer, or tammy cloth.
Pâte.	Pastry or dough.
Pâté.	Paste, e.g. *Pâté d'anchois*, anchovy paste.
Pâté.	Raised pie. Patty case of puff pastry with a rich filling. Diminutive *petites pâtés*.
Patisser.	To make pastry.
Patisserie.	Pastry of a dainty, attractive character.
Patissier.	Pastrycook.
Petites Caisses.	Small shapes of baked pastry with a rich savoury filling; or the cases may be made of paper, china, or silver.
Pilau, Pilaff.	An Indian or Turkish dish, prepared from rice, onions, meat, and raisins or sultanas.
Piqué(e).	Larded—a term used in Braising (see p. 60).
Plat (*M*.).	Dish.
Pluche (*F*.).	Leaves of aromatic herbs—parsley, tarragon, or chervil divided into tiny pieces, or lettuce or sorrel finely shredded —used as a garnish.
Poché(e).	Poached.
Pointes d'Asperges (*F*.).	Asparagus tips.
Potage (*M*.).	Soup.
Poussin (*M*.).	Baby chicken.
Praline (*F*.).	A mixture of caramel sugar and browned almonds, pounded and used for flavouring in confectionery.
Purée (*F*.).	A smooth pulp, frequently obtained by passing materials through a sieve. The term is also applied to thick soups which have been sieved.

Râper.	To grate or to shred.
Ravioli.	Nouille paste rolled very thinly, and enclosing a mixture of spinach, cheese, etc. Boiled and mixed with sauce, used as a garnish or meatless dish.
Réchauffé—	Literally, re-warmed. Food which has been cooked, and is re-dished.
Recherché.	As applied to cookery, or to a meal, means very choice and dainty.
Réduire.	To reduce.
Remouillage (*F*.).	Second, or Household, stock.
Renversé(e).	Turned out, as from a mould on to a dish.
Repassé(e).	Strained more than once.
Rhum.	Rum. A powerful spirit of rich flavour. A few drops are excellent used as an essence for flavouring sweet dishes, and it has good keeping power for rich cakes, Christmas pudding, etc.
Rissoler.	To brown.
Rissoles.	Minced meat mixture enclosed in thinly rolled pastry, egged, crumbed, and fried. Diminutive—*Rissolettes*.
Ruban.	Ribbon. *Rubanée*—a mixture arranged in layers of different colours.
Saignant.	Underdone.
Saisir (faire).	To cook meat briskly to seal in the juices.
Saladier (*M*.).	Salad bowl.
Salami.	Italian sausage used as an hors d'œuvre.
Salmis.	A rich game stew.
Salpicon.	Chopped chicken or veal, mixed with a rich white sauce, seasoned, and flavoured with chopped truffles and champignons.
Sauternes.	Sauterne, a French white wine of claret character, used largely in the preparation of dishes served "au vin blanc."
Sec, Sèche.	Dry.
Sirop (*F*.).	Syrup.
Sommelier.	Wine Steward.
Suprêmes.	Best, delicate portions of food.
Tambour (*M*.).	A fine sieve.
Tamis (*M*.).	Tammy cloth.
Tartine (*F*.).	A slice (as of bread and butter). Sometimes used to denote a sandwich.
Tasses (*F.pl*.).	Cups. En Tasses—served in cups, e.g. Bouillon en Tasses.

Timbale (*F*.).	Literally, cup or beaker. Applied in cookery to a light mixture of fish, game, or poultry, cooked or moulded in cup- or timbale-shaped moulds.
Tournedos.	Beef fillets, grilled or fried quickly.
Tourte.	A shallow open tart.
Truffe (*F*.).	Truffle.
Tutti-Frutti.	Italian term for a mixture of fruits, also applied sometimes to vegetables.
Vanille (*F*.).	Vanilla.
Velouté(e).	Velvety and smooth.
Vin (*M*.).	Wine.
Zeste (*M*.).	Zest, or thinly cut or grated rind of orange or lemon.

FRENCH FOR MENU MAKERS

THE "Bill of Fare" has a hearty sound and our wholesome British foods described in plain terms by the process used in cooking them has a sincerity beyond doubt. At the same time it tends to monotony and is not entirely suited to modern needs—when kitchens are small, fuel expensive, and the number in the family often few.

There is the great disadvantage that the English language becomes clumsy in describing more fanciful dishes, and it is extremely difficult to avoid the use of foreign terms—usually French, which language has become the Esperanto of the kitchen. Civilized cookery, as now understood, originated in Italy, but was developed by the French, to whom the art much appealed.

A menu should be written entirely in French (or entirely in English), though occasionally a "mongrel" menu is found—possibly with the idea of helping those who do not understand French well.

In order to write a Menu in French correctly, it is not essential to have a deep knowledge of the language or to speak it fluently, though naturally such accomplishments make the matter easier. Certain rules, given below, must be followed strictly, and an extensive vocabulary of foods and culinary terms is also essential.

The dating of menus is important, and conversion tables of weights and measures, which are appended, are useful for translating French Recipes.

THE QUESTION OF GRAMMAR

The French do not use the same definite article for masculine, feminine, and plural, as we do in England, but use le, la, and les respectively for these three. Similarly their "of the" is not formed by prefixing a word to their definite article (except in the feminine), but it is "du," "de la," and "des." Also "to the" or "with" is "au," "à la," or "aux." There is, however, in modern menu-making a tendency towards the omission of "au," "à la," etc., except when reference is made to the style of cooking of a particular country. Thus, *Filets de sole à l' Américaine*, but *Filets de sole Princesse*. "A la" in menus is often short for "à la mode de," and in such cases "la" is always used.

As regards the formation of plurals in French, this is usually done by adding "s" to the singular. There are, however, the following exceptions: words ending in S, X, or Z, do not change; words ending in AU and EU add X; words ending in AL make

AUX. Whether compound words make both parts plural depends on the nature of the parts. Thus Chou-fleur, Cauliflower, makes Choux-fleurs, but Chou-de-mer, Sea-kale, makes Choux-de-mer.

It is important to note that in French the adjective must agree with the noun in number and gender, and in most cases adjectives follow the same rules as nouns for such formations. Also, THE ADJECTIVE USUALLY FOLLOWS ITS NOUN.

DATES

In most French menus the date, written in full, appears at the foot of the card, and a few points as to the designation of dates would be useful here.

1. The day of the week comes first, with a capital initial. These are—

Sunday.	Dimanche.	Wednesday.	Mercredi.
Monday.	Lundi.	Thursday.	Jeudi.
Tuesday.	Mardi.	Friday.	Vendredi.
	Saturday.	Samedi.	

2. Next comes the day of the month, written out in full (see paragraph of numbers below), with the definite article.

3. This is followed by the month, written with a *small* initial. The months are—

January.	*janvier.*	July.	*juillet.*
February.	*février.*	August.	*août.*
March.	*mars.*	September.	*septembre.*
April.	*avril.*	October.	*octobre.*
May.	*mai.*	November.	*novembre.*
June.	*juin.*	December.	*décembre.*

4. Lastly comes the year. This is usually written in numbers; but if it is written in full it takes the form of " one thousand, nine hundred, and forty-six," using the form " mil" (*not* mille) for the thousand. Thus, 1946 is Mil neuf cent quarante-six. An alternative method is to use " Nineteen hundred and forty-six," or dix-neuf cent quarante-six.

Thus, the menu of a dinner served on 6th May, 1946, would be dated "Lundi, le six mai, mil neuf cent quarante-six."

TEMPERATURE CONVERSION

To convert Degrees Fahrenheit to Degrees Centigrade—

Multiply the number of degrees Fahrenheit, *less* 32°, by 5, and divide the result by 9.

E.g. What is 59° Fahrenheit in Centigrade degrees?

$(59-32) \times 5 \div 9 = 5 \times 27 \div 9 = 135 \div 9 = 15°$ Centigrade.

To convert Degrees Centigrade to Degrees Fahrenheit—
Multiply the number of degrees Centigrade by 9, and divide the result by 5; then add 32°.

E.g. What is 18° Centigrade in Fahrenheit degrees?

$(18 \times 9 \div 5) + 32 = 32\frac{2}{5} + 32 = 64\frac{2}{5}°$ F.

METRIC CULINARY MEASUREMENTS

Measure of Capacity

10 decilitres make 1 litre.
10 litres make 1 Dekalitre.
10 Dekalitres make 1 Hectolitre.
1 Litre equals 1·76077 pints.
1 Litre equals 1000 cu. cm.

Measure of Weight

10 decigrammes make 1 Gramme.
10 grammes make 1 Dekagramme.
10 Dekagrammes make 1 Hectogramme.
10 Hectogrammes make 1 Kilogramme.
1 gramme equals 564 drams, and 1 kilogramme equals 2 lb. 3 oz. 4·4 grains.

CONVERSION TABLES

To Convert	To
Centimetres	Inches Multiply by 2 and divide by 5.
Cu. Centimetres	Cu. Inches Multiply by 3 and divide by 50
Cu. Inches	Cu. Centimetres Multiply by 50 and divide by 3
Gallons	Litres Multiply by 9 and divide by 2.
Grammes	Ounces Divide by 28.
Grammes	Pounds Divide by 248.
Inches	Centimetres Multiply by 5 and divide by 2
Kilograms	Pounds ,, 12 ,, 5
Litres	Gallons ,, 2 ,, 9
Ounces	Grammes ,, 28
Pounds	Kilograms 5 ,, 12

CARDINAL NUMERALS

1. un, une.
2. deux.
3. trois.
4. quatre.
5. cinq.
6. six.
7. sept.
8. huit.
9. neuf.
10. dix.
11. onze.
12. douze.
13. treize.
14. quatorze.

CARDINAL NUMERALS—*(contd.)*

15. quinze.	60. soixante.
16. seize.	61. soixante et un.
17. dix-sept.	70. soixante-dix.
18. dix-huit.	71. soixante-onze.
19. dix-neuf.	80. quatre vingts.
20. vingt.	81. quatre vingt-un.
21. vingt et un.	90. quatre vingt-dix.
22. vingt-deux.	91. quatre vingt-onze.
30. trente.	100. cent.
31. trente et un.	101. cent un.
40. quarante.	200. deux cents.
41. quarante et un.	1000. mille.
50. cinquante.	1001. mille un.
51. cinquante et un.	2000. deux mille.

VOCABULARY OF FOOD MATERIALS

Note. In this vocabulary the "Le" and "La" has only been added to indicate gender.

Meat—La Viande

ENGLISH.	FRENCH.	ENGLISH.	FRENCH.
Beef.	Le Bœuf.	Mutton.	Le Mouton.
Brains.	Les Cervelles (*F.*)	Ox-Tail.	La Queue de Bœuf.
Calf's Head.	La Tête de Veau	Pork.	Le Porc.
Ham.	Le Jambon.	Sausage.	La Saucisse.
Kidney.	Le Rognon.	Sausage (Breakfast).	
Lamb.	L'Agneau (*M.*).		Le Saucisson.
Liver.	Le Foie.	Suet.	La Graisse.
Marrow, Beef,		Sweetbread.	Le Ris (de Veau).
	La Moëlle de Bœuf.	Tongue.	La Langue.
		Veal.	Le Veau.

Joints—Relevés

ENGLISH.	FRENCH.	ENGLISH.	FRENCH.
Aich-bone.	La Culotte.	Neck.	La Carré.
Breast.	La Poitrine.	Rib.	La Culotte.
Cushion (of veal).		Saddle (of mutton).	
	La Noix (de veau).		La Selle (de mouton).
Fillet.	Le Filet.	Shoulder.	L'Épaule (*F.*).
Head.	La Tête.		L'Éclanche (*F.*).
Knuckle.	Le Jarret.	Sirloin.	L'Aloyau (*M.*)
Leg.	Le Gigot.	Wing.	L'Aile (*F.*).
Loin.	La Longe.		

Poultry and Game—La Volaille Et Le Gibier

ENGLISH.	FRENCH.	ENGLISH.	FRENCH
Blackcock.	Le Coq de Bruyère.	Partridge.	La Perdrix.
Capon.	Le Chapon.	Pheasant.	Le Faisan.
Chicken.	Le Poulet. } La Volaille.	Pigeon.	Le Pigeon.
		Plover.	Le Pluvier.
Chic-Chicken.	Le Poussin.	Ptarmigan.	Le Perdreau Blanc
Duck.	Le Canard.	Pullet.	La Poulette.
Duckling.	Le Caneton.	Quail.	La Caille.
Goose.	L'Oie (*F*.).	Rabbit.	Le Lapin.
Goose Liver.	Le Foie d'Oie.	Snipe.	La Bécassine.
Gosling.	L'Oison (*M*.).	Teal.	La Sarcelle.
Guinea-Fowl.	La Pintade.	Turkey (cock).	Le Dindon.
Hare.	Le Lièvre.	Turkey (hen).	La Dinde.
Hazel-Hen.	La Gélinotte.	Wild Duck.	
Leveret.	Le Levraut.		Le Canard Sauvage.
Lark. La Mauviette (Alouette).		Woodcock.	La Bécasse.
Ortolan.	L'Ortolan (*M*.).		

Fish—Le Poisson

ENGLISH.	FRENCH.	ENGLISH.	FRENCH.
Anchovy.	L'Anchois (*M*.).	Mackerel.	Le Maquereau.
Bass.	Le Bar.	Mussel.	La Moule.
Bream.	La Brème.	Oyster.	L'Huître (*F*.).
Brill.	La Barbue.	Perch.	La Perche.
Carp.	La Carpe.	Pike.	Le Brochet.
Caviare.	Le Caviar.	Plaice.	La Plie.
Cod.	Le Cabillaud.	Prawns.	Les Écrevisses (*F*.).
Crab.	Le Crabe.	Red Mullet.	Le Rouget.
Crawfish.	La Langouste.	Roe.	La Laitance.
Crayfish.	L'Écrevisse (*F*.).	Salmon.	Le Saumon.
Dab.	La Limande.	Salmon Trout.	
Dory (John Dory).			La Truite Saumonée.
	Le Saint Pierre.	Salt Cod.	La Morue.
Eel.	L'Anguille (*F*.).	Sardines.	Les Sardines (*F*.).
Flounder.	Le Carrelet.	Scallop.	Le Pétoncle.
Grey Mullet.	Le Mulet.	Shad.	L'Alose (*F*.).
Gudgeon.	Le Goujon.	Smoked Haddock.	
Haddock.	L'Aigrefin (*M*.). } La Merluche.		La Merluche Fumée.
		Shrimps.	Les Crevettes (*F*.).
Hake.	Le Merlus.	Skate.	La Raie.
Halibut.	Le Flétan.	Smelt.	L'Éperlan (*M*.).
Herring.	Le Hareng.	Soft Roe.	See "Roe."
Lamprey.	La Lamproie.	Sole.	La Sole.
Lobster.	Le Homard (*M*.).	Sturgeon.	L'Esturgeon (*M*.).

Fish—Le Poisson—(contd.)

English.	French.	English.	French.
Trout.	La Truite.	Whiting.	Le Merlan.
Turbot.	Le Turbot.	Young Turbot.	Le Turbotin.
Whitebait.	La Blanchaille.		

Vegetables—Les Légumes

English.	French.	English.	French.
Artichoke.	L'Artichaut (M.).	Kale.	Le Chou Frisé.
Asparagus.	L'Asperge (F.).	Leek.	Le Poireau.
Broad Bean	La Fève de Maru.	Lentil.	La Lentille.
Brussels Sprout.		Lettuce.	La Laitue.
	Le Chou de Bruxelles.	Mushroom.	Le Champignon.
Broccoli.	Le Brocoli.	Onion.	L'Oignon (M.).
Beetroot.	La Betterave.	Parsley.	Le Persil.
Cabbage.	Le Chou.	Parsnip.	Le Panais.
Caper.	La Câpre.	Peas.	Les Petits Pois (M.).
Cardoon.	Le Cardon.	Potato.	La Pomme (de terre).
Carrot.	La Carotte.	Pumpkin.	La Citrouille.
Cauliflower.	Le Chou-Fleur.	Radish.	Le Radis.
Celery.	Le Céleri.	Salsify.	Le Salsifis.
Celery Knobs.	Le Celeriac.	Sea-kale.	Le Chou-de-mer.
Cos Lettuce.		Sorrel.	L'Oseille (F.).
	La Laitue Romaine.	Spinach.	L'Épinard (M.).
Cress.	Le Cresson.	Tarragon.	L'Estragon (M.).
Cucumber.	Le Concombre.	Tomato.	La Tomate.
Egg Plant.	L'Aubergine (F.).	Truffles.	La Truffe.
Endive.	L'Endive (F.).	Turnip.	Le Navet.
Garlic.	L'Ail (M.).	Vegetable Marrow.	La Courge.
Gherkin.	Le Cornichon.	Vegetable Herbs.	
Horseradish.	Le Raifort.	(aromatic).	
Haricots.			Les Aromates (M.).
	Les Haricots Blancs (M.).		

Fruit—Le Fruit

English.	French.	English.	French.
Apple.	La Pomme.	Date.	La Datte.
Apricot.	L'Abricot (M.)	Fig.	La Figue.
Brambleberry.	La Ronce.	Gooseberry.	La Groiselle Verte.
Cherry.	La Cerise.	Grape-fruit.	La Pamplemousse.
Cranberry.	L'Airelle (F.).	Grape.	La Grappe.
Currant—		Greengage.	La Reine Claude.
Black.	La Groiselle Noire.	Lemon.	Le Citron.
Red.	La Groiselle Rouge.	Mandarine.	La Mandarine.
White.	La Groiselle Blanche		

Fruit—Le Fruit—(contd.)

ENGLISH.	FRENCH.	ENGLISH.	FRENCH.
Medlar.	La Néfle.	Pineapple.	L'Ananas (M.).
Melon.	Le Melon.	Plum.	La Prune.
Mirabelle.	La Mirabelle.	Prune.	Le Pruneau.
Mulberry.	La Mûre.	Quince.	Le Coing.
Nectarine.	Le Brugnon.	Raspberry.	La Framboise.
Orange.	L'Orange (F.).	Rhubarb.	La Rhubarbe.
Peach.	La Pêche.	Strawberry.	La Fraise.
Pear.	La Poire.	Tangerine.	La Mandarine.

Butter, Cream, etc.—Le Beurre, La Crème, etc.

English	French	English	French
Bacon.	Le Lard.	Dripping.	La Graisse de Rôti.
Butter.	Le Beurre.	Egg.	L'Oeuf (M.).
Cheese.	Le Fromage.	Lard.	Le Saindoux.
Cream.	La Crème.	Milk.	Le Lait.

Grocery—L'Epicerie

English	French	English	French
Almond.	L'Amande (F.).	Jam.	La Confiture.
Arrowroot.	La Fécule De Marante.	Jelly.	La Gelée.
Barley.	L'Orge (F.)	Macaroni.	Le Macaroni.
Barley, finely ground.	La Crème D'Orge.	Mustard.	La Moutarde.
Buckwheat.	Le Sarrasin.	Nutmeg.	La Noix de Muscat.
Candied Orange Peel.	L'Orangeat (M.).	Oatmeal.	L'Avoine (F.).
Candied Peel.	La Peau de Citron.	Oil.	L'Huile (F.).
Carraway Seed.	Le Carvi.	Olive.	L'Olive (F.).
Chocolate.	Le Chocolat.	Paste.	La Pâte.
Clove.	Le Girofle.	Pepper.	Le Poivre.
Cocoa.	Le Cacao. / Le Cacao en Poudre.	Pistachio.	La Pistache.
Coconut.	La Noix de coco.	Raisin.	Le Raisin Sec.
Coffee.	Le Café.	Rice.	Le Riz.
Currant.	Le Raisin de Corinthe.	Rice, finely ground.	La Crème de Riz.
Fig.	La Figue.	Sago.	Le Sagou.
Flour.	La Farine.	Salt.	Le Sel.
Gelatine.	La Gélatine.	Semolina.	La Semoule.
Ginger.	Le Gingembre.	Spice.	L'Épice (F.).
Honey.	Le Miel.	Sugar.	Le Sucre.
Icing Sugar.	La Glace de Sucre.	Sultana.	Le Raisin de Damas.
		Tapioca.	Le Tapioca.
		Tea.	Le Thé.
		Vermicelli.	Le Vermicelle.
		Vinegar.	Le Vinaigre.
		Yeast.	La Levure.

TABLE OF FOODS IN SEASON

SPECIAL SEASONS

Now that transport has improved so much, most foods are obtainable all the year round. The following list notes when foods (mainly English) are at their best and cheapest.

Apples.
English. Aug.–Mar.
New Zealand } Apr.–Jul.
Australian
Oregon and Canadian. Oct.–Mar.
S. African. Mar.–Apr.

Apricots.
English. Jul.–Aug.
S. African. Dec.–Jan.
Spanish. June.

Artichokes.
Globe. Aug.–Oct.
Jerusalem. Oct.–Mar.

Asparagus. English. Apr.–Jun.

Blackcock. Oct.–Dec.

Beans, Broad. June–Aug.

Beans, Runner. Jul.–Nov.

Blackberries. Sep.–Oct.

Brussels Sprouts. Sep.–Feb.

Capsicums. Sep.–Oct.

Carrots, young. May–Aug.

Cauliflowers. Mar.–Nov.

Celeriac. Oct.–Mar.

Celery. Sep.–Feb.

Cherries. Jun.–Aug.

Crabs. May–Sep.

Cranberries. Oct.–Feb.

Cucumbers. May–Sep.

Currants. Jun.–Aug.

Custard Apples. Oct.–Dec.

Damsons. Sep.–Oct.

Ducks (wild). Aug.–Mar.

Ducklings. Mar.–May.

Ducks. June–Jan.

Endive. Nov.–Mar.

Figs. Outdoor. Aug.–Sep.

Flageolets. May–Aug.

Flounders. Aug.–Apl.

Golden Plover. Aug.–Mar.

Geese. Sep.–Feb.

Gooseberries. May–Aug.

Goslings. May–July.

Greengages. July–Sep. (beg.).

Grouse. 12th Aug.–12th Dec.

Guinea Fowl. Jan.–Mar.

Hares. 1st Aug.–28th Sep.

Hazel Hen. Jan.–Jun.

Herrings. Jul.–Feb.

Kale. Dec.–Mar.

Lamb. Jan.–Jul.

Leeks. Nov.–Mar.

Lettuce, English. May–Nov.

Leverets. Aug.–Mar.

Loganberries. Jul.–Aug.

Mackerel. Nov.–Jun.

Mandarines. Dec.–Apr.

Mangoes. Oct.–Dec.

Marrows. Jul.–Nov.

Medlars. Sep.–Nov.

Melons, Hothouse. May–Nov.

Mulberries. Aug.–Sep.

Mushrooms, Field. Jul.–Oct.

Nectarines, Hothouse. Aug.–Oct.

Oranges, Seville. Feb.–Mar.

Oysters. Sep.–Apr.

Parsnips. Sep.–Apr.

Partridges. 1st Sep.–31st Jan.

Passion Fruit. Oct.–Jan.

Peaches. Jun.–Dec.

Pears.
  Avocado. Oct.–Mar.
  English. Aug.–Jan.
Peas. Jun.–Sep.
Perch and Pike. Jul.–Feb.
Persimmons. Oct.–Dec.
Pheasant. 1st Oct.–31st Jan.
Plums. Jul.–Oct.
Pomegranates. Oct.–Apr.
Pork. Sep.–Mar.
Ptarmigan. 20th Aug.–20th Dec.
Pumpkins. Sep.–Oct.
Quinces. Oct.–Nov.
Rabbits. Sep.–Mar.
Radishes. May–Nov.

Raspberries. Jul.–Sep.
Red Cabbage. Sep.–Jan.
Rhubarb.
  Garden. Apr.–Oct.
  Forced. Dec.–May.
Salmon, Scotch. Feb.–Sep.
Salsify. Oct.–Jan.
Savoy Cabbages. Oct.–Mar.
Scallops. Oct.–Apr.
Sprats. Nov.–Apr.
Strawberries. Jun.–Aug.
Swedes. Sep.–Apr.
Tangerines. Nov.–Feb.
Turkeys. Sep.–Feb.
Whitebait. Feb.–Aug.

FOODS IN SEASON THROUGHOUT THE YEAR

Fish.
Bream. Brill. Dory. Eels. Hake. Halibut. Mullet. Plaice. Salmon (imported). Soles. Turbot. Whiting.

Shellfish.
Crayfish. Lobsters. Mussels. Prawns. Shrimps.

Meat.
Beef. Mutton. Veal.

Vegetables and Salads.
Beetroot. Cabbages. Carrots. Globe Artichokes. Horseradish. Lettuces. Mushrooms (cultivated). Mustard and Cress. Onions. Potatoes. Spinach. Tomatoes. Turnips.
Note. Cucumbers, Asparagus and French Beans, can be obtained all the year round, but they are expensive.

Fruit.
Apples. Bananas. Grape-fruit. Grapes. Lemons. Oranges. Pineapples.

INDEX OF RECIPES